Welcome

Jonathan has been writing about his experiences with computers, gadgets, games and technology for more than 15 years. He has written for many popular consumer magazines and is the author of several MagBooks.

I'll freely admit that, before I began researching this book, I knew next to nothing about robotics or electronics, beyond what I could (barely) remember from science lessons at school. At first, I was intimidated by the vast gaps in my knowledge. But then a friend of mine, who makes electronic projects as a hobby, introduced me to something called Arduino.

Arduino is a platform that many hobbyists and beginners use for their electronic projects. It's based around a small credit card-sized computer, not unlike a Raspberry Pi, but even simpler to use. It doesn't have (or need) an operating system, but you can write and upload programs to it and get it to do all kinds of things.

Arduino makes it incredibly easy to start building projects on your own. It comes with a simple software environment, complete with sample programs for you to upload to the device. And it's incredibly cheap, too. Arduinos can be bought for £20 – even less if you shop around – and you can pick up a selection of electronic components to play with for only a few pounds.

But the really great thing about working with Arduino compared to other computer projects is that you can see the results of your programming directly affecting or physically interacting with the world around you. Instead of making graphics appear on a screen, for example, you can program a real light to switch itself on and off, or your programs can receive and interpret information about the real world via a sensor.

Individually, these functions might not sound Earth-shattering. But when you start combining them together and adding others – a distance sensor to interpret the environment, say, and some motors for autonomous motion – suddenly you're starting to build a robot.

And that's exactly what you'll be doing if you follow the projects in this book. We'll start by making simple projects and gradually build it all together until we've created a complete robot. You won't need to learn anything massively complicated or use any unfamiliar equipment. And if you're still feeling daunted, remember if the author of this book can go from knowing almost nothing to building his own robot, then anyone can.

JONATHAN PARKYN
Author

CONTENTS

56

72

86

94

112

132

IN THIS CHAPTER

HOW TO BUILD A ROBOT

FIRST STEPS

For those who've never worked with electronics before, the idea of building a complete robot yourself may seem like an impossible task. What do you need? Where do you get it from? And how do you put it all together? We'll be answering a lot of those questions over the next few chapters. But before then, we're going to answer the most important question of all – why build a robot in the first place? While we're at it, we'll give you a beginner's guide to electronics, and we'll have a little fun building our first basic bot, into the bargain.

WHY BUILD A ROBOT?

Robots aren't just science fiction – they're all around us and, as we'll explain, you have the power to construct one yourself

WHAT YOU'LL LEARN

- **What robots are and where you'll encounter them**
- **The basic principles behind how robots work**
- **How easy it is to start building your own robots**

Whether you're a little kid or a big one, there's something undeniably exciting about robots. Even the most unglamorous assembly line robot can hold a special appeal. It's hard to define, but perhaps it's the thrill of seeing a man-made device reacting to its environment and carrying out tasks without the need for human interference. Or maybe it's the excitement of seeing science and technology seemingly evolving before our very eyes. Either way, robots aren't just about some far-off future. Robots already live and work among us – they're everywhere.

In this book, we're going to find out what makes many of the robots around us tick. Not only that, but we're also going to show you how to build your own robot from the ground up – an artificially intelligent device that will be able to sense its environment, move around independently and respond in a variety of different ways. By the time you've finished reading, you'll have everything you need to build a robot yourself, even if you've never had any experience of electronics or computer programming before.

EVERYDAY ROBOTS

If we asked you to draw a picture of a robot, the likelihood is that you might draw something similar to the robots we often see in popular science fiction: C3-Po from *Star Wars*, perhaps, or Robby the Robot from *Forbidden Planet*, or

▲ **Samsung SR8855 NaviBot Robotic Vacuum Cleaner.**

maybe even the Terminator. But, contrary to popular belief, robots don't have to be hyper-intelligent synthetic beings or ruthless killing machines from the future. In fact, they don't even need to be humanoid at all. Characters like these might make for dramatic stories, but real robots are – by definition – much simpler and much less theatrical. Essentially, a robot is any machine that can carry out a range of actions on command, according to a pre-programmed set of instructions. And when you think about robots in those terms, you soon realise that they're a lot more common than you might have imagined. In fact, you could argue that almost any autonomous or semi-autonomous system, from your motion-controlled porch light to your bank's cash machine, is a type of robot.

Robotic devices make life easy for us, by opening supermarket doors automatically when they sense our presence, for example, or by taking on tasks that would otherwise be repetitive and boring, such as lifting and welding. They can perform jobs that are dangerous or difficult – or even impossible – for humans to carry out, such as remotely disabling explosive devices, or aiding surgeons to carry out complex medical procedures, or travelling to Mars to carry our research on our behalf.

THE ORIGINS OF MODERN ROBOTS

Somewhat fittingly, the term 'robot' was coined not by scientists but by a work of science-fiction – Karel Capek's 1921 play, 'Rossum's Universal Robots'. The first recognisable 'modern' robots predate the existence of the word by over 120 years. The mechanical loom invented by Joseph Marie Jacquard in 1801, for instance, was an automatic machine that used punched cards to control the pattern of the textile with minimal human involvement. This loom is widely recognised as one of the forerunners of modern digital computing, partly because it was an early demonstration that machines could be programmed to carry out a range of tasks. But if you look at one of Jacquard's punchcards, you'll see the pattern is a series of zeros and ones – in other words, binary data. For many, William Grey Walter is the father of modern robotics. He created a number of autonomous electronic machines in Bristol in 1948, including tortoise-shaped robots Elmer and Elsie, which were able to 'learn' simple behaviours.

Robots come in all manner of shapes and sizes, from little, round robotic vacuum cleaners made by Samsung and LG, to quadrupeds designed for military use, like BigDog, made by pioneering robotics firm Boston Dynamics. Many industrial robots look like one big metal arm. And, yes, there are even some robots that are human-shaped, such as Honda's famous ASIMO. But, regardless of their outward appearance, most robots share a number of basic key characteristics. They usually have some kind of sensory input – microphones to 'hear' or cameras to 'see', for example – so they can sense the environment around them. They usually have some logic programming to interpret and process the information they gain from their sensors, even if the logic is as simple as 'if this, then that'. And they'll usually have the ability to generate some type of output – a function that they perform once the criteria of their programming has been met. On the most basic end of the spectrum, your porch light has motion and light sensors (input). It will intelligently establish whether it's dark enough and whether there has been any motion (logic) and, if the criteria has been met, it will switch on the light for a specified time (output).

Robots can, of course, be much more complex and much more intelligent than that. Samsung's £300 SR8855 NaviBot Robotic Vacuum Cleaner, for example, has 38 separate sensors that all work together to provide the machine's input. Its logic includes not only anti-collision and anti-fall programming but also mapping technology, so that it learns the layout of your home. And its output functions include autonomous movement, vacuuming and the ability to recharge itself when it senses its battery is low.

Some of the robots currently in development make devices like the NaviBot seem pretty basic in comparison. Scientists in Switzerland, for instance, are developing small robotic modules, called roombots, which can self-assemble into different types of 'intelligent' furniture. Meanwhile, Google's driverless cars have notched up more than 500,000 miles to date – all without any major accidents. Google has recently bought up a lot of robotics companies, too, including the aforementioned Boston Dynamics. Bionics, nanotechnology and even hands-free lawn mowing are all areas where innovations are happening thick and fast. If you're a fan of robots, now is a pretty exciting time to be alive.

A robot is a machine that can carry out a range of actions on command, according to a pre-programmed set of instructions

EARLY ROBOTS

Amazingly, it's known that the Ancient Greeks created simple 'programmable' robots using a system of string and weights in around 60 AD. Some historical texts suggest that autonomous mechanical statues – or automata – may have existed in Ancient China hundreds of years earlier than that. Similar accounts tell of moving mechanical people and animals used for entertainment throughout Medieval times and into the Renaissance. The Banu Musa brothers from Baghdad published a fascinating book called *The Book of Ingenious Devices* in 850 AD, which details the designs for dozens of automated and robotic devices. And, amongst his many other ingenious inventions, Leonardo da Vinci designed a mechanical knight in 1495 that could sit, stand and move its arms. One of the most famous examples of automata is the Turk, an 18th century robot that could apparently play chess. Sadly, the Turk was revealed to be an elaborate hoax, with a human 'director' cleverly concealed within. It wasn't until 1997 that a genuine chess-playing machine, IBM's Deep Blue, was able to take on a human world champion, Garry Kasparov. And win.

MiP is a very clever, ready-made robot toy.

1 First steps

Robots can perform jobs that are dangerous for humans, such as disabling bombs.

The Arduino Uno has revolutionised the world of DIY electronics.

MICRO CONTROL

Okay, so we've cleared up some common misconceptions and now we have a better idea of what a robot actually is. But building one yourself? Surely you'd have to be a scientist or an engineer to do something like that, right? In fact, that's another popular fallacy – almost anyone can have a go.

Until fairly recently, putting together your own robots would have been something only engineering students or highly experienced enthusiasts might have attempted. But the availability of cheap components and the ability to construct reasonably sophisticated electronics projects without the need for skills such as soldering has broadened this area out so that people with little or no prior experience can get started easily and inexpensively.

Key to this is the emergence of cheap, mass-produced microcontroller devices, such as the amazingly versatile Arduino Uno. We'll be looking at the Uno in much more detail a little later on in this chapter, but it's worth briefly explaining what it is and why this type of technology is revolutionising the world of DIY electronics. Basically, the Uno is a tiny computer, and it comes on a printed circuit board about two-thirds of the size of a credit card, which houses not only the microcontroller itself, but also power regulation, USB connection and input/output pins that allow you to attach components such as sensors, motors and more. Simple programs can be written on your PC, then uploaded to the board via USB, where you can see your programming come to life as various real-world interactions. An official Arduino Uno will cost you less than £20. Opt for one of the many unofficial boards, however, and you're looking at as little as £8.

Robby the Robot is a popular science-fiction robot.

You may already be familiar with the Raspberry Pi and, in some ways, the Uno is conceptually similar to the Pi – just much, much simpler. The Pi is more like a full-blown PC and is vastly overqualified for the purposes of building simple electronic projects – even robots. That hasn't stopped a lot of Raspberry Pi owners from using the device as the basis for some great hardware-based projects, and we'll be involving the more popular mini-computer in some of our own projects later on in this guide. But for the majority of our projects, including everything from our 'first steps' guides right up to the construction of our main robot, which we've called Magbot, we'll be using an Arduino Uno.

In short, the Uno, and devices like it, have made experimenting with electronics cheaper and more accessible than ever.

JUST FOR FUN

We still haven't tackled the question we asked in the headline – why build a robot in the first place? Ready-made robot toys have been available for many years, and some of the latest ones are pretty sophisticated. MiP (**www.wowwee.com/mip**), for example, is a robot that balances on two wheels, responds to gestures and can be 'programmed' using a mobile phone app. MiP is a very clever toy, but it also costs £100 and you don't get any of the enjoyment or satisfaction of putting it together yourself.

THE MARS ROVER

Right now, around 225 million miles away, a robot the size of a Ford Fiesta is wending its way across the surface of Mars. The robot you're going to build yourself over the course of this book may never travel to another world, but he actually has a great deal in common with the Curiosity Mars Rover. Controlling Curiosity is a computer less powerful than a Raspberry Pi. This computer, the RAD750, created by a subsidiary of British company BAE Systems, contains over 2 million lines of code written in a programming language called C, which is pretty much the same language we'll use to code our own Magbot. This code controls everything from sensing the environment to navigating the Rover through the Martian landscape. Since radio waves take more than 12 minutes to travel between Mission Control and Mars, the Rover can't be driven like a remote-control car. So it includes software that uses its cameras (input) to determine where rocks and other obstructions are, calculates a safe path (logic) and turns the wheels (output). And that's almost exactly how Magbot will work when you've finished making him.

Making your own robot can certainly work out cheaper than buying one off the shelf. Our three-wheeled Magbot might not be quite as sophisticated as MiP, but he'll also cost you a lot less – under £18 if you source the cheapest possible components.

Building robots and other electronic projects has an obvious educational side. Complete the step-by-step guides in this book, for example, and not only will you have a fully functioning robot by the end of it, but you'll have learned how many of the electronic devices you use every day work, too. On top of that, you'll find that you've picked up a good understanding of computer programming, as well as the ability to construct electronic circuits, even if you've never had any previous experience of either discipline.

The main reason for building a robot, however, is that you'll get a great deal of fun and enjoyment out of doing so, whether you're working on your own or with a family member or friend. Programming software, such as an app for a mobile phone, is one thing. But building and programming a physical object to respond or interact with the real world can be infinitely more satisfying.

MY FIRST BOT

This book has been designed for the young and not-so-young alike as a step-by-step guide to building and programming your first robot. As we've said, you don't need to be an electronics expert or a computer whizz to complete our projects. Everything you need to know can be found within the pages of this book, and it's all explained in easy-to-understand language.

As well as our 'main' project – building Magbot – we've opted to include a number of practice projects and quick guides throughout, so that you can see various key concepts in action, put what you learn into practice and hone new skills as you go. We'll start with basic projects, such as making a light blink on and off, and work our way up to more complex stuff, such as programming your robot to evade obstacles and communicate wirelessly. We'll provide all the programming code required and describe in simple terms how it all works. We'll tell you exactly all the parts and equipment you'll need and show you where you can get it from. And we'll explain how to stay safe whilst working on your projects and what to do when something goes wrong. ☼

Some robots are human-shaped, such as Honda's famous ASIMO.

MAKE A MINI ROBOT IN MINUTES

We demonstrate how easy it is to build your own electronic projects by making a simple robot in just six steps

WHAT YOU'LL NEED

- An old toothbrush
- A Stanley knife
- A chopping board
- A small 1.5V battery
- A vibration motor
- Some Sellotape
- Some Blu-tak

If you have kids or grandkids of a certain age, you may have already heard about Hexbugs. They're a popular brand of ready-made robot toys, all of which are modelled after types of insects. Hexbug sets are great fun, but they can be pretty expensive – anything up to £40 – and some of the robots themselves are actually pretty basic. In this workshop, we're going to show you how to make a Hexbug Nano-type robot from scratch using mostly basic materials you have lying around your house, such as an old toothbrush. Unlike the robot we'll be building later on in this guide, Bristlebug won't be a very intelligent device, but it will move around on its own using the physics of vibration and explore its environment just like the Hexbugs you buy in the shops. You'll also learn how easy it is to start creating electronic projects.

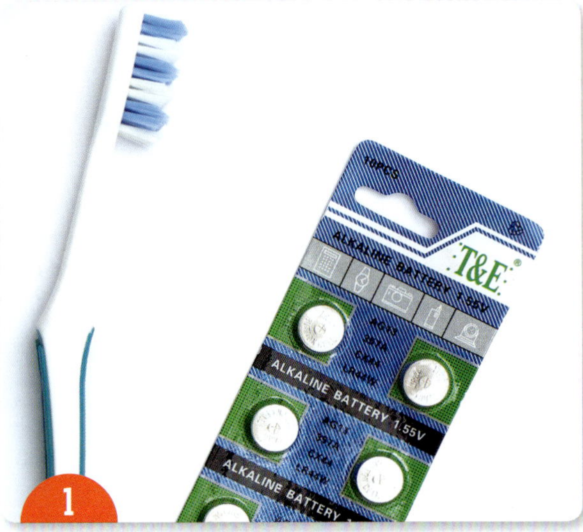

1

2

3

TIP

Bristlebug should move around and navigate by bouncing off obstacles. But depending on the type of toothbrush you use, you may want to experiment with your design to get the best results. Try rebalancing the body by placing the battery further forward along its back, for example.

1

Before you start building anything, you'll need to amass your components and equipment. There's a list of what you'll need for this project opposite, but a few items need a little explaining. For the old toothbrush, any non-electric toothbrush will do, but if the bristles are too worn Bristlebug might not move very well. Toothbrushes with angled bristles are ideal, but not essential. The 1.5V battery should be the small, flat silver type, such as an LR44. If you don't have any spares lying around, you can order them in strips of 10 for about £1 from Amazon.

2

The vibration motor we're using is a device designed for a mobile phone – the component that buzzes and vibrates when the phone's in silent mode. These can be bought from Amazon for about £1 each. If you're feeling brave and there's an old, unused handset lying around, you could open it up to see if you can find its vibration motor – it should look like the one shown. Make sure you have the owner's permission first. Cracking open the mobile's case can be difficult, however, and it's unlikely that you'll be able to put it back together again.

3

Once you've got all the various bits and pieces, you can put them together. For Bristlebug's body, we just need the head of the toothbrush. We're going to cut off the handle using a Stanley knife, but you could use wirecutters. In either case, younger readers should get parents to help them, as the tools will be sharp. Place the toothbrush on a chopping board and saw off the majority of the handle, leaving a very short 'tail'. You may not need to saw all the way through, as once you've made a deep enough incision you can probably snap off the remainder.

4

The vibration motor we bought from Amazon came with a self-adhesive sticker on one side. If yours did, too, simply peel this off and stick the motor to the back of the toothbrush head, towards the top of the brush, the opposite end to the tail. If your vibration unit didn't come with an adhesive layer, or if you salvaged your motor from inside an old phone, you'll have to find another way to stick it onto the brush. Double-sided Sellotape is ideal, but you could fold a piece of normal Sellotape into a loop and use that instead.

5

The motor should have two very small wires. Both ends should be bare, but we needed to remove a bit more plastic coating to successfully make contact with the battery. You could use wirecutters, but the wires are so thin it's easy to accidentally cut right through them. The easiest way is to use your teeth and bite off about 5mm of coating. Next, take a small piece of double-sided Sellotape (or loop some single-sided tape) and place it so it runs down Bristlebug's back, then stick the red wire down so the bare end is facing up towards the tail end.

6

Take the watch battery and stick it flat side down to the back of the toothbrush head towards the 'tail' end – this will give Bristlebug some balance. The sticky tape you used will hold the battery in place. It's important to place the battery so that the flat surface makes contact with the bare end of the wire you stuck down. To complete the circuit, just touch the other wire to the top side of the battery and Bristlebug should start vibrating immediately. Use a small blob of Blu-tak to hold the top wire in place, then put him on a flat surface and watch him go!

EASY ELECTRONICS

We explain some of the basic principles behind working with electronics in simple terms to help you get started with your own practical projects

WHAT YOU'LL LEARN

- What electric circuits are and how they work
- Why an electric current flows around a circuit
- How Ohm's Law works and why it's useful

Building Magbot is going to involve using two main disciplines: writing programming code and working with electronics. Don't worry if you're not familiar with either, as we'll explain most of the important bits as we work though our projects. But before we start putting together any electronic parts, you might find it useful to wrap your head around one or two underlying principles first.

Even if you've never worked with electronics before, you may already have a grasp of some of the basics without realising it. You'll know from magnets, for example, that like poles repel and opposite poles attract, and the same principle is central to the way electronic circuits work.

Over the next few pages, we're going to explain some of the key concepts behind electronics in simple terms. We won't be able to cover all aspects or go into masses of detail, so think of this as a crash course in theory to help you get onto practical stuff as quickly as possible. You should find that most of it is surprisingly straightforward. We're not university professors or professional engineers, so we've tried to make everything as accessible as possible. But, equally, don't worry too much if you find some of it confusing at this stage. Those who already have a good idea about how current, voltage and resistance work could skip ahead. Everyone should familiarise themselves with the rules for working safely, however, so we've dedicated a separate section later in this chapter.

WHAT'S AN ELECTRIC CIRCUIT?

All electronic devices basically work in the same way: an electric circuit is created, which causes a current to flow through various components. To create a circuit, you need a power source (such as a battery), a conductor (the wiring that carries the electricity from one place to another) and a load (the device the electricity is powering, such as a light bulb). The circuit may also include a control device, a simple example of which would be a switch. When the switch is on, it will connect the circuit to let electricity flow; when it's off, it will break the circuit to stop the flow of electricity. So why does electricity flow in the first place?

WHAT'S AN ELECTRIC CURRENT?

In very basic terms, electronics is the manipulation of something called electrons. These are tiny particles that all have a negative electric charge. On a power supply, such as a battery, you'll find a negative terminal containing lots of electrons and a positive terminal containing far fewer electrons. Since like poles repel and opposite poles attract, the negatively charged electrons will always try to find the quickest way to get away from each other and move over to the positive terminal, and they will travel through anything that can provide them with a path to get there. This flow of charged electrons is called an electric current.

Now we definitely don't recommend doing this, but let's say you connected a wire from the negative terminal on your battery directly to the positive one. In this case, the electrons would flow straight down the wire from negative to positive. Not only would that be a bit of a waste, it would also create the ultimate short circuit (see below for more on these) and you could even end

JUST TO CONFUSE YOU

So, remember when we told you that electrons flowed from negative to positive? Well, just to confuse matters, many circuit diagrams found in textbooks or engineering schematics will include arrows that show the flow of electric current going from positive to negative. This is called 'conventional flow' and it's something of a hangover from the early days of electricity when it was thought the flow went the opposite way round to what we know today – blame Benjamin Franklin and his pioneering experiments with electricity in the 1750s! Thankfully, it doesn't make much difference which way electricity is shown to flow, and we won't be using many circuit diagrams in this guide anyway.

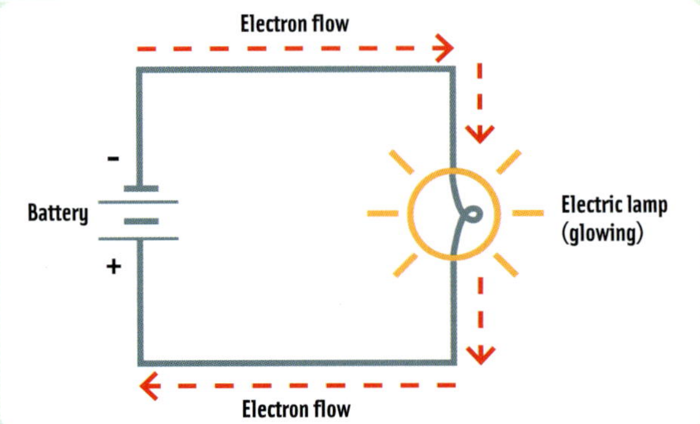

The key thing to understand is that voltage, current and resistance are always directly proportional to each other

up with a fire on your hands. Instead, you could put the flow of electrons to much better (and safer) use by including other components in the circuit between the negative and the positive terminals – components that are able to take advantage of the electrical current passing through them. A simple example might be adding a light emitting diode (LED). Now, the electrons need to rush through the LED on their way from negative to positive. The LED responds to the electrical current passing through it by releasing energy in the form of light and heat. Different types of components respond to or interact with current flow in different ways.

MEASURING AND CALCULATING

In any electrical circuit, there are three important factors in play – current, voltage and resistance – and each one has a direct relationship with the other two. As we said above, current is the flow of electricity. It's measured in amps (A). Voltage (measured in volts, or V) is the 'pressure' of the electrical flow. Resistance, in ohms (or by the symbol Ω), is the measure of how difficult or easy it is for electricity to flow through a circuit. The relationship these three share is often likened to the flow of water through pipework – voltage 'pumps' the flow of current through any resistance it encounters in the pipes on its way.

The key thing to understand is that voltage, current and resistance are always directly proportional to each other, and this is essentially what Ohm's Law is. Ohm's Law states that current is equal to voltage over resistance and is often represented by the formula **I = V/R**, where 'I' is the current in amps, 'V' is the voltage in volts, and 'R' is the resistance in ohms. The same formula can also be written **V = IxR** or **R = I/V**, meaning that it's always possible to calculate one of the values as long as you know the other two. Likewise, if you make a change to any of the three values in a circuit, you can easily calculate the effect it will have on the others. Have a look at the triangle diagram right. This will help you remember how Ohm's Law works.

Don't worry – we won't be testing you on this later! But, should you wish to continue working with electronics beyond the main projects in this book, you'll often find you need to refer back to Ohm's Law to help you build circuits.

OTHER KEY CONCEPTS

With those main principles under your belt, you should have a good grasp on the main ideas behind how electronics function. There are loads of other important concepts and rules that we could explain here, but we don't want to overload you at this stage. We'll explain other ideas as and when we need to in our projects. There are also many related topics that you won't need to know to build your first robot, so we won't be covering these at all. If you're interested, though, have a look at our 'Further reading' box on p16 for more information. Before we start making our own circuits, however, there are a few

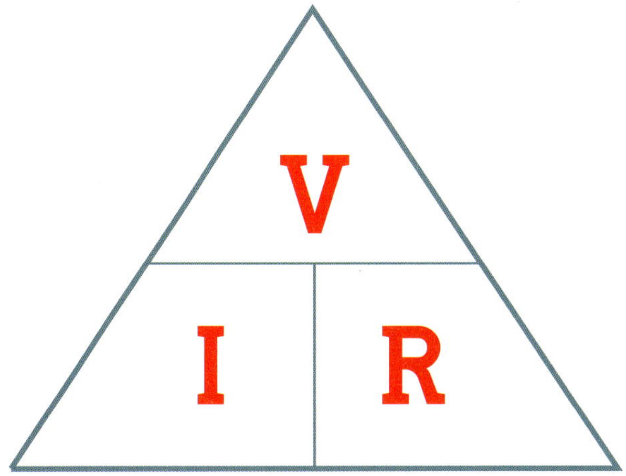

▲ Ohm's Law states that current is equal to voltage over resistance.

LEMON BATTERY

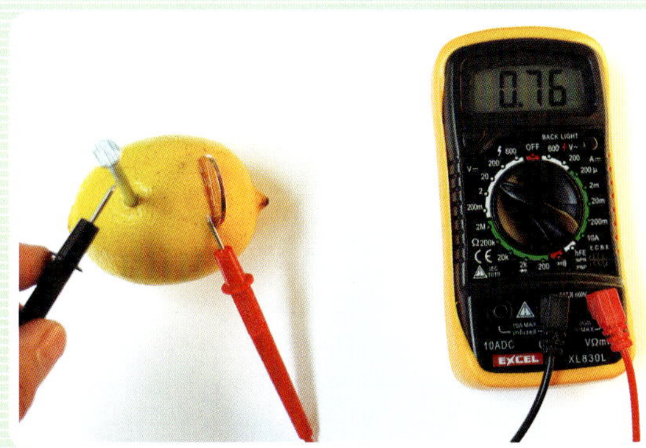

Batteries work using an electrochemical reaction to produce an electric current. In very basic terms, a battery has two electrodes – one is made of a material that has lots of electrons (negative) and the other is made of a material that has very few electrons (positive). These two electrodes are isolated from each other internally by a chemical called an electrolyte that blocks electrons. So, it's not until the electrodes are connected externally via a circuit that the electrons can flow from negative to positive, providing a current as they go.

You can carry out a brilliant experiment at home to demonstrate how batteries work – all you need is a galvanised (zinc-coated) nail and a copper coin for the electrodes, and a lemon for the electrolyte.

Stick the nail into one side of the lemon and insert the copper coin into the other side – and that's it. To prove the lemon battery is producing an electric current, test it with a multimeter (see chapter 2) and you should see a low voltage being produced. This isn't enough to power anything much, but if you link three or four lemon batteries together in series by connecting the copper coin on one to the galvanised nail on the next with crocodile clips, you could increase the voltage enough to illuminate an LED.

further related concepts you might want to bone up on, and we've summarised these below. You'll find even more definitions of electronics terms in our glossary on p142.

AC versus DC

There are two types of electric current – direct current (DC), which is the type usually supplied by a battery and alternating current (AC), which is the type supplied via a mains socket. The main difference is that with DC, the current flows in one direction only, while with AC, the current continually switches between flowing in one direction and the other. AC can be very dangerous indeed, so we'll be avoiding it altogether in this book. All the circuits we'll be creating use DC.

Conductors and insulators

Conductors are components that are capable of allowing an electric current to flow freely, while insulators are the opposite – components that block the flow of electricity. Certain types of material make ideal conductors and insulators. Metals are good conductors. Copper is used in most electrical wiring. Plastic, rubber, glass and ceramic, meanwhile, are often employed as insulators – mains wiring is always housed in a plastic coating to insulate it.

Resistors

Resistors are vital components in electronic circuits – they literally resist the flow of current. And why would you want that? Well, basically it's a way of controlling the current. In a simple circuit with a 5V power supply and a single LED, for instance, connecting the power directly might pass too much current through the LED and damage your components. Pop a resistor into the circuit, however, and you can lower the current in your circuit accordingly. We'll be explaining more about using resistors in chapter 3.

Ground

The term 'ground' can refer to several slightly different things in electronics, depending on the context. In our projects, all ground (GND) means is the connection to zero volts in the circuit.

Series and parallel

When your components are connected in a consecutive chain, this is described as 'in series'. In series, the current can only flow in one straight path. When components are connected parallel to each other, this is called 'in parallel' and the current will flow in several paths.

Open and short circuits

Two of the most common problems with electronics are open and short circuits. Current won't flow at all if the path of the circuit is open at any point, so check your power supply, conductors and components are all connected properly and returned to ground.

A short circuit, on the other hand, is where the current finds an unintended path through your circuit, potentially bypassing key components, such as resistors or loads. Current will always seek the shortest path through the circuit. But if there's little or nothing to resist current flow, this will result in a much higher current than intended, which could be dangerous, burning up any components along the way. Many electronic devices have built-in circuit breakers or fuses that will intentionally create an open circuit and stop all current flow as a safety measure, if it detects a current that's too high.

Mains wiring is housed in a plastic coating.

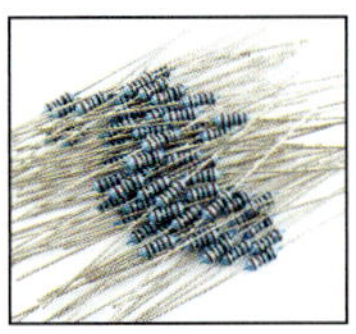

Resistors resist the flow of current.

WIRE COLOUR

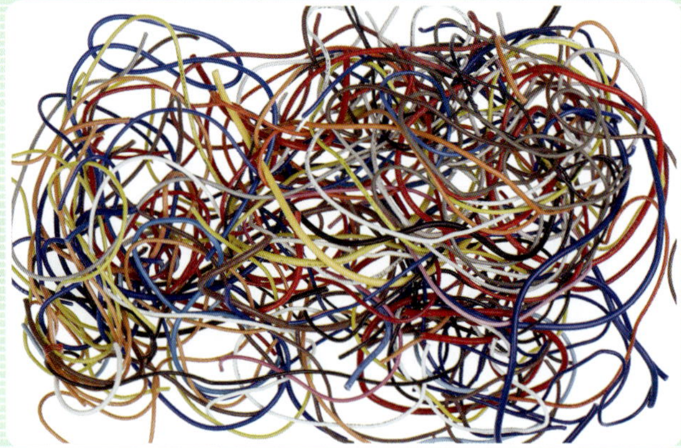

In the diagrams throughout our practical projects, we'll be sticking to a specific colour coding for the wires we use. In each project, we'll be using red wires for power and black wires for ground, as these are generally considered the standard colours associated with these concepts. For other types of connections, we've used mainly yellow and blue wires in our diagrams, for no other reason other than for clarity and continuity. In truth, the colours you use yourself won't matter in the slightest, though using similar colours for similar types of components – all orange wires for resistors, for example – can help you recognise and learn about how the various types of connection work. If you buy a component kit like the one we recommend in the next chapter, however, you'll probably find that you're somewhat restricted by whatever colours come in the box.

FURTHER READING

If you're keen to learn more about electronics, there are dozens of great websites with information aimed at beginners. Here are a few of our favourites to get you started:

- **Electronics Club** www.snipca.com/12719
- **All About Circuits** www.snipca.com/12720
- **Sparkfun** www.snipca.com/12721
- **Adafruit** www.snipca.com/12722
- **Electronics Teacher** www.snipca.com/12723
- **Collin's Lab** www.snipca.com/12724
- **Circuit Lab** www.snipca.com/12725

INTRODUCING ARDUINO

At the heart of the robot you're about to build is a very clever piece of hardware – a microcontroller. We're going to explain what it is and how it works

WHAT YOU'LL LEARN

- How we can make electronic devices 'intelligent'
- What a microcontroller is and why it's useful
- Why we're using an Arduino Uno for our robot

The Bristlebug we built earlier is a lot of fun, but it's also quite possibly one of the most unintelligent types of robot that you can create. It doesn't have any real way of sensing its own environment, other than randomly bumping off anything it comes into contact with. And it doesn't have any logic to interpret its surroundings, or the ability to perform anything other than one single, simple function: to vibrate around the place until either its battery runs out or it gets stuck behind the fridge.

But what if we could give a robot like Bristlebug a brain? What if we could attach sensors to it so that it could see and hear? What if we could program it so that it can react to its environment intelligently and 'think' for itself? And what if we could provide it with a way to carry out more than one task? You 'd need something bigger and more manoeuvrable than Bristlebug for all this, but suddenly you're starting to make something that's more like a 'proper' robot. So where exactly do we get a brain from?

The Uno's designers have included a number of key features on the circuit board that make it easy for beginners.

WHAT'S A MICROCONTROLLER?

In theory, we could use a small PC – such as a Raspberry Pi – for our robot's brain, but we don't really need all the processing power of the CPU, or the memory or the advanced capabilities of a full-blown computer. It would probably consume power too quickly for our needs, and we certainly won't need the ability to run a complex operating system. So, instead of a PC, we're going to use something called a microcontroller.

A microcontroller is a type of chip that you'll often find being used in many 'embedded' systems – that's to say low-powered computerised systems that are built into devices and are designed to carry out a particular task or tasks. An example of this might be a washing machine, which obviously doesn't need an entire PC powering it, but which requires a computer chip to allow it to perform certain automatic functions. And for that, a microcontroller is ideal. Most modern appliances these days use multiple microcontrollers in order to operate.

The main equipment you'll need to get started on your first projects.

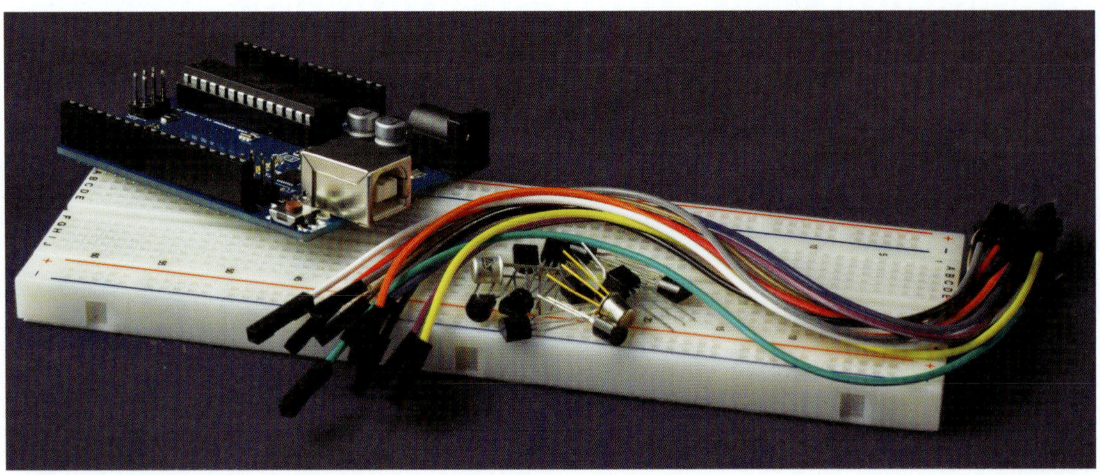

WHAT'S ONBOARD?

The Arduino Uno isn't just a microcontroller – it has lots of other useful features built in. Here, we offer a brief guided tour of the main parts of the device we'll be using for Magbot's 'brain'. Note that if you're using an unofficial (or 'clone') Arduino, the layout of the board may look different

1 Reset button This lets you reboot the Arduino and restart any program that is loaded onto it without having to disconnect the board from a power source.

2 USB port Provides an easy way to upload programs to your Uno – simply connect it to your PC. USB can also supply power to the Arduino board.

3 Power socket An external DC power supply, such as a battery pack or an adaptor, can be attached to power the board when it's not being powered by a PC.

4 Power pins These are used to provide either 5V or 3.3V of power to the other components in your circuits. There's also a GND pin here to ground your circuit.

5 Analog input pins These six pins can read a constantly varying signal from an analog input (such as a temperature sensor) and convert it into a digital value.

6 Microcontroller The microcontroller is the Uno's main integrated circuit; the brains of the board. The Arduino Uno uses an Amtel ATmega328 chip.

7 Power LED This onboard LED illuminates when a power source (including USB) is connected to your Arduino Uno. If it doesn't light up, it's likely there's a problem.

8 Digital pins These 14 pins (numbered 0 to 13) can connect both inputs and outputs. The ones with the tilde (~) symbol are PWM pins, which can 'simulate' analog output.

9 TX, RX and L TX and RX are LEDs that illuminate to show when the Uno has transmitted (TX) or received (RX) information. L is an onboard LED associated with pin 13.

10 GND pin One of several ground pins on the Uno board. This can be used to ground (in other words, provide a return path for) your circuits.

1 First steps

▸ This Arduino Ethernet shield adds networking.

Microcontrollers look like other integrated circuits (ICs) – usually a small black square or oblong with a number of metal legs. Essentially, they're tiny, simplified computers with their own CPU, memory, and input/output connections, just like your desktop or laptop PC. Except with microcontrollers, all of this is housed on one small, often inexpensive chip.

Every microcontroller has a series of digital input/output pins via which it interacts with other components. Some of these pins can be switched to either 'High' (or '1') or 'Low' (or '0') through programming instructions. For example, if you wanted to switch an LED on and off, you could connect it to one of the microcontroller's digital pins, then program the pin to output 'High' (on) followed by a 'Low' (off) in a continuous loop.

If that sounds a bit simple, that's because it is. And it's this simplicity that makes starting out with your own electronics projects much easier and more enjoyable than you might assume. Once you get a bit more practice, you'll discover that you can use a microcontroller's pins in lots of clever combinations in order to achieve some fairly complex actions. And, in addition, some microcontrollers feature something called an analog-to-digital converter (ADC), which allows them to measure the full range of a constantly varying (analog) signal, rather than just high or low.

▾ The ATMEGA 328 Microcontroller.

From our perspective, microcontrollers can be very useful for making robots. Indeed, many 'real' robots, such as those you find on industrial assembly lines, are built using microcontrollers.

WHY ARDUINO?

Certain types of microcontrollers are more suitable for beginners and hobbyists than others. In this book, we'll be using an Arduino Uno

ARDUINO HISTORY

Like the Raspberry Pi, the Arduino Uno has its roots in an educational background. Before Arduino came along, many electronics students and hobbyists used a microcontroller called BASIC Stamp, made by an American company Parallax Inc (www.parallax.com). The trouble was, the BASIC Stamp was neither very powerful nor particularly affordable. So, in 2005, a group of Italian academics and engineers designed a microcontroller board that was intended to make it much easier and cheaper for beginners and enthusiasts to get started. The board was dubbed 'Arduino' (allegedly named after a bar in the Italian town of Ivrea) and was quickly adopted as the platform of choice by thousands of users. It's estimated that there are at least 700,000 Arduinos currently 'in the wild' – and that's only counting official boards.

ARDUINO VARIANTS

There are at least 20 different types of official Arduino board, including ones with built-in networking (such as the Arduino Ethernet) and others that are designed for wearable use (such as the tiny, round Arduino LilyPad). There are also various revisions of some products – the R3 version of the Uno that we're using, for example, offers a number of small improvements over the R2 version. On top of that there are numerous shields and accessories that can be added. See arduino.cc/en/Main/Products for more details on the official products available. As we've already mentioned, there are also lots of unofficial copycat alternatives on the market, many of which are considerably cheaper than their official counterparts. We'll be looking at these more in the next chapter.

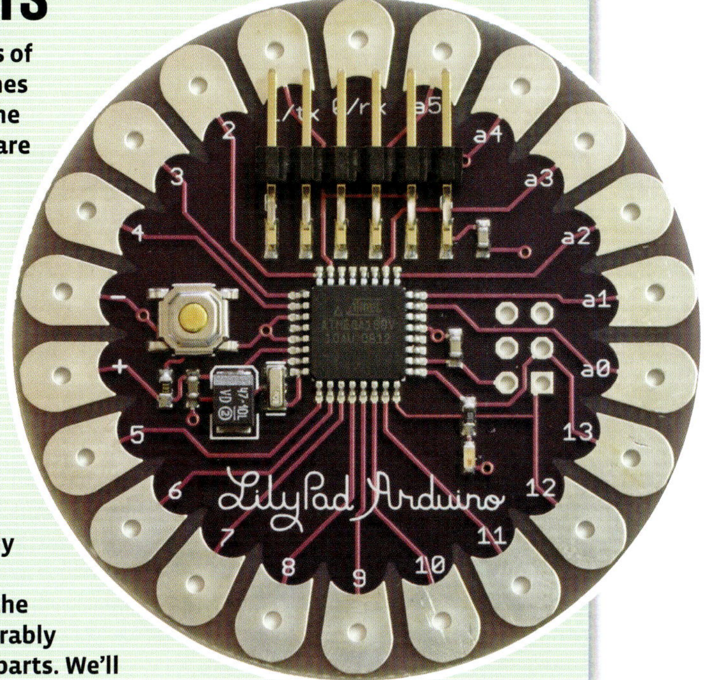

(arduino.cc), and there are a number of reasons why the Uno is the best candidate for the job. Here are five of them:

1 It's designed for beginners

First of all, the Arduino Uno is a 'single-board' microcontroller. All this really means is that the microcontroller chip itself – an Amtel ATmega328 on the most recent official models – comes built onto a circuit board. But the big difference is that the Uno's designers have elected to include a number of other key features on the circuit board that make it easier for beginners to get started, such as a USB port for connecting to a computer, a power socket, a reset button and solder-free connectors for all its input/output pins, so you can just plug in wires and pull them out again as needed. See the diagram on p19 for more about the board.

2 It's easy to program

The Arduino comes with its own software – or 'integrated development environment' (IDE) – which makes it easy to write and upload programming code to the microcontroller. The programming language it uses is C++, but the Arduino software makes it easy to understand and learn this by providing lots of examples and 'real' English comments (see chapter 3 for more on programming). Better still, the Uno's microcontroller chip is pre-programmed with a boot loader, which allows you to upload new code to it without the need for any external hardware.

3 It's open source

The Arduino platform is designed to be completely open source, which means that anybody can adapt and share both the hardware design and the software. There are many benefits to this, including the fact that Arduino is supported by a large, helpful community of fellow users – just go to **forum.arduino.cc/** to see them in action. The schematic for the Uno board is freely available, too, so you can even build your own. In fact, we'll be showing you how in chapter 8.

4 It's expandable

Another great thing about Arduino devices is that you can add accessories, such as 'shields' – expansion boards that add specific functions, such as wireless communication. We'll be using a motor shield later on (see chapter 5) when we build Magbot. Shields slot into the existing board easily and allow you to carry on using all the Arduino Uno's pins as usual.

5 It's cheap

You can pick up an official Arduino Uno for less than £20 online. They cost a little more (about £25) if you buy one from a high-street shop, such as Maplin. But because the hardware is open source, there are a lot of unofficial Arduino boards around, some of which cost as little as £8, or even less if you shop around. There are pros and cons to going the unofficial route, however, as we'll be explaining in chapter 2.

TAKE MICRO-CONTROL

As well as the Arduino Uno itself, we'll need a number of other components for our robot. In the next chapter, we'll show you exactly what you need and where to buy it from. Remember to check our safety tips later in this chapter as well. Don't worry if the business of microcontrollers still feels like a bit of a mystery at the moment. Everything will begin to fall in place once we've started attaching components and trying out our first few projects.

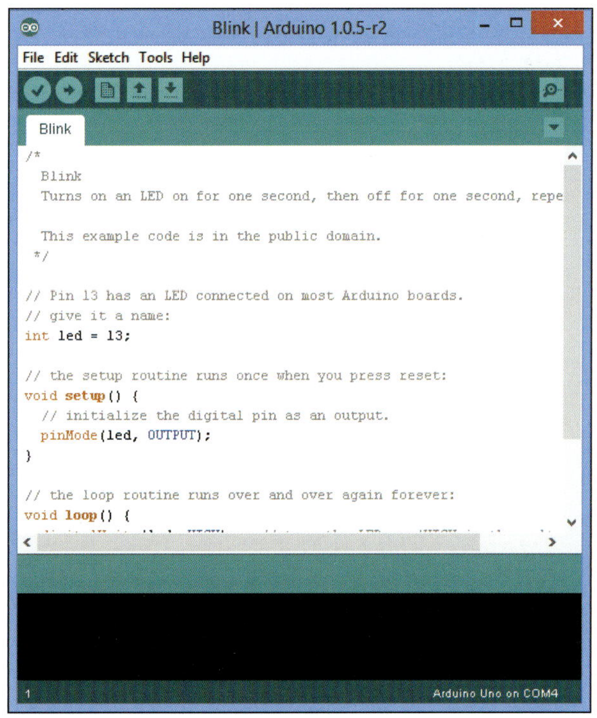

▲ **The Arduino comes with its own IDE software.**

GETTING STARTED WITH ARDUINO UNO

It's time to plug in, power up and program your Arduino microcontroller for the very first time

WHAT YOU'LL NEED

- An Arduino Uno board
- A USB cable
- A computer

One of the major benefits of the Arduino Uno is how easy it is to get started. With just a handful of cheap components and some free software, you can set yourself up and start programming within a few minutes. To prove it, we're going to get you started in six easy steps and take you right up to the point where you upload your first simple program – or 'sketch' – to the board. You won't need all the items from our shopping list in chapter 2 for this workshop – just the Arduino Uno board itself, a PC and a USB cable. This will need to be an 'A' plug to 'B' plug type cable, like those used by many printers, rather than a standard USB cable. We're going to assume you're using a Windows PC, though instructions will be all but identical for anyone using a Mac or a Linux system.

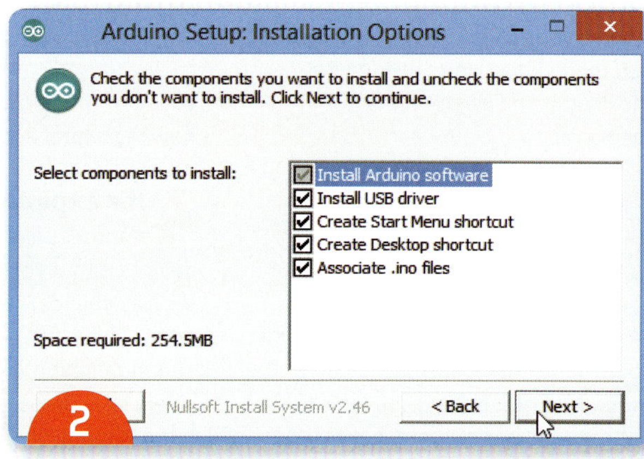

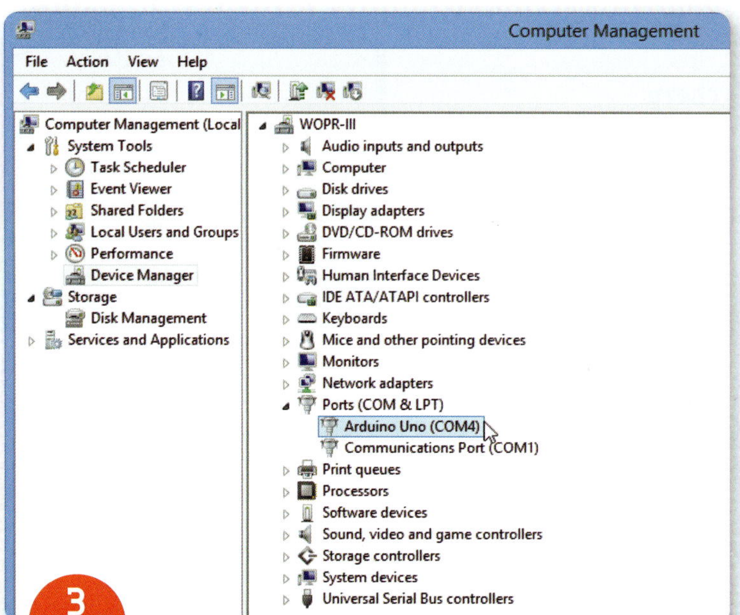

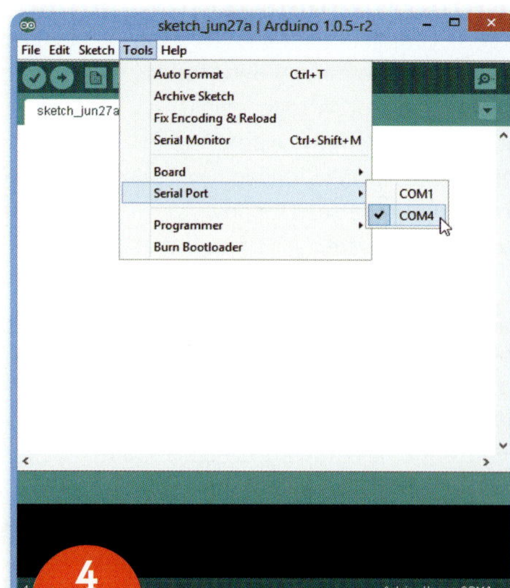

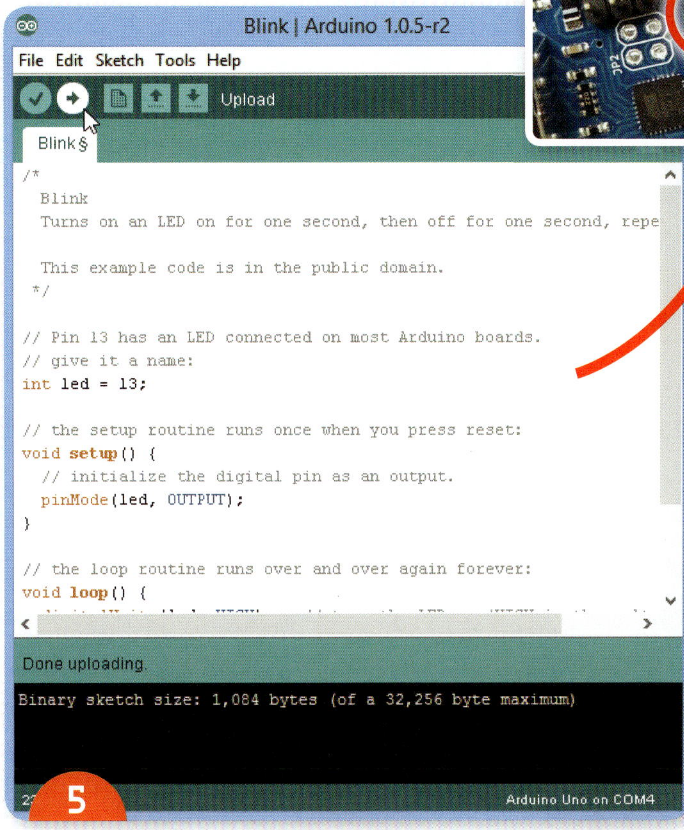

TIP

Sometimes, the Arduino device driver may fail to install when you first plug the Uno into your PC. And if you're using a cheap Arduino clone instead of a genuine board, you may encounter other installation problems. Turn to our troubleshooting section in chapter 9 for solutions.

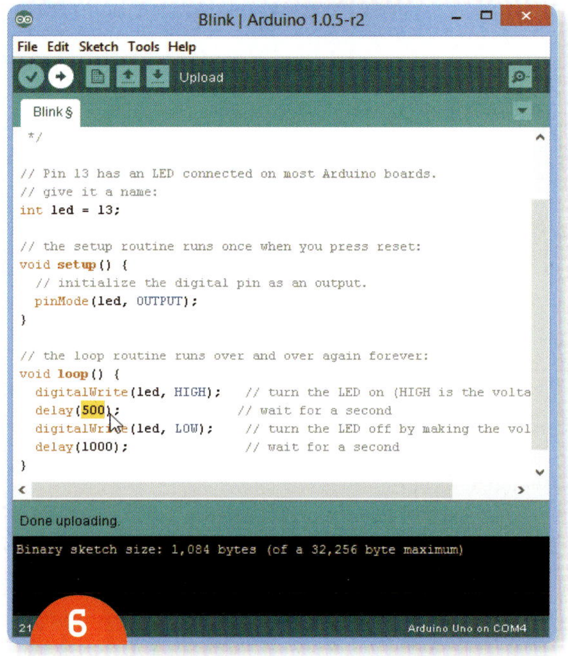

1

First, you'll need to download the Arduino Uno drivers and IDE software. Windows users should go to **arduino.cc/en/Main/Software**, scroll down to the 'Arduino IDE' heading and click on the Windows Installer link. The current version is 1.0.5 and we recommend downloading this even if a newer version becomes available, as it's the version we've used in this book. Mac and Linux versions can be found here, too. Save the software, then double-click the file to begin installation and agree to the licence terms.

2

On the next screen, leave all the components ticked and click Next followed by Install. During installation, you'll be prompted to install the driver software – click Install then Close. Now, get your USB cable. The square 'B' plug fits into the socket on your Uno and the more familiar flat 'A' plug goes into your PC. We recommend plugging the Uno directly into your computer rather than a USB hub or a USB port on your keyboard, as the board needs to draw power over USB. When you plug the Uno into your PC, the Uno's green power light will switch on.

3

Your PC should automatically recognise the new hardware and install the necessary device driver for it. Make a note of the COM port number shown in the Setup window. If you miss this message, you can find out which COM port your Uno is associated with by right-clicking My Computer and selecting Manage (Windows XP) or by pressing the Windows key, typing **device manager** and pressing Enter on your keyboard (Windows 7 and 8). Click 'Ports (COM & LPT)' and you should see an entry for Arduino Uno with a COM port next to it. In our case, it's COM 4.

4

Open the Arduino software – there should be a shortcut on your desktop but, if not, press the Windows key, type **arduino** and press Enter (or look under Start, All Programs if you're using Windows XP). A small, blank window will open. You'll need to specify which type of board you're using, so click the Tools menu, then click board and select Arduino Uno. You'll also need to specify the COM port the board is using. Click Tools again, then click Serial Port and select the COM port that you noted down. Now, we're ready to upload our first program to the Arduino

5

Click File, Examples, '01 Basic' then Blink. Another Arduino window will open with some code in the main area – a simple sketch designed to make an LED blink. To upload this to your Uno, click the right-pointing arrow button in the top toolbar. On the board, the TX & RX lights will briefly flash to show communication has occurred. When the upload is finished, the message 'Done uploading' will appear near the bottom of the Arduino window and the LED marked 'L' should blink. You've just done the electronics equivalent of running your first 'hello world' PC program!

6

Arduino boards often ship with the Blink sketch pre-loaded, meaning the 'L' LED may start blinking as soon as you plug it into your PC and you won't see any change after uploading the code in the previous step. So to prove we're uploading a program, let's adapt the sketch by changing the frequency of the blink. Scroll down to where it says 'void loop' and you'll see 'delay (1000)' listed twice – this is the number of milliseconds that the Uno will wait before executing the next line of code. Change both values to 500 and upload the sketch again – now the 'L' LED will blink faster.

IN THIS CHAPTER

HOW TO BUILD A ROBOT

WHAT YOU NEED

Robots don't build themselves, which means it's up to us humans to put all the parts together. But before we do, we need to know which parts to get and where we can get them from. In this chapter, we'll be providing lots of buying advice for anyone interested in building robots and tinkering with other electronic gizmos. We'll explain how to get everything at the cheapest possible prices. Not only that, but we'll also tell you what tools you should gather together and how to stay safe when working on your electronics projects.

BUYER'S GUIDE

We explain what you'll need to build your robot, where to buy it from and how to save money

WHAT YOU'LL LEARN

- **Where to find the items you need for your projects**
- **How to save money when shopping for components**
- **How to recognise counterfeit Arduino products**

If you're going to set about building a robot, you're going to need something to build it from. And if you're new to electronics, you might well be wondering exactly what parts you need and where on earth you're going to get them from. Well, that's where this section of our book comes in.

Over the next few pages, we're going to be talking about what your robot will be made of and where you can purchase the things you need and the best prices. Then, on p30, we'll provide you with a custom-designed shopping list of everything you'll need to follow the projects in this book.

BUYING THE BRAIN

We've already talked about the most important part of your robot – its brain. Back in chapter 1, we introduced you to the Arduino Uno. Pretty much every project we'll be carrying out in this book relies on having an Uno to hand. You can pick up an Arduino board from a variety of online or high-street stores and prices can vary. In the UK, Maplin is probably the biggest bricks-and-mortar retailer selling the Uno. Walking in off the street to buy an Uno is one of the more expensive ways to get hold of one – it will cost about £25 – but you'll also be able to browse all the other electronic goodies the store has while you're there.

Amazon is a great source for electronic components and we'll explain why in a moment. The retailer is currently selling the Arduino Uno for about £22 including delivery.

▼ A breadboard allows you to construct projects without any soldering.

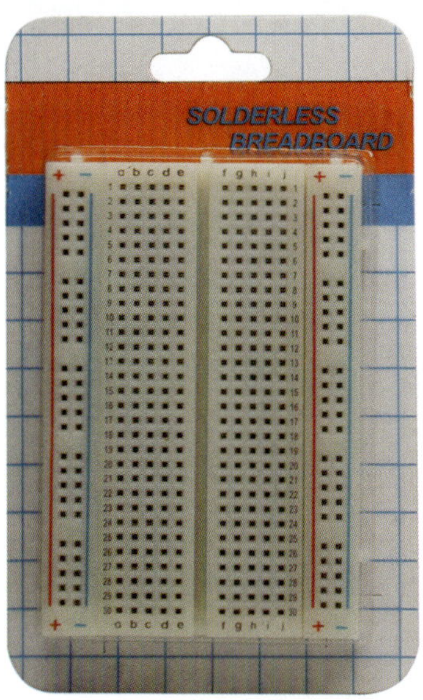

▲ The Adafruit Boarduino clone acts like an Arduino, and works with the latest Arduino software.

The Arduino store itself (**store.arduino.cc**) is currently selling the device for £20 including VAT, but you'll then need to factor in roughly another £4 (and up to six days) for delivery.

One way to save more than just a couple of pounds is to opt for a non-official Uno board. We mentioned these back in the previous chapter and they can provide an extremely cheap way for beginners to get going with their own projects. You might wonder about the legality of such products. But because of the open source nature of Arduino hardware, people are encouraged to use, improve upon and build their own hardware. And this means that lots of companies have produced their own devices based on the original Uno design. Most of these companies are legitimate and their products are designed to adapt or improve on the Uno in some way, whether that's via adding features, altering the aesthetics or lowering the cost. For example, Adafruit (**www.adafruit.com**) is a US-based website aimed at helping people to learn about

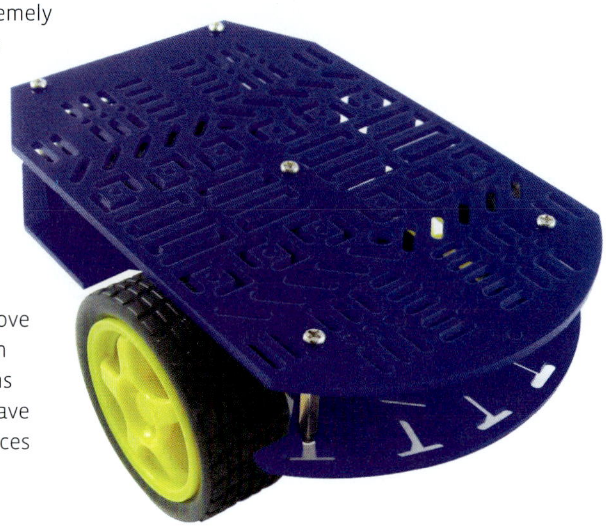

▶ Magbot's chassis and wheels.

electronics. It also has its own online store where, alongside official Arduino products, it also sells something called a Boarduino – an £10 Arduino-compatible device that users can build themselves onto a breadboard. We'll be showing you how to do something similar yourself in chapter 8.

Run a search for 'Arduino compatible' on Amazon and you'll find dozens of Uno-like boards for sale, many for less than £10. Some of these require you to assemble the board yourself, others are pre-built for you but look somewhat different to the official board. In most cases, however, if it claims to be 'compatible' this usually means that it's built around the same microcontroller as the Uno and will work with the Arduino IDE software.

If you do decide to go this route, you'll need to take into account the fact that your unofficial board will look different and may even work a little differently to the ones we'll be using in this book.

HOW TO TELL A FAKE

The flip side of this is the slightly sleazy world of counterfeits. Buying a cheap product that describes itself as Uno-compatible is one thing, but paying for something that claims to be a genuine Arduino product, only to later discover it's a fake is another issue entirely.

While Arduino itself actively encourages users to experiment and build upon its products, the company understandably takes a pretty dim view of anyone who attempts to pass its products off as the genuine article.

One of the more compelling reasons for buying an official Arduino device is that you're ensuring that some of the money spent will go back into supporting the ongoing development of the technology. Inadvertently buy a fake, on the other hand, and your cash could be hurting, rather than helping, the company. In addition, just like a fake Rolex watch, fake Arduinos often originate from the Far East. They're usually made from substandard components and are much more likely to break. Some may not even work properly with the Arduino IDE software.

So, if you prefer to go the official route rather than the 'compatible' one, how can you tell whether the Uno you're buying is the real deal and not a cheap knock-off? Well, buying from a respected retailer is always a good place to start. Obviously, if you get your Uno from Maplin or – better still – the official Arduino store, you'll have very little to worry about. Amazon is pretty safe, too, as long as you're buying from Amazon itself, as opposed to a private seller. See p29 for a list of other respected vendors.

The trouble is, some fakes can be pretty convincing, complete with official-looking logos, trademarks and so on. There are some giveaways to look out for, though. Does it say 'made in Italy' on the front and rear of the board? If not, it could be fake. Counterfeit Unos also tend to be deeper blue rather than the distinctive greeny-blue of the original. Some of the components may look different or might be located in a

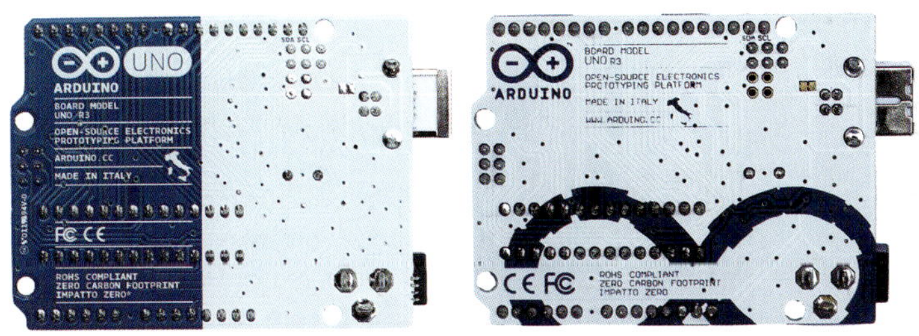

▲ A real Uno left, and a fake Uno right.

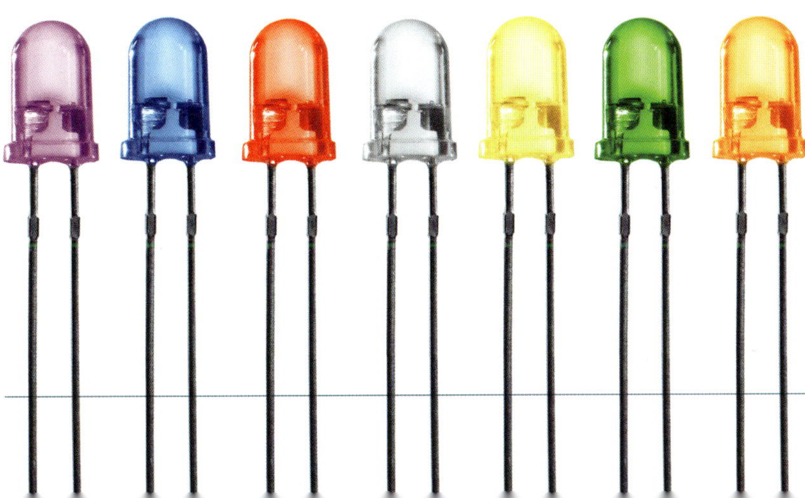

◀ LEDs - you'll use lots of these!

SALVAGE AND RECYCLE

Later in this chapter, we've provided a shopping list of items you can buy for the projects in this book, but part of the fun of working with electronics is the way in which many of the materials you use can be salvaged from other devices. Wires are a very good example. The component kit we've recommended comes with a big bundle of jumper wires that you can use to connect your circuits, but you could just as easily use wires you've appropriated yourself from discarded electronic devices, such as old toys that no longer work. For Magbot, we repurposed the thumbstick from a broken Xbox controller and used it as his nose. We're not suggesting that you take to pieces any devices that are currently in use, but if, say, you have an old PC sitting in a garage or loft waiting to go to the dump, it can be cannibalised for all kinds of components, including its wires. Bear in mind that there are some devices, such as old CRT televisions, that are not safe to take apart. For more on safety, head to the end of this chapter.

2 What you need

Your unofficial board will look different and may work differently to the ones we'll be using in this book.

non-standard place, like the reset button, for example. On most genuine Arduino Unos, the onboard power LED is green and the 'L' LED is yellow. If you're using a clone board, you may find that some or all of the LEDs are different colours – often red. For more clues and comparisons, have a look at **arduino.cc/en/Products/Counterfeit**.

OTHER COMPONENTS

The other component we'll be using in almost all our projects is a breadboard – sometimes known as a protoboard. This humble device is the cornerstone of home electronics, as it allows you to construct projects without the need for any soldering. Their name comes from the fact that early electronics enthusiasts made their own prototypes using wooden breadboards with rows of nails hammered into them. We'll be explaining more about how breadboards work in the next chapter, but a basic half-sized breadboard like the one we'll be using throughout this book shouldn't cost you much more than about £2 if you shop online.

Amazon is a great place to buy breadboards and most of the other electronic components you'll be needing, as it provides you with access to a large community of private sellers via its Marketplace. Prices are highly competitive and it's usually very easy to find what you need. As with the Arduino hardware, some of the general electronic components that are for sale originate from China and the Far East, and these are often incredibly cheap. Items ordered from distant sources can take much longer to be delivered, so if you want something in a hurry, check the seller's details to see where the items are being shipped from. Usually the product page will say 'shipped from the UK' or 'shipped from Hong Kong' or similar. Buying anything from independent foreign sellers over long distances always carries a certain risk factor. But because components are so cheap, if they get lost or break quickly, you won't have wasted anything more than a pound or two.

Other good places to shop include online stores that cater for Raspberry Pi users, as there's a lot of crossover when it comes to building hardware projects. Sites like **thepihut.com** and **www.modmypi.com** sell lots of useful components and accessories, and many have started selling Arduino boards, too.

WHAT YOU DON'T NEED

There are a few items associated with electronics that you might assume you need, such as a soldering iron. But our aim is to keep things simple and cheap, so we've made it possible to carry out all of the projects in this book without having to go anywhere near a soldering iron, or, indeed, any solder wire.

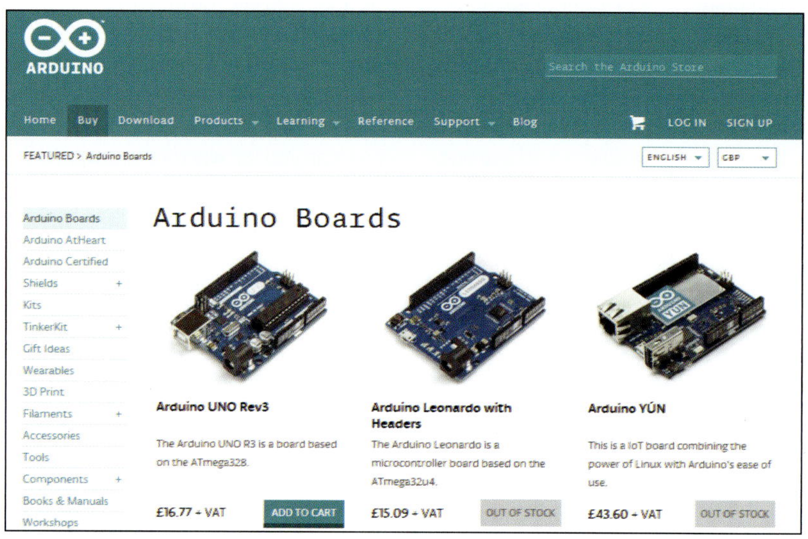

The official Arduino store is currently selling the Uno for £20 including VAT.

▲ The motor shield: third-party build it yourself.

THINGS WILL BREAK

You'll need to face up to the fact that, when you start out experimenting with electronics, you'll break things. It's inevitable. Even when you start gaining more confidence in your own abilities, you'll occasionally cause a short circuit or misplace a resistor and accidentally blow an LED or melt a wire. These things happen, so don't feel too bad about it. Almost all your components will cost less than a pound to replace, unless you damage the Uno itself. Even if you have to replace your Arduino with a new official board, £20 probably isn't going to break the bank. You'll need to be a little careful with your PC, but we'll explain more about this at the end of the chapter.

Key components that we'll be using in our projects include LEDs – light emitting diodes – resistors, buttons, jumper wires and various sensors. You could buy all these items separately, but when you're starting out it makes much more sense to get hold of an electronics component kit. These are aimed at hobbyists and beginners, and they tend to bundle together lots of common components in one box. They're often pretty good value for money, too, compared to buying items individually. And if you get one that's specifically designed to be used with an Arduino, you'll often find it comes with a CD containing sample sketches – programs for your microcontroller that you can try out and adapt yourself. That's why we've put one on our shopping list for making Magbot – a £20 box of tricks from a UK company called Hobby Components Ltd, which trade via Amazon. It includes a great selection of bits and pieces, and we'll be using a lot of the components it contains throughout this book.

ANYTHING ELSE?

To get Magbot moving, we'll need some wheels, motors and a chassis to carry him around. Again, you can buy all these parts separately, but it's usually easier (and often cheaper) to buy a pack that includes all the components you need. See our shopping list for specific examples. Finally, there's one last major piece of the puzzle – the motor shield. Shields are accessories designed to add a function of some kind to your Arduino Uno; in this case, it will drive the motors that power our robot's wheels. We'll explain more about how shields work in chapter 5 of this book. The key thing to know when buying them, however, is that, like the Uno itself, they come in official and unofficial varieties. Official shields cost more money; the motor shield made by Arduino itself costs about £28 on Amazon, for example, but third-party equivalents can be bought for as little as £5. A word of warning – some cheap motor shields require you to build the board yourself. This is usually relatively straightforward, but it will require the use of a soldering iron.

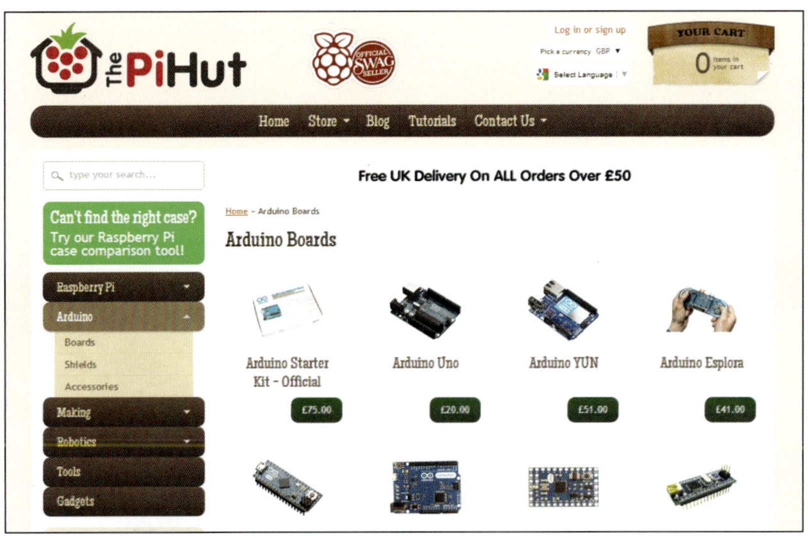

▲ The PiHut sells lots of useful components and accessories.

TOP OF THE SHOPS

There are dozens of great places to buy electronic components on the web, as you'll discover once you start exploring for yourself. Here's a list of URLs for our favourites to get you started:

- **Amazon** www.amazon.co.uk
- **Arduino** store.arduino.cc
- **Bitsbox** www.bitsbox.co.uk
- **Farnell UK** uk.farnell.com
- **Maplin** www.maplin.co.uk
- **ModMyPi** www.modmypi.com
- **The Pi Hut** thepihut.com
- **RS Components** uk.rs-online.com
- **Mouser Electronics** uk.mouser.com

SHOPPING LIST

Find out exactly what you need to buy in order to build your robot and how much it will cost you

On these pages, we've listed all the components you'll need to complete the main projects in this book, including your completed robot. We've split it into two lists. In the first, we've gone the 'official' route, buying a genuine Arduino Uno and sourcing all our other parts from UK-based suppliers. This has the benefit of fast delivery and will mean that all your components will look and work exactly like they do in this book, as well as on the many websites you may find yourself referring to should you take your new hobby further. We've saved a few bob by buying online rather than in a bricks-and-mortar store, but this option is still the more expensive at £99.27 in total, plus optional extras.

The official Arduino Uno will look and work exactly like they do in this book.

CHEAP AS CHIPS

For the second list, we've gone for the ultimate budget option. We've opted for an Arduino 'compatible' board and sourced many of the components from Chinese suppliers (via Amazon Marketplace) to get the cheapest prices. As you can see, the total cost is just £17.70, but you may have to wait a few weeks for your parts to arrive in the mail, and you'll find there are a few differences in the way they look and function compared to those used in this book. For example, we've gone for an Arduino-compatible Nano, as it was by far the cheapest. This is much smaller than the Uno and the board has a different layout, as you can see from the image below. Also, the cost we've listed only covers the essentials required to make a basic version of the robot. If you want to complete all our practice projects, as well as add all of Magbot's bells and whistles, you'll need to buy in the optional extras we've mentioned, too. When it comes to putting the budget bot together, you'll need to read the special instructions in chapter 7.

PRICES ARE RIGHT

For both lists, we've included links to suggested web pages where each item can be bought at the price we've quoted, but since prices and stock levels change you may find some of the components are more expensive (or possibly cheaper) when you buy them – or they may no longer be available, in which case you may need to source your own equivalents from one of the retailers recommended in the previous section. All prices include VAT, but in some cases you may need to add delivery charges.

Also note that we haven't included the cost of the equipment you'll need to use when building your projects, such as screwdrivers and pliers, nor have we included the cost of consumables, such as batteries, sticky tape and so on.

This Nano-compatible board is smaller than the Uno.

ADVANCED PROJECTS

Bear in mind that we haven't included the cost of any of the components required for the projects in the 'Advanced' section of this book (chapter 8) in either of the shopping lists on this page. When we get to them, we'll be detailing the items required and explaining how much they're likely to cost on a project-by-project basis.

SHOPPING LISTS *Compare our lists and decide whether to take the 'official' or budget route*

MAGBOT (OFFICIAL)

All the items in the main list are essential for completing the full version of Magbot and the other main projects. To keep costs down, we've put the USB cable as an extra, as you may already have one. We've also put the switched battery pack as an extra, as it's a bit of a luxury – the robot chassis kit we've suggested comes with a battery holder but it doesn't have an on/off switch. Also, the micro servo is optional, as it's not needed for Magbot – just for a short project to show how servos work.

Essentials

Arduino Uno R3 microcontroller **£22.19**
www.snipca.com/12859

Arduino motor shield R3 .... **£28.24**
www.snipca.com/12860

Dagu Magician Robotics 2WD robot car chassis **£19.98**
www.snipca.com/12861

Hobby Components Microcontroller Experimenter's Kit **£19.99**
www.snipca.com/12862

Ultrasonic module HC-SR04 .... **£1.99**
www.snipca.com/12863

Arduino-compatible analogue joystick **£2.39**
www.snipca.com/12864

Male-to-female jumper wires (40pk) **£3.50**
www.snipca.com/12870

5.5mm male DC plug to 9v battery clip connector **£0.99**
www.snipca.com/12867

TOTAL £99.27

Optional extras

USB 2.0 A to B cable (1.8m) £1.18
www.snipca.com/12866

Switched 4 x AA battery pack £0.85
www.snipca.com/12869

Towerpro SG90 micro servo 9g £2.99
www.snipca.com/12865

TOTAL (WITH OPTIONAL EXTRAS) £104.29

BUDGET BOT

The items in the 'Essentials' list are all you'll need to complete a budget version of Magbot, though there will be several differences compared to the 'official' version of the robot – see chapter 7 for more information. If you want to complete all the main projects in the book and add whiskers, LEDs, remote control and sound to the Budget Bot, you'll need to either add the items from the optional extras or source all the individual parts you need yourself and look for the best price in each case.

Essentials

Arduino-compatible Nano (with free USB cable) **£4.99**
www.snipca.com/12904

L293D motor drive chip **£1.49**
www.snipca.com/12905

Buyincoins 2WD Motor Smart robot car chassis kit **£7.99**
www.snipca.com/12906

Ultrasonic module HC-SR04 .... **£1.05**
www.snipca.com/12856

Breadboard **£2.18**
www.snipca.com/12907

Wire (scavenged) .... **Free**

TOTAL £17.70

Optional extras

Hobby Components Microcontroller Experimenter's Kit **£19.99**
www.snipca.com/12862

Arduino compatible analogue joystick **£2.39**
www.snipca.com/12864

Male-to-female jumper wires (40pk) **£3.50**
www.snipca.com/12870

9V battery clip connector **£0.99**
www.snipca.com/13041

TOTAL (WITH OPTIONAL EXTRAS) £44.57

WHAT'S IN THE BOX?

If you can't – or don't want to – get the Hobby Components microcontroller kit we've recommended here, it might be useful to know what individual components it contains. We'll be using almost all of these in our projects in one way or another:

1 x 8 x 8 LED matrix display
1 x 4-digit 7-segment display
1 x shift register
65 x jumper wires
4 x push buttons
1 x active buzzer
1 x passive buzzer
1 x pp3 battery clip
1 x 400-point solderless breadboard
1 x 10k potentiometer
1 x light dependent resistor (light sensor)
1 x infrared LED (5mm)
1 x infrared sensor
1 x temperature sensor (lm35)
1 x tilt sensors / switches
2 x red LED (3mm)
2 x blue LED (3mm)
2 x green LED (3mm)
2 x yellow LED (3mm)
10 x 220R resistors
5 x 10k resistors
1 x infrared remote control
4 x 4 16-key matrix membrane keypad

PREPARING YOUR WORKSPACE

We show you what tools you'll need and how to get your workbench ready for your robot-building projects

WHAT YOU'LL LEARN

- What you can do to prepare for your projects
- What tools and equipment you'll need
- Tips for storing and working with your components

In addition to buying all the components that physically make up your robot, you'll need to gather together some tools and clear a space to carry out your work. Ideally, you need a decent-sized surface to work on – obviously not everyone has a dedicated workbench for home projects, but almost any surface will do. Things can get messy and electronic components can have a lot of sharp parts, so steer clear of expensive mahogany dining tables. Use a tough tablecloth or similar covering to prevent scratches. Once you have somewhere to work, you'll need to get your tools. Thankfully, many of the items you'll need are things that should be readily available in your home. If not, most of the equipment required can be bought cheaply online.

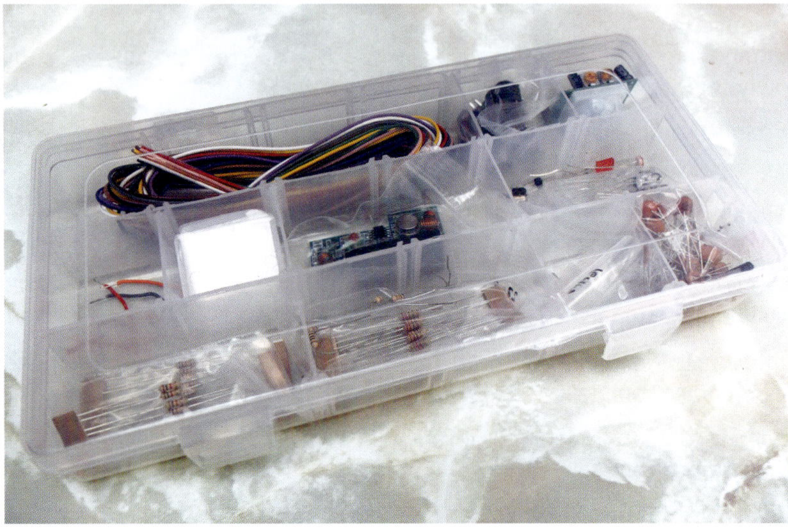

▲ You don't need a fancy component box like this - jam jars will do.

A MAGNIFYING GLASS

Some of the components you'll be working with can be quite small and fiddly. A magnifying glass is essential for identifying parts and checking your circuits. It doesn't have to be big or expensive – whatever you have around the house will be fine.

▼ Needle-nose pliers are very useful for twisting wires.

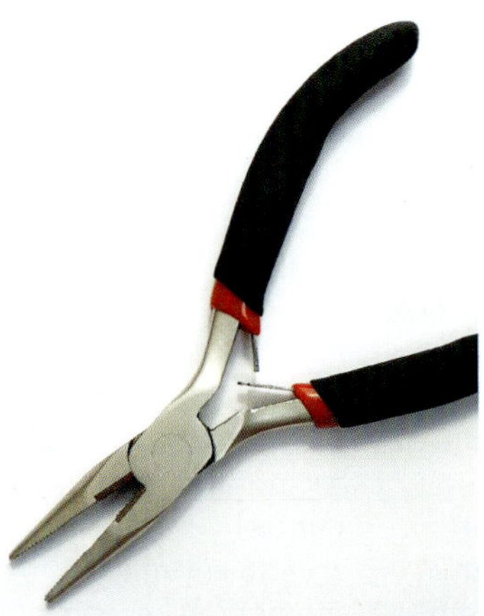

NEEDLE-NOSE PLIERS

Normal pliers will do if you don't have a pair of needle-nose pliers at home. But the type with slimmer jaws are ideal for getting into tight situations, grabbing stubborn components and pulling them out of circuits, as well as for bending and twisting wires. You can get these for about £3 online.

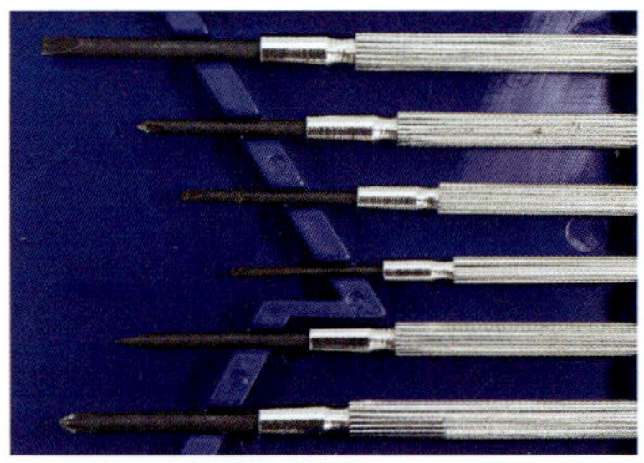

▲ A precision screwdriver set is necessary.

A PRECISION SCREWDRIVER SET

A lot of the parts we'll be using later on – robot chassis kits, battery packs and so on – will require you to screw various bits and pieces together. And, in the majority of cases, the screws themselves will be pretty small. Normal-sized screwdrivers will be too big, so precision screwdrivers are necessary. You'll need both flat-head and Philips varieties, but precision screwdrivers can usually be bought in a set if you don't already have them. If you shop around you can get a set for around £5 online.

JAM JARS

You'll need something to store your components in. You'll probably want to separate out your bits and pieces by type – resistors, sensors, wires and so on – and you'll need to be able to identify which parts are in which container so you can access them quickly and easily. You can buy special clear plastic component cases that are neatly divided up into compartments. But you don't need to splash out on one of these – we found that old jam jars were ideal for storing components, as they were transparent and you can tip the contents into the lid to sift through for the part you want without spilling everything onto your work surface. Plus, we happened to have a load of them in the house. Use whatever equivalents you have available – beauty cream pots, beakers and the like are also good.

USING A MULTIMETER

In most cases, you can get away with using tools you probably already have around you home. But one dedicated item we highly recommend buying – especially if you think you might end up pursuing electronics as a hobby beyond this book – is a multimeter. This is a single device that lets you measure voltage, current and resistance. Multimeters have a wide variety of uses – you can test whether a battery is dead or not, for example, and you can measure the current around your circuits. One really useful ability it provides is a quick and easy way to work out the value of a resistor. The colour-coded bands on resistors are supposed to let you know their value, but they're very hard to see and you'll never remember one from the other. One way to work out a resistor's value is to use an online calculator like the one at www.snipca.com/12782, which lets you select the number and colour of the bands. But even this is a bit of a hassle. If you have a multimeter, simply set the dial to 20 k Ω (or 2k Ω), then touch the end of one probe onto the left leg of the resistor and the other probe onto the right, and it will tell you the resistance value onscreen. You can get a decent multimeter from Amazon for less than £10.

Thankfully, many of the items you'll need are things that should be readily available in your home

A TRAY

Keeping a tray on your desk or table underneath you as you work is a very good idea. Components, cables and screws are all liable to drop out of your hands as you try to fit them together and having something below to catch them when they do will save you from scrabbling around on the floor with a torch looking for them underneath furniture. Although having a torch handy just in case is probably a good idea, too.

A STANLEY KNIFE

It doesn't have to be an official 'Stanley'-branded knife, obviously, but a very sharp DIY knife of some kind is essential for trimming rough edges off components and so on. We already used one in chapter 1 to help build our simple Bristlebot. And, later on, we'll be using one for cutting accessories for Magbot.

CHOPPING BOARD

This one goes with the Stanley knife – or any other cutting, trimming or slicing job that involves sharp implements. Unless you have a dedicated DIY workbench at your disposal, it's more likely you'll be using the kitchen table or your desk and you don't want that pockmarked with dozens of little scratches. A wooden (or plastic) chopping board is a must for these tasks.

WIRECUTTERS

Even if you buy a load of pre-cut jumper wires, there will be moments when you'll need to trim one or expose more of the conductive wire by stripping off some of the plastic insulator. Ideally, you'll have both a set of wirecutters and a wire stripper, but you'll find there are tools available that combine both tasks. Armed with one of these, you'll be able to convert almost any wire or cable into a connector for your electronics projects.

BLU-TAK, TAPE AND VELCRO

When it comes to making anything like a robot, you'll soon find that you need a way to stick things together quickly and easily without the mess and permanence of glue. Blu-tak (or similar) is absolutely the best stuff for this. You can use it in thin, flat layers to stick battery compartments to robot chassis or use it in big blobs to protect yourself against something sharp. It's an insulator, too, so you can use it on the bottom of the Arduino board or on the bare end of a wire. And it's easy to pull things apart again later on. Double-sided sticky tape (or normal tape folded over on itself) is a good substitute and preferable in certain situations, so it's best to have both if possible. Having a roll of electrical tape is useful, too. And Velcro – specifically the self-adhesive variety – can also be useful for fixing bits together.

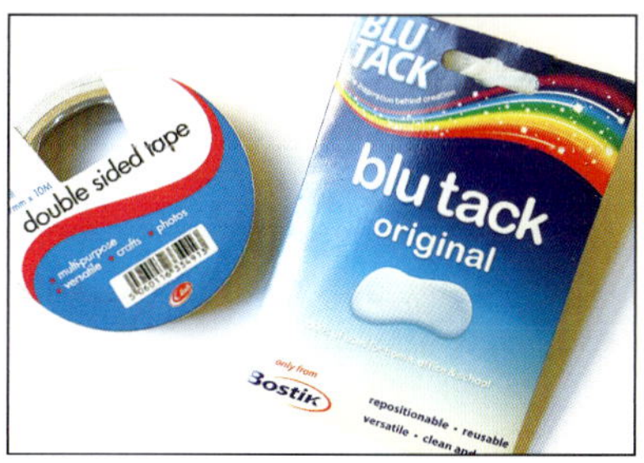

▲ Blu-tak and double-sided tape are your friends.

CORKS, WIRE TIES, SMALL SCREWS

Start saving these now. We're not joking. Corks can be used for all kinds of robot parts – necks, feet and more. We'll be using one as Magbot's nose, among other things. Wire ties are those little things that you find twisted around the cables of any new electronic products you buy (headphones, power cables and so on). Scavenge a load of these and you'll find they have a wide variety of uses in your projects, from taming your robot's tangle of wires to fixing bits and pieces together.

SAFETY FIRST

Working with electronics isn't without its risks, so follow our advice to help prevent damage to your components and, more importantly, to yourself

WHAT YOU'LL LEARN

- How to prevent injury from electric shocks
- How to make sure you don't damage your equipment
- How to use your tools and components safely

You probably already know that messing about with electricity can be dangerous. But that shouldn't stop you from enjoying working on your robot and carrying out other electronics projects. In fact, it's relatively easy to stay safe, as long as you keep a few key rules in your mind as you go. Reading our safety tips before you start will help prevent any serious problems.

1 Avoid AC current

Electricity is dangerous – there's no getting round it. But mains electricity in particular can be deadly. Not only is its voltage high (230V), but it also uses alternating current (AC), which can have a devastating effect on the human body (see the box opposite). So one way to limit the potential damage to yourself and your equipment is to avoid using mains electricity altogether. There are plenty of other ways to power your projects – such as via batteries or via the USB port of your PC, both of which use DC current – so there's really no need to go anywhere near it.

2 Be careful with batteries

Batteries are safer than mains electricity, because their voltage is lower and because they work on DC current rather than AC. But that's not to say that they aren't still dangerous. The Darwin Awards (**www.darwinawards.com**), for example, tells the sad story of a young naval officer who managed to kill himself with a 9V battery whilst attempting to measure the resistance of the human body. He decided to use himself as a subject and he held the positive and negative probes of a multimeter in his left and right hands, which would normally be fine – except he somehow managed to puncture the skin on both hands with the sharp ends of the probes. The man's blood supply suddenly became a conductor and the current from the 9V battery powering the multimeter travelled across his heart, killing him.

That's a pretty extreme example, but another, more common way that batteries can become dangerous is if they short circuit. If you have, say, four AA cells in a battery pack, you need to be very careful that the wires coming from the pack don't touch each other. If the bare end from the red (power) wire touches the bare end of the black (ground) wire,

▲ Avoid AC current as it can have a devastating effect on the human body.

▲ 9V batteries are fine, but don't use anything more than 12V.

the electrons will rush from negative to positive without any resistance, which can not only damage the batteries themselves, but also melt any nearby equipment, possibly even starting a fire. Some types of battery – including NiCad cells – have even been known to explode when a short circuit like this occurs.

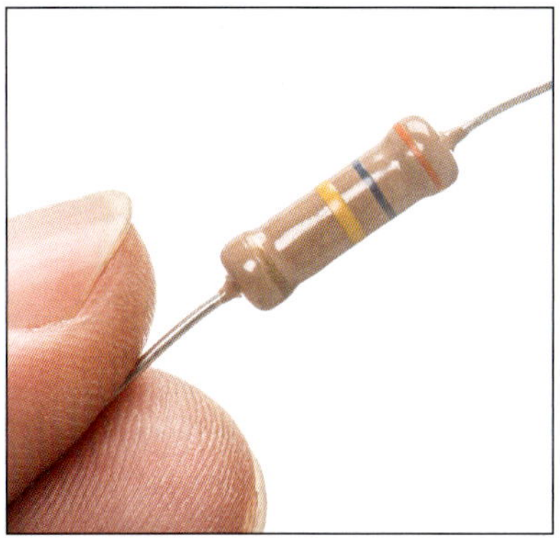

▲ Use resistors to protect your components.

3 Use resistors

Resistors are very good at protecting your equipment, so it's a good idea to use them wherever possible. Putting a resistor between the power source and an LED, for example, can limit the current going to the component and, therefore, prevent it from burning out. Similarly, it's possible to use resistors to protect the pins on your microcontroller. An example of this might be a circuit with a switch in it, where the switch is connected to a pin on your Arduino board as an input device. You could probably get away with connecting the switch to the pin directly, but by using a resistor you're adding a layer of safety that limits the current, thereby protecting the pin in case of, say, errors in the programming code.

4 Stay dry

This might sound like an obvious one, but when you're experimenting with electronics try to make sure you keep clear of liquids. Water conducts electricity, which means you shouldn't work in damp or moist environments (bathrooms, conservatories, garages) and you should try to keep tea, coffee and soft drinks far away from your workbench. It also means you need to keep yourself moisture free. If you've just been to the toilet and washed your hands, for example, make sure you dry them properly afterwards. And if you're working somewhere hot, watch out for sweaty hands.

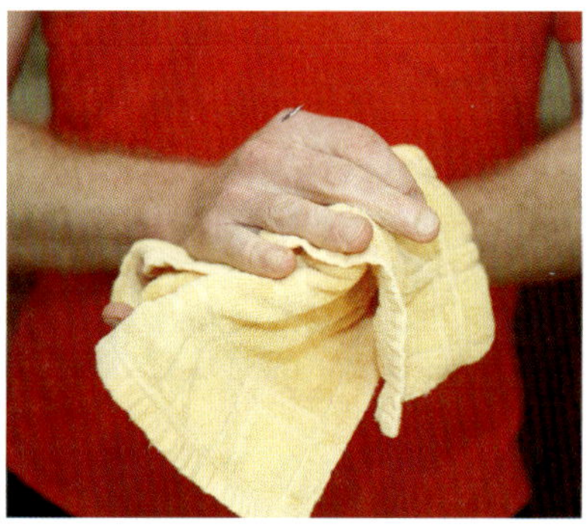

▲ Try to keep your hands dry.

5 Stay away from metal surfaces

Metal is another good conductor, so you should avoid placing your Arduino Uno board on anything metal – especially if it's connected to a power source, such as a battery or your PC – as this can quickly create a short circuit. So where we've recommended using a tray underneath your projects as you work, make sure the tray is made of wood or plastic, not metal.

Resistors are very good at protecting your equipment, so it's a good idea to use them

6 Double-check your circuits

Before you plug in a battery pack or connect your Arduino to your PC, it's wise to do one last check to make sure that all the components and wires you've used are connected correctly. In all our projects, for example, we'll provide you with easy-to-understand diagrams of all the circuits we're building. Compare these to your work to double-check everything's right before you add any power to the mix.

WHAT WILL AN ELECTRIC SHOCK DO TO ME?

There are various ways that electrocution can affect the human body and none of them are particularly good. The precise effect will depend on the type of current you come into contact with, the strength of the voltage, along with certain other conditions, such as how much moisture is present and how long you're exposed. It's actually the amount of current that does the damage – the more current flowing through your body, the worse the outcome is likely to be for you. But high voltage electricity can break down the human body's natural resistance to current, making it more likely for a shock to occur. Low-voltage electrocution can occur in wet conditions, where your skin's resistance is dramatically reduced.

At low levels, the effects of an electric current may be nothing more than a barely perceptible tingling sensation. Increase the current and you could receive painful shock and lose control of your muscles. At high levels, you can end up with nerve damage, cardiac arrest and, eventually, death. AC current has the added bonus of playing havoc with your heart. Its alternating nature means that it's likely to induce ventricular fibrillation (uneven, uncoordinated pumping), which is often fatal. Remember, though – we'll only be working with low-voltage DC current in our projects, so the risk of injury is fairly low.

2 What you need

Watch out for telltale signs - like magic blue smoke.

Some people wear anti-static wristbands to protect delicate components.

7 Don't rewire anything while powered

Once your circuit is connected to a power source – or to your PC – make sure you don't change any of the connections. It's very easy to create a short circuit at this point, so just avoid doing so. It's much better to disconnect the power, make your changes, double-check them, then plug the power back in. Similarly, don't ever attempt to mount an accessory, such as a motor shield (see chapter 5), onto your Arduino board whilst it's connected to your PC or a power source.

8 Learn warning signs

When something's not right, there will often be some obvious telltale signs and you'll soon get to know what these are. If anything in your circuit is getting too hot, for example, there's almost certainly going to be a problem somewhere. Similarly, if you notice a caustic burning smell then something's up. Most worrying of all is the appearance of something that electronics enthusiasts fondly refer to as 'magic blue smoke'. In all cases, you should pull the plug on the power as soon as you spot the symptom before trying to establish the cause.

9 Use a USB hub

You might, understandably, have some concerns about the safety of your PC. After all, damaging a bunch of cheap components is one thing, but frying several hundred pounds worth of computer – not to mention all the irreplaceable data on it – is another matter altogether. Thankfully, your PC has a lot of built-in protection against power surges and suchlike, but we've heard several stories about people who've managed to kill their computer's USB ports. One way to eliminate this issue is to use a powered USB hub. That way, you can still transfer data to and from your PC, but you'll be getting power from the hub rather than the computer. Most good powered USB hubs provide built-in current protection.

11 Don't use more than 12V

The Arduino Uno board operates at 5V, but it has its own built-in voltage

THERE WILL BE BREAKAGE

It's worth bearing in mind that you can't protect everything all of the time. While you obviously need to take good care of yourself, many of the electronic bits and pieces you work with will perish for one reason or another. It's unavoidable, but it's all part of the process. Even experienced electronics enthusiasts will cause inevitable casualties. The good thing is that most of the parts you'll be working with are cheap and easy to replace. Plus, you'll learn from every mistake, so remember that the components you inadvertently fry along the way have all died in a good cause.

Protect your PC's ports with a powered USB hub.

regulator that allows you to connect an external power supply of up to 12V. We'll be using a 9V battery for most of our projects and that will be fine. But connecting a power source that supplies anything more than 12V can cause your Uno to overheat, so we don't recommend it.

12 Don't rush or force things

When connecting components or making things for your projects, the best advice we can offer is to take your time and do the job properly, rather than rushing it. You're much more likely to make a mistake if you're hurrying, and that could cost you a valuable component. Likewise, don't try to force a connection if something doesn't seem to fit. Apply firm but careful pressure and, if necessary, disassemble other components so that you can see more clearly whether or not there's some kind of obstruction.

12 Take care with your tools

It goes without saying that you need to be careful when using anything sharp, such as a Stanley knife, for example. When you're cutting, use a chopping board or a piece of old wood underneath. Accidents happen when you least expect them, so you'll need to take care when wielding anything from a screwdriver to wire strippers. You can do a lot of damage to yourself and your equipment with a soldering iron, too. Luckily, we won't be using one for our projects, but you can read more about soldering (and related safety issues) in chapter 8.

13 Wear safety glasses

You might think this one is overkill, but it's all too easy for the clipped end of a wire or something similar to fly up and hit you in the eye while you work. This is especially the case when working on electronics projects, as the small size of the components means that we tend to lean in and get our eyes up close to the action. It might seem unlikely but, again, anything can happen, so the best advice we can offer is to provide your eyes with some insurance by wearing safety goggles while you work.

Use safety glasses to protect your eyes.

14 Protect against static

Static electricity can build up in your body for a number of reasons, including friction. You've probably noticed that sometimes when you walk on carpet, then touch someone, you can give them an electric shock. That's called a static discharge, when the current flows from you to something – or someone – else. A static discharge isn't normally harmful to humans, but it can be devastating to sensitive electronic components, such as integrated circuits. As such, some electronics enthusiasts use anti-static wristbands or use special anti-static mats while they work. Most of the components we'll be using in our own projects are pretty hardy – including the Arduino board – so protection against static is optional. Don't say we didn't warn you, though.

15 Keep help at hand

The low-voltage DC current that we'll be working with is mostly harmless as long as you remember to take the precautions we've outlined in this section. But accidents can happen in any kind of practical project, whether it's a scratch from a sharp edge or a burn from a component that's overheated. As such, it makes sense to keep a well-stocked first aid kit nearby, just in case.

Keep a first aid kit handy – just in case.

IN THIS CHAPTER

HOW TO BUILD A ROBOT

FUN WITH LEDS

Making things out of simple components, such as LEDs, buttons and resistors, is a great way to start learning about how both the hardware and the software sides of building a robot work – and have a bit of fun at the same time. In this chapter, we'll explain the basics of both physically putting components together and programming your creations using a series of easy-to-understand projects to demonstrate how each new concept works in practice. And, by the end of the chapter, you'll have built the very first part of your finished robot, too!

BUILD AND PROGRAM YOUR FIRST PROJECTS

We're about to make our very first electronic projects – before we do, let's explain how to work with breadboards and programming code

WHAT YOU'LL LEARN

- **How to use a solderless breadboard**
- **The basics of writing and editing programming code**
- **How to compile and upload programs to the Uno**

So far, a lot of our advice has been theoretical. All that's about to change, however. In this chapter, we're going to introduce a number of key concepts that you'll need to know for building robots or any other type of electronic device. Not only that, but now's also the time for us to start getting hands-on. We're going to build our first simple projects using basic components and home-made circuits. And we're going to learn how to understand, modify and write code ourselves so that we can upload our own programs to the Arduino Uno microcontroller.

▲ Breadboards let you put together components without the need to mess about with soldering irons.

BUILDING BLOCKS

There are two basic elements of any microcontroller project – the hardware and the software. The hardware is the microcontroller itself, along with all the other components you're using – LEDs, or sensors, for example, and the wires, resistors and circuit boards you use to connect them. The software is the program that you upload to the microcontroller. At its most basic, you might have a simple circuit containing an LED and some code that tells your microcontroller to switch the LED on and off at timed intervals. That's what was happening in Chapter 1 when we first connected the Arduino Uno to our PC and uploaded the example sketch Blink to make the onboard LED flash.

Explaining how to control LEDs is one of the best ways to start learning about building and programming electronic devices. So, in the early projects we're about to embark on, we'll be expanding on what we learned in Chapter 1 by adding in some other essential hardware components and making simple LED-based circuits, which we'll program with software to carry out a variety of tasks. By the end of this chapter, you'll have learned a number of skills and created some of the parts for our finished robot. First, let's find out more about the hardware and software we'll be using.

There are two basic elements of any microcontroller project: the hardware and the software

USING A BREADBOARD

As we've already said, breadboards are great for anyone starting out with their own electronic projects, as they let you put together components without the need to mess about with printed circuit boards or soldering irons. But if you've never used a breadboard before, there are some things you'll need to know first.

A breadboard is a rectangular slab of plastic, the surface of which is covered with a grid of small holes. These holes are sockets and they're linked together under the surface by conductive metal strips in horizontal and vertical rows. Hold the breadboard vertically and you'll see a notch or gutter running down the middle of the board – this is sometimes referred to as the centreline. The rows of sockets immediately either side of the gutter are linked horizontally but aren't linked across the gutter itself. These are called terminal strips. The sockets are usually numbered in a grid format: so, A1-A5 are linked, B1-B5 are linked and so on. You'll also see two separate columns of sockets running down either side of the board – often labelled positive (+) and negative (-). These are the power and ground rails and they're linked vertically.

The terminal strips are used to add components – diodes, LEDs, sensors, resistors and so on – as well as the jumper wires to connect them. Integrated circuit chips can also be plugged into terminal strips, straddling across the centreline so that each of its legs has its own unique connection. The power rails are usually used to supply voltage and ground connections.

ANATOMY OF A SKETCH

Here's a very basic sketch – the Blink example that comes with the Arduino software. Here, we're going to break it down into its component parts to help demystify the programming code

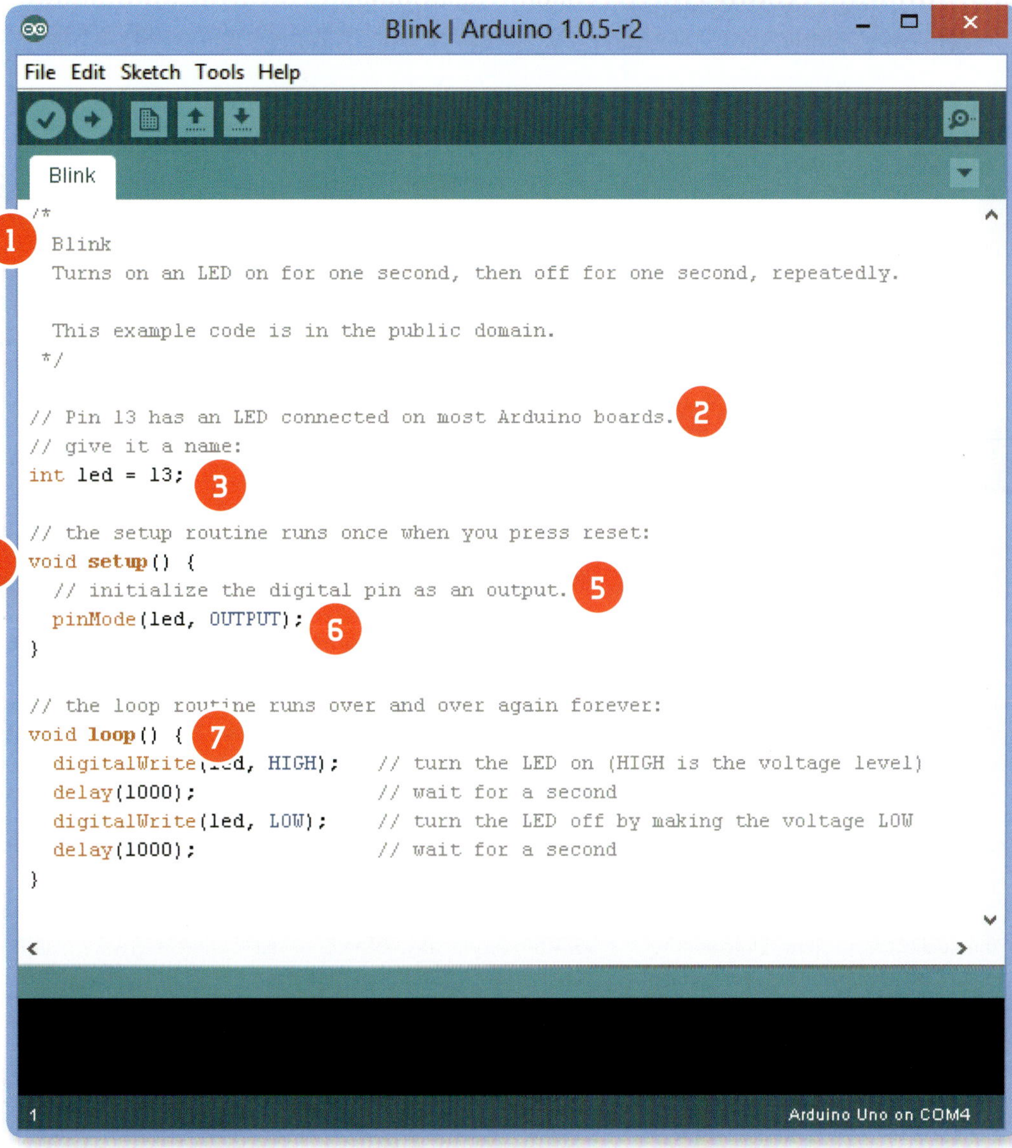

1 Comments
Anything between `/*` and `*/` is a comment – a block of text included within the code to help you understand what's going on. The `/*` part tells the Arduino to ignore all the text from that point onwards until the `*/` closes the comment.

2 In-line comments
Similar to the `/*` text, in-line comments are descriptions that are sometimes inserted into code to help explain what's happening. Any text that's immediately preceded by `//` is an in-line comment and is ignored by the Arduino.

3 Variables
Variables are used to store and define data. Each variable has a type, a name and a value. Here, the type is `int`, meaning integer, the name is `led` and the value is `13`.

4 Setup function
The `void setup()` function is required in every Arduino sketch – it's the first function that the microcontroller will run when it's powered on or reset. The 'void' part means that no information is reported back to the program.

5 Body
All the code included between the curly braces `{}` defines the function. The open brace marks the beginning of a function's definition and the closed brace indicates the end.

6 Semicolons
All commands or statements in the Arduino programming language need to end with a semicolon – this is a common factor of many programming languages.

7 Loop function
The `void loop()` function is executed after the setup function is complete. The Arduino will continue to execute this function in an endless loop until the board is powered down or a new sketch is uploaded.

3 Fun with LEDs

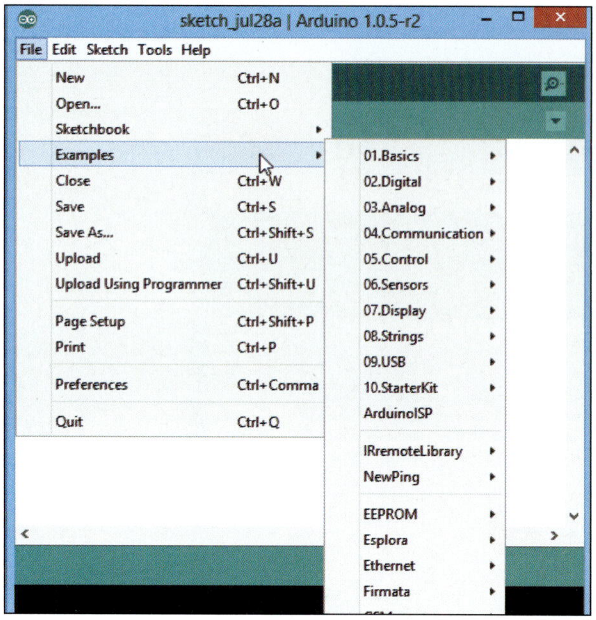

▲ **Lots of example sketches are available in the Arduino IDE.**

In all cases, components and wires are held in place by metal spring clips – just push the bare end of a wire or the metal legs of a component into a socket and the clip will hold it in place. If you're making long-term devices, breadboard clips are no substitute for soldering things permanently into position, but the clips will keep your components in place reasonably securely while you build and experiment. If you get something wrong, fixing it is as easy as pulling the wire or component out of one socket and pushing it into another. And when you've finished, you can easily disassemble your breadboard creations and build something new.

If that still sounds a bit confusing, don't worry – things will become clearer once you start building breadboard circuits yourself in the workshops. In the meantime, have a look at the diagram opposite to get a clearer idea of the breadboard's layout.

▼ **A sketch read-only error message.**

CRACKING THE CODE

In any robot or electronic device, hardware is usually only half the story. Programming code of some sort controls the functions of virtually any electronic device you care to think of, from the automatic doors at your supermarket to the operating system that runs your PC. And all of that code was, at some point, written by a programmer using a specific programming language.

In terms of our robot and the other projects we're going to make, we'll be using programming code to write programs – or 'sketches' – for the Arduino Uno microcontroller, which will be at the heart of almost all our creations, including our robot.

All the sketches used to program the Arduino Uno are written in a programming language called C++. If you're not familiar with C++, don't panic. It's not essential to learn an entire programming language if you just want to experiment with your own robotic or electronic creations. For the main projects in this book, we'll supply you with all the finished code you need from our online repository. And many of the examples we'll be using come built into the Arduino software.

Arduino sketches can often be easier for newcomers to understand than you might assume, however. They tend to be written very clearly, with lots of 'real' English and additional comments included to help beginners see what all the various lines of code are for. In the workshops throughout this chapter and beyond, we're going to make sure we explain a great deal of the code that we use as we go, too. So, even if you know nothing about programming languages to begin with, you're likely to pick things up fairly quickly.

PROGRAMMING BASICS

Whether or not you're interested in learning more about programming, it will help to have a grasp of some of the fundamental theories behind writing and compiling programs for your electronics projects.

The simplest way of looking at Arduino sketches is to see them as a kind of list of instructions that tell the hardware what to do. Even the most basic sketch needs to contain two specific functions: the 'setup' and the 'loop'. The setup function is run once, immediately after the device is switched on or reset, while the loop function is run continuously from that point onwards. So, if you wanted to program an LED to blink on and off, the setup function might initialise a pin on the Uno to output to an LED, while the loop will tell the Uno to switch the LED on and off over and over again at specific intervals.

Sketches can be written using the Arduino software, the posh name for which is 'integrated development environment', or IDE for short. This is the program we downloaded and set up back in chapter 1. Have a look at the annotated screen on p41 for an idea of what a sketch looks like in the Arduino code editor window and find out what the main bits of code refer to.

To write a sketch from scratch, simply launch the Arduino software on your PC, then start typing up the code in the empty part of the window. Once you've saved your work, you can access it again by clicking File, then Sketchbook. As we've already said, you don't have to be fluent in programming languages to get started. There are dozens of sample sketches included with the Arduino software. Click File, then select Examples to get an idea of what's available. One of the best ways for beginners to gain an understanding of coding is by modifying existing code, which is what we'll be doing throughout this book. The built-in Arduino examples are a great place to start, but if you do modify any of them and you want to save the results you'll need to use the File, Save As option and save the file under a different name.

Once you've written or modified your code, getting it onto the Uno is easy – just connect the board via your USB cable, then click the right-pointing arrow at the top of the editing window. This will compile your program and upload it to the Uno in a single step. We'll be doing this a lot over the next few chapters. Right – theory class is over for the time being. Let's start building stuff!

BREADBOARD LAYOUT

One of the main benefits of breadboards is their simplicity, but if you've never used one before you'll need to know what's what. Here, we point out the main features

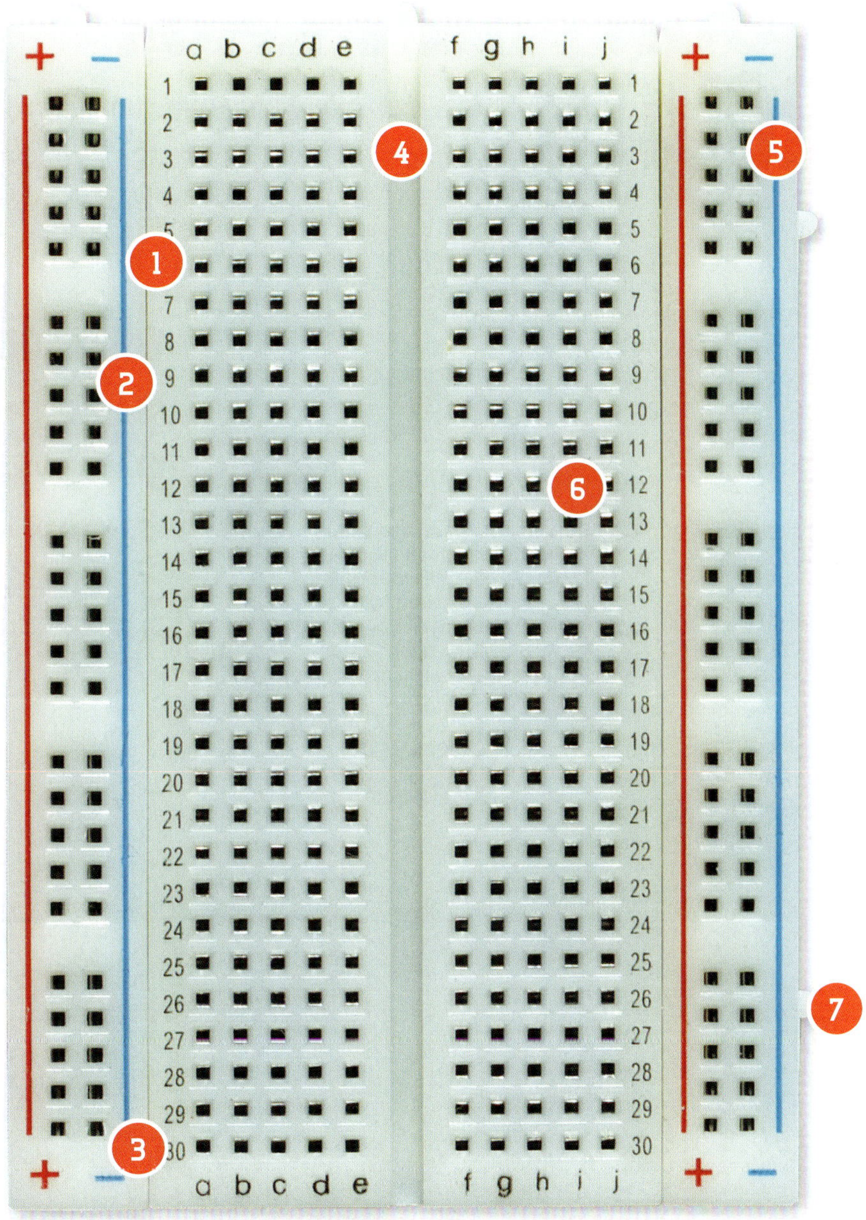

1 Terminal strips The horizontal rows of sockets are linked together by conductive metal strips (usually nickel-plated phosphor bronze) under the plastic, but they aren't lined across the middle groove (or centreline).

2 Contact sockets The sockets on a breadboard are almost always laid out in a 2.54mm matrix, allowing for standardised components, such as integrated circuit (IC) chips, to slot in snugly.

3 Grid numbers The numbers and letters around the edges of the terminal strips provide each socket with its own unique alphanumeric grid reference – we'll be referring to these a lot.

4 The centreline The groove running down the middle of the board isolates the left and right terminal strips from each other. Integrated circuits chips can be placed across the centreline to prevent a short circuit.

5 Power rails The two columns running down either side are usually for connecting a power supply. These are connected vertically; plug a current into the top hole and all the holes below it will be powered.

6 Spring clips With a breadboard, you don't need to solder anything – components and wires are held in place by pushing them into spring clips inside the board's sockets.

7 Slots Running out of space on your breadboard? If so, just add another one. Most breadboards have slots and nubs on the top, bottom and side edges, letting you slot them into further boards.

MAKE YOUR FIRST EASY LED CIRCUITS

Make LEDs blink, fade and more with our beginner's guide to working with electronic circuits

In chapter 1, we demonstrated how to upload a simple example sketch called Blink to your Arduino Uno board to make its onboard LED blink at different speeds. Now, we're going to take things one stage further by introducing additional components and creating our first simple circuits, putting many of the fundamental principles of electronics into practice. We're going to use a breadboard, LEDs, resistors and jumper wires in conjunction with various pins on the Uno board, which we'll program to carry out different types of function. First, we're going to make a single LED blink on and off, then we're going to use one of the Arduino's pulse width modulation (PWM) pins to make the LED fade on and off gently. All the components required are included in our shopping list in chapter 2.

TIP

It doesn't matter what colour jumper wires you use but, for your own sake, we heartily recommend that you should at least try to be consistent,as using randomly coloured wires could lead to confusion later on when your wiring gets more complicated.

WHAT YOU'LL NEED

- **An Arduino Uno board**
- **A USB cable**
- **A computer**
- **1 x LED**
- **1 x 220 Ohm resistor**
- **2 x jumper wires**
- **A breadboard**
- **A battery pack**

1

First, grab your breadboard and one LED – we're using a red one, but the colour isn't important at this stage. The LED has two connectors: a positive leg (anode) and a negative leg (cathode). You can usually tell these apart by the fact that the negative leg is slightly shorter than the positive one. Also, if you run a finger along both sides of the LED body, you should find that one side is flatter, while the other has a slight ridge at the base. The flat side is negative and the ridged side is positive. Insert the negative leg into socket E11 on the breadboard and the positive leg into socket E12, as shown in the diagram.

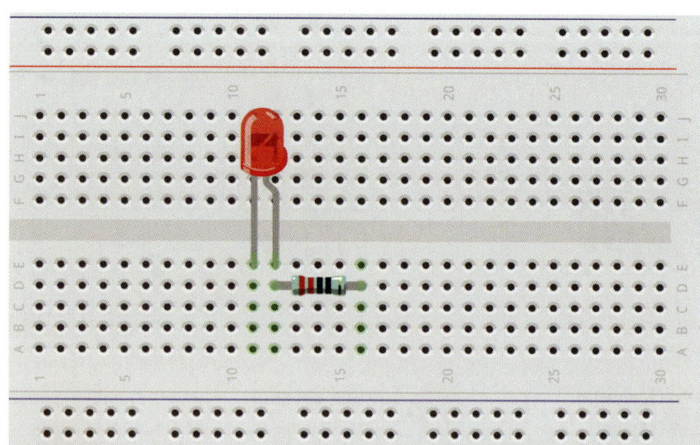

2

Next, we're going to add a resistor – go back to chapter 1 to find out why resistors are so important. If you've bought a starter pack of components, you probably have a selection of resistors with different values to choose from. You'll need a 220 Ohm resistor for this,so refer to our section on using a multimeter in chapter 2 to find out how to tell the value of a resistor. Unlike the LED, it doesn't matter which way round you insert the resistor into the breadboard. Simply put one leg into socket D12 (so that it's lined up with the positive pin of the LED) and the other leg into socket D16.

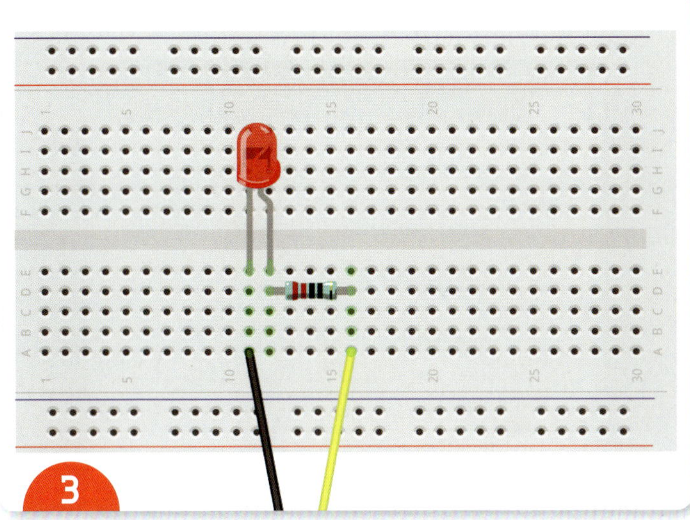

3

Component kits like the one in our shopping list come with jumper wires of varying lengths and colours. Plug one end of a black wire into socket A11 so that it's in the same horizontal terminal strip as the negative pin of the LED, and push one end of a yellow (or other coloured) wire into A16 so that it's lined up with the lower leg of the resistor. Generally speaking, black wires are used for the ground wire and red is used for power, but since we're only connecting a single LED in this circuit it will get power directly from the Arduino's output pin, which is why we've used yellow.

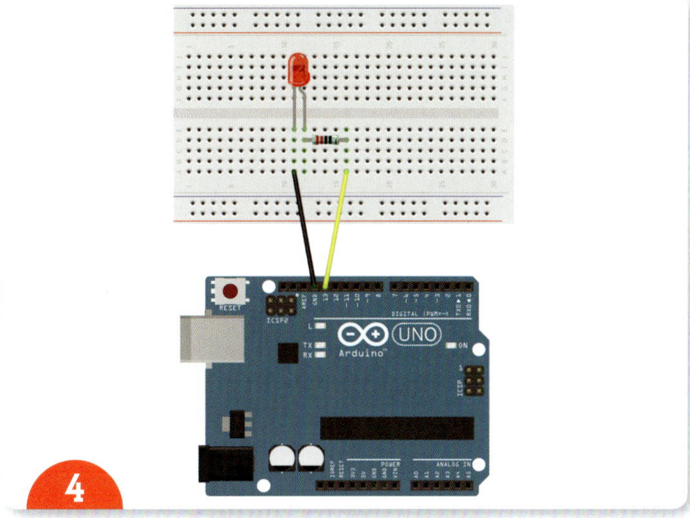

4

Before connecting the wires to the Arduino Uno, make sure it's unplugged from your PC and/or a power supply – you should always do this whenever you're connecting a circuit for the first time. The Uno has two rows of pins: one running down the left-hand side of the board and the other down the right-hand side. Each pin should be clearly marked, though some cheap non-official clone boards aren't always as well labelled. Connect the black wire from socket A11 on the breadboard to the top GND (ground) pin on the Uno, and the wire from socket A16 on the breadboard to pin 13 on the Uno, as shown.

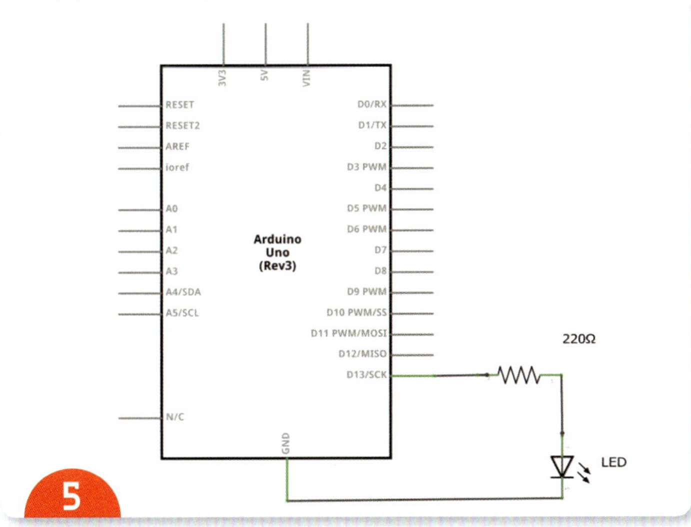

5

Circuit diagrams or schematics are used by electronics professionals and experts to represent physical circuits. Since this guide is aimed at beginners, we're won't be using many schematics, which require learning lots of symbols and conventions, but it's useful to get an idea of what they look like. The image above is a schematic of our current circuit. You'll see the Uno and its various pins; wires are connected to GND (Ground) and pin 13. The zigzag line represents our 220 Ohm resistor, and the down arrow with the line under it represents a diode. The arrows pointing away from it mean it's a light emitting diode, or LED.

6

Double-check that all the components in your circuit are wired up correctly before you connect your Uno to your PC, to avoid damaging components. If you've followed our instructions carefully so far, your simple circuit should look similar to the one pictured above. When you connect the Uno to your computer, don't be surprised to find that the LED on the breadboard starts blinking straight away. This is because the Uno is still running the Blink sketch that we uploaded back in chapter 1. Launch the Arduino software and click File, Examples, then 01 Basics, and select Blink to launch the Blink sketch.

3 Fun with LEDs

7

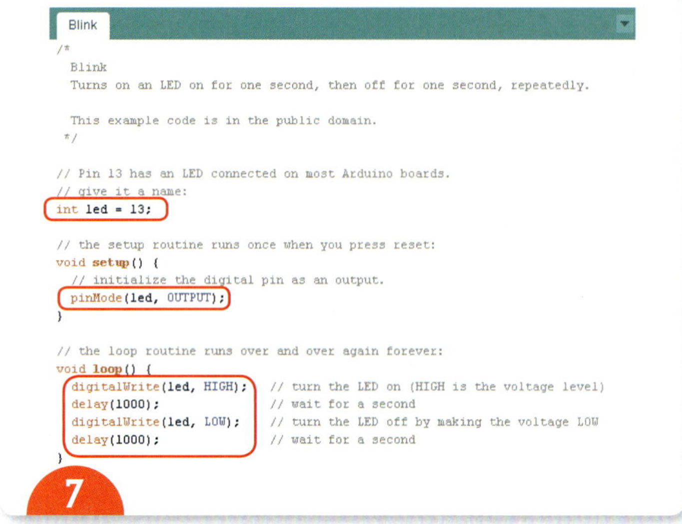

```
Blink
/*
  Blink
  Turns on an LED on for one second, then off for one second, repeatedly.

  This example code is in the public domain.
 */

// Pin 13 has an LED connected on most Arduino boards.
// give it a name:
int led = 13;

// the setup routine runs once when you press reset:
void setup() {
  // initialize the digital pin as an output.
  pinMode(led, OUTPUT);
}

// the loop routine runs over and over again forever:
void loop() {
  digitalWrite(led, HIGH);   // turn the LED on (HIGH is the voltage level)
  delay(1000);               // wait for a second
  digitalWrite(led, LOW);    // turn the LED off by making the voltage LOW
  delay(1000);               // wait for a second
}
```

Before we upload it, let's examine the code. Underneath the comments at the top is the line **int led = 13;** – this is a variable with the name **led** and a value of 13, referring to pin 13 on the Uno board. Next, the setup function **pinMode(led, OUTPUT);** initialises the pin as an output, meaning it's ready to provide current. Finally, the loop function defines the sketch's ongoing actions, which are to turn the LED on (**digitalWrite(led, HIGH);**), wait for a second (**delay(1000);**), turn the LED off (**digitalWrite(led, LOW);**), wait for another second (**delay(1000);**), then repeat the process ad infinitum.

8

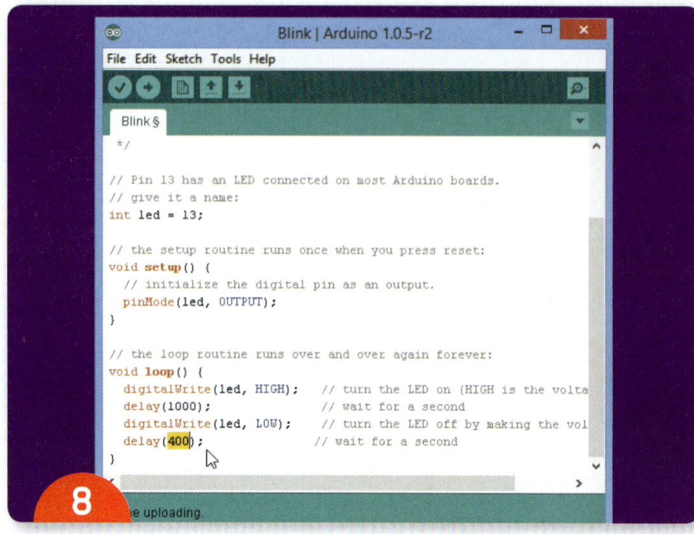

```
Blink | Arduino 1.0.5-r2
File Edit Sketch Tools Help
Blink §
 */

// Pin 13 has an LED connected on most Arduino boards.
// give it a name:
int led = 13;

// the setup routine runs once when you press reset:
void setup() {
  // initialize the digital pin as an output.
  pinMode(led, OUTPUT);
}

// the loop routine runs over and over again forever:
void loop() {
  digitalWrite(led, HIGH);   // turn the LED on (HIGH is the volta
  delay(1000);               // wait for a second
  digitalWrite(led, LOW);    // turn the LED off by making the vol
  delay(400);               // wait for a second
}
e uploading
```

Let's alter the frequency of the blink by modifying the code ourselves and then re-uploading it to the board. Scroll down to the **void loop ()** section and look for the line of code beneath where it says **digitalWrite(led, LOW)**, where it currently reads **delay(1000)**. Change the value 1000 to 400 so that the line now reads **delay(400)**, then click the Upload (right arrow) button at the top of the window. Once the modified code has been uploaded, you'll see the LED remains on for longer than it stays off, providing a kind of rhythmic 'pulsating' effect.

9

The LED is still just blinking – this is because it's connected to one of the Uno's digital pins, which can only switch between on or off. But by using one of the Uno's PWM pins, we can gently fade the LED instead. The PWM pins are still digital, but they're capable of using something called 'pulse width modulation' to generate analog-like output. Basically, you can change, or modulate, the duration of the signal's 'on time', or pulse width. Repeated fast enough, this will create the impression of a continuously varying, or analog, value. In this way, you could gradually vary the brightness of an LED or the speed of a motor.

10

Unplug the Arduino board from your PC, then disconnect the yellow jumper wire from pin 13 on the Uno, leaving all the other wires and components plugged in as before. The Uno's PWM pins are denoted by the tilde (~) symbol in front of the number. There are six PWM pins in total – in this case, we're going to use pin ~9. Plug the yellow wire into this, as shown. Double-check that everything in your circuit is connected properly, then plug the Uno into your PC again. You'll notice that the LED is no longer blinking – this is because the Uno is still running the Blink sketch, which uses pin 13.

TIP

While you're working with your components, remember not to put your Arduino Uno down on a metal surface, and never change any wires or components while your Uno is powered. Refer back to chapter 2 for more tips on staying safe while working on electronics projects.

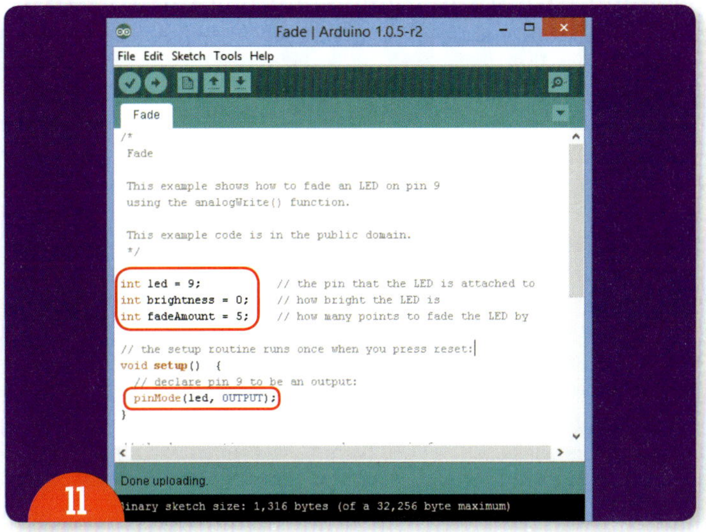

11

In the Arduino software, click File, Examples, then 01 Basics, and select Fade. This is another of the Arduino program's built-in sketches and it's designed to fade an LED on and off. At the top of the code, you'll see three variables: `int led = 9;` defines pin 9 as the one the LED is attached to, `int brightness = 0;` defines how bright the LED is and `int fadeAmount = 5;` defines how many steps we're going to fade the LED by. In the setup function, `pinMode(led, OUTPUT);` sets the pin as an output, exactly as it did when we used Blink.

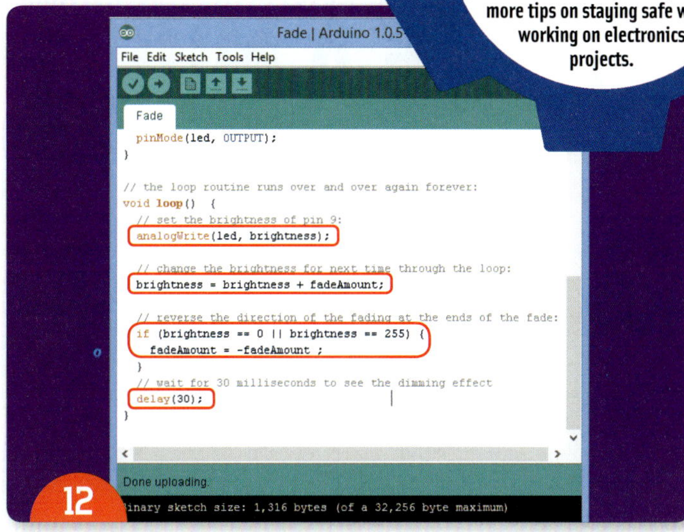

12

Scroll down to the loop function and you'll see a bit more going on here. For a start, the `analogWrite(led, brightness);` function tells us that we're going to use PWM on the pin and the brightness values indicated in our `int brightness` variable above – i.e. pin 9 at a brightness of 0. The next two lines introduce the `fadeAmount` variable, which gradually increases the brightness value from 0 (all the way off) to 255 (all the way on). And the `fadeAmount = -fadeAmount ;` line changes the fade amount to negative when it reaches maximum, reversing the fade effect. The `delay(30);` line at the end controls the speed of the fade.

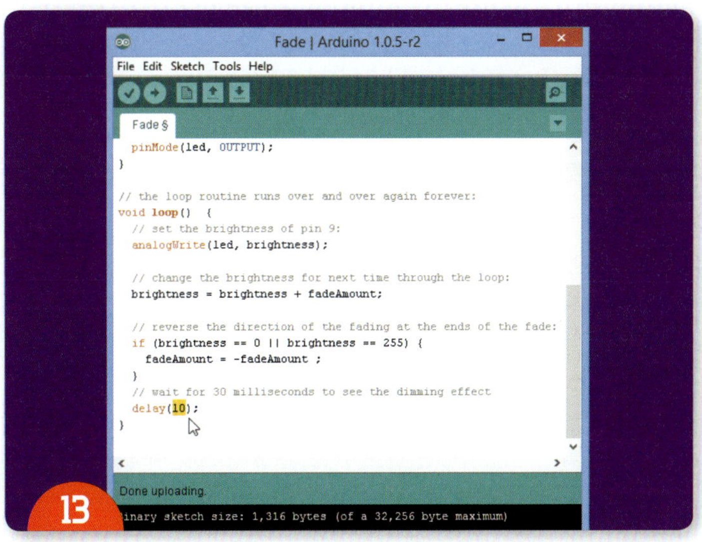

13

Click the Upload (right arrow) button in the Arduino toolbar; this will replace the Blink sketch on the Uno with the Fade one. After a second or two, the LED on your breadboard should start to fade gently on and off. At this point, you could experiment by modifying the code to see what effect it has. For example, you could change `delay(30);` to `delay(10);`, which will speed up the fade. Alternatively, you could change the minimum and maximum brightness values in the loop function to see what effect this has. Make your changes, then re-upload the sketch to watch the difference.

14

For the final step here, we're simply going to prove that you don't need your Arduino Uno board plugged into your computer for the sketch you've uploaded to run. So far, our circuits have only been powered when they've been plugged into our PC's USB port, but now we're going to untether our creation and use an independent power source instead. Unplug the USB cable from the Uno and get your battery pack. Connect the battery to the power socket on your Arduino board and your circuit should spring back into life. You'll see that the LED fades on and off, exactly as before.

CREATE A MULTI-LED ARRAY

Learn two slightly different ways to switch six LEDs on and off in a sequence

WHAT YOU'LL LEARN

- An Arduino Uno board
- A USB cable
- A computer
- 6 x 220 Ω resistors
- 6 x LEDs
- 7 x jumper wires
- A breadboard

So far, we've only been working with single LEDs, but it's possible to build projects that include multiple LEDs, too. In this project, we'll be creating a circuit with six LEDs in a row, and we'll then program our microcontroller to use a type of function called a 'for' loop to cycle back and forth through the LEDs in sequence. This project is often referred to as Knight Rider, after the 1980s television series, since it emulates the way the 'futuristic' LED display on the bonnet of KITT, the robot car. We'll also demonstrate how to alter the sequence by modifying the code and blink our LEDs in any order we want. Carrying out this project sets us up neatly for the following one, where we'll be making an LED battery meter that we'll use on our finished robot.

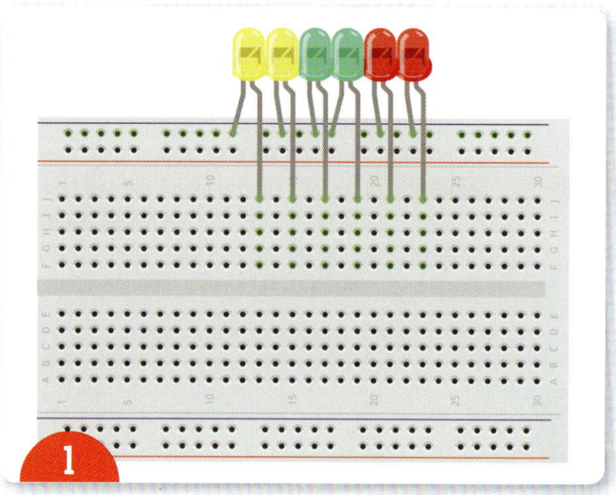

1

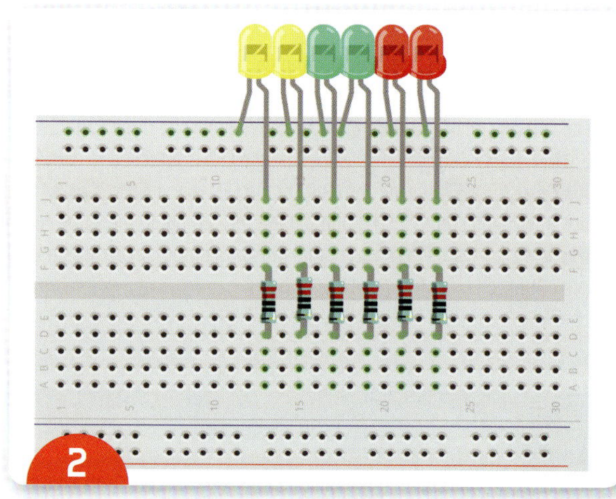

2

3

ForLoopIteration

```
void setup() {
  // use a for loop to initialize each pin as an output:
  for (int thisPin = 2; thisPin < 8; thisPin++)  {
    pinMode(thisPin, OUTPUT);
  }
}

void loop() {
  // loop from the lowest pin to the highest:
  for (int thisPin = 2; thisPin < 8; thisPin++) {
    // turn the pin on:
    digitalWrite(thisPin, HIGH);
    delay(timer);
    // turn the pin off:
    digitalWrite(thisPin, LOW);
  }

  // loop from the highest pin to the lowest:
  for (int thisPin = 7; thisPin >= 2; thisPin--) {
    // turn the pin on:
    digitalWrite(thisPin, HIGH);
    delay(timer);
    // turn the pin off:
    digitalWrite(thisPin, LOW);
  }
}
```

4

TIP

The trouble with both methods we've shown here is that they take up a lot of pins on your Uno – one per LED. Later (chapter 8) we'll show you a way to make a similar project with many more LEDs but only using only three pins.

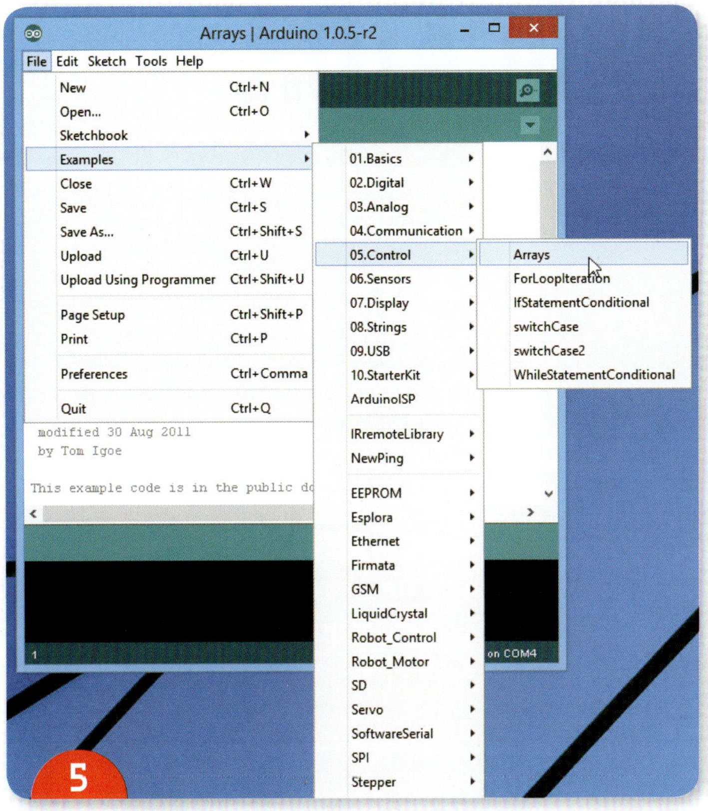

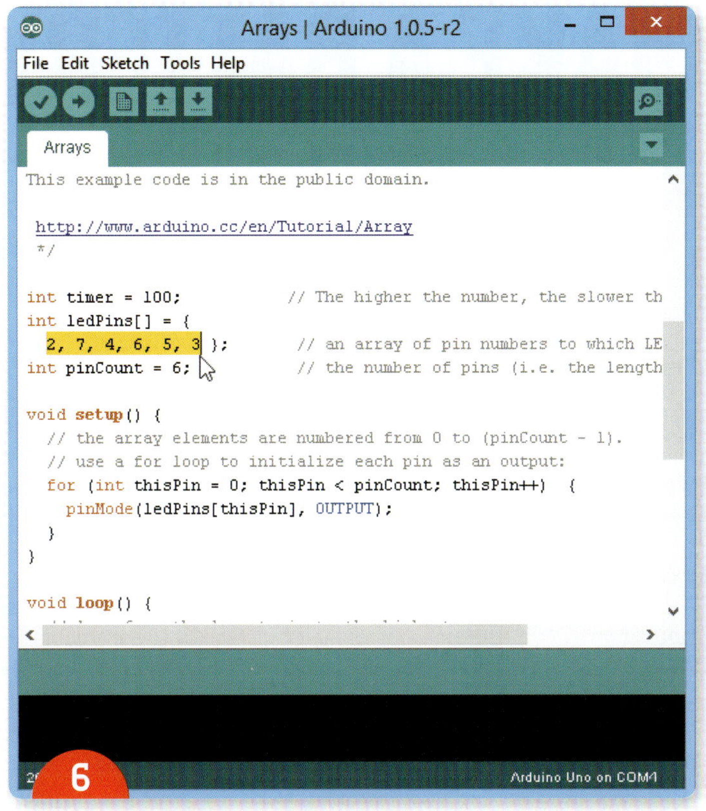

1

Take your breadboard and insert six LEDs into it. You don't necessarily need to put them in the same colour order as we have in the picture above. Just make sure that all the positive (anode) legs are inserted into sockets in column J spaced two sockets apart – so, J13, J15, J17, J19, J21 and J23. As you go, insert the negative (cathode) leg for each LED into the corresponding sockets in the ground rail (usually marked with a minus '-' sign) just above. Then, get a black jumper wire and insert it into the top left-hand socket on the upper ground rail.

2

Locate six 220 Ω resistors among your components. You can use a multimeter (see chapter 2) or online calculator, such as **www.snipca.com/12782**, to identify which resistors you need by their colour coding. Insert each resistor into your breadboard so that their legs straddle the centreline, and the upper leg of each one is linked across the same row as an LED. So, the first resistor slots into sockets E13 and F13, the next one slots into E15 and F15 and so on until the last one, which slots into E23 and F23. Unlike LEDs, it doesn't matter which way around they go.

3

Finish off the circuit as shown with six coloured jumper wires (we've used yellow ones). Insert one end of each wire into a socket in the same row as the lower leg of each resistor – A13, A15, A17, A19, A21 and A23. Make sure your Arduino Uno isn't plugged into your PC or a power source, then insert the other end of your coloured wires into pins 2 to 7 in sequence. Pin 2 on the Uno should connect to socket A23 on the breadboard, pin 3 to socket A21, pin 4 to socket A19 and so on. Connect the other end of the ground wire to the GND pin on the upper edge.

4

Connect your Uno to your PC via USB and start the Arduino IDE software. Click File, Examples, then 05 Control and select ForLoopIteration from the list. Look at the code, and in the `void setup()` section you'll see that it begins by defining a for() loop that initialises each of the digital pins 2 to 7 as outputs. In the main loop function of the code, two for() loops are used to continuously loop through the LEDs, one by one – first from lowest to highest (pin 2 to pin 7), and then from highest to the lowest.

5

Click the Upload icon and you should see the LEDs light up in a left-to-right sequence. That's great, but with the ForLoopIteration sketch you're stuck with some limitations – the pins need to be numbered in sequence and the LEDs need to be turned on in the same sequence. For a little more freedom of choice, let's try another sketch, called Arrays. Leave all the LEDs, resistors and jumper wires and so on as they are and, in the Arduino software, click File, Examples, then 05 Control and select Arrays. Click Upload to see the effect.

6

You'll notice that the LEDs now light up in a non-sequential order. If you look at the code, you can see what's going on and modify the sequence. Scroll down to the variable that begins `int ledPins[] = {` and you'll see a sequence of numbers – this defines the order in which the pins will output a High signal and light the LED. Click in the code and change the sequence from `2, 7, 4, 6, 5, 3` to `2, 3, 4, 5, 6, 7`, then re-upload the sketch. Now, the LEDs should light up in a left-to-right sequence, as in Step 5. Change this sequence to anything you like.

MAKE A BATTERY INDICATOR FOR MAGBOT

Build the very first part of your robot – an LED indicator that will show Magbot's battery level

WHAT YOU'LL NEED

- An Arduino Uno board
- A USB cable
- A computer
- 3 x LEDs
- 3 x 220Ω resistors
- 4 x jumper wires
- A breadboard
- A battery or battery pack

In order for Magbot to move around on his own without being tethered to a PC, we'll be running him off a battery. But batteries run out, so it would be useful to know how much juice Magbot has left at any point. And that's why we're going to put what we've learned about LEDs to good use by building a battery indicator for him. We'll be using the part we're about to create for our finished robot (see chapter 7). Before you begin, you'll need to download our code for Magbot. Go to **www.pcpro.co.uk/links/robot** and download the magbot.zip file. Extract the ZIP to the Arduino program's sketch folder. If you're using Windows, this should be C:\Users\yourusername\Documents\Arduino. This project will also introduce another useful feature of the Arduino – its serial monitor. This is a utility that allows us to monitor certain aspects of the Uno's operation via our PC.

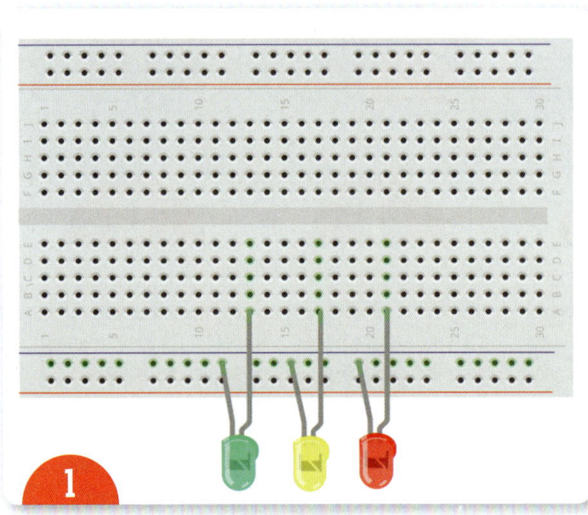

1

2

TIP

The Arduino Uno's serial monitor tool will come in particularly handy in the next chapter when we start using sensors, since it provides a quick and easy way for us to find out exactly how the sensors are reacting to their surroundings.

3

```
/*********************************************
Battery functions
*********************************************

void batteryLevel()
{
  // Check battery level
  long vcc = readVcc();

  Serial.print("Battery: ");
  Serial.println(vcc);

  if (vcc > 4500) {
    digitalWrite(A0, HIGH);
  } else {
    digitalWrite(A0, LOW);
  }

  if (vcc > 4000) {
    digitalWrite(A1, HIGH);
  } else {
    digitalWrite(A1, LOW);
  }

  if (vcc > 3500) {
    digitalWrite(A2, HIGH);
  } else {
    digitalWrite(A2, LOW);
  }

}
```

4

```
void setup() {

  // Open serial monitor at 9600 baud to see debugging messages.
  Serial.begin(9600);

  // Battery indicator leds
  pinMode(A0, OUTPUT);
  pinMode(A1, OUTPUT);
  pinMode(A2, OUTPUT);

}

void loop() {

  batteryLevel();
  delay(1000);

}

/*****************************************************************
Battery functions
*****************************************************************

void batteryLevel()
{
  // Check battery level
  long vcc = readVcc();

  Serial.print("Battery: ");
  Serial.println(vcc);
```

5

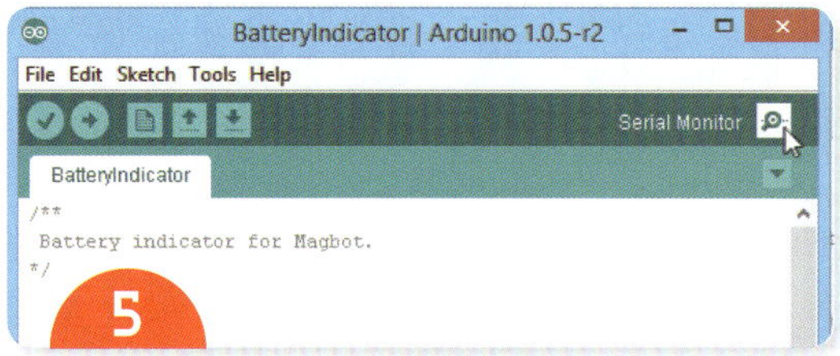

5

6

1

First, take your three LEDs and insert them into your breadboard. Put the anode (positive leg) of the first one in socket A13, the anode of the next one in A17 and the anode of the third one in A21. Now, insert the cathodes (negative legs) of each LED in the corresponding socket on the ground rail (-) below. We're using a traffic light-style system to show how much charge remains in the battery, so we're placing the LEDs in the order shown (green, yellow, red from the left), although the colours won't actually make any difference, so feel free to use what you have available.

2

Use your multimeter (or an online calculator) to identify three 220Ω resistors and then insert them into the breadboard so that they straddle the centreline in the same row as each of the LEDs. The first one will go in sockets E13 and G13, the second in sockets E17 and G17 and the third in sockets E21 and G21. Wire up the Arduino Uno to the breadboard as shown, with a black cable going from the GND pin next to pin 13 to the bottom ground rail, and three coloured wires attaching pins A0, A1 and A2 to sockets J13, J17 and J21 respectively, so that they're all lined up with the resistors and the LEDs.

3

It's important to note that, while we've connected three analog input pins on the Arduino Uno, we won't actually be using them as analog inputs. There are two main reasons why we're using these pins. First, it's a good way to demonstrate that the Uno's analog inputs can also be used as digital in/out pins if you need them to. Here, for example, all they're going to do is switch between High (on) or Low (off), depending on how much voltage is detected. The second reason is that, when it comes to building our battery meter into Magbot later on, these will be the only pins left for us to use.

4

Plug the Uno into your PC and start the Arduino program. Click File, then Sketchbook. If you extracted the ZIP file earlier, you should find 'magbot' listed here. Click this, then select BatteryIndicator. In the `setup` function, you'll see pins A0, A1 and A2 are set as outputs. In the loop is a `batteryLevel` function. The line `long vcc = readVcc();` effectively tells the Uno to check its internal voltmeter. Below this are three `if...else` statements – these state that if the voltmeter (vcc) reading is greater than a specific value, the LED attached to the pin specified will be switched on (High); if not, it will be switched off (Low).

5

Also in the code are some lines beginning with the word `Serial`. These refer to the Arduino's serial communications – a way for the Uno and your PC to talk to each other over USB. Serial communication is initialised with the setup line `Serial.begin(9600);`. In the loop, you'll see two more `Serial` lines, as shown. These basically tell the Arduino to keep sending your PC the latest voltmeter reading. Click Upload and all three LEDs on your breadboard should light up. In the Arduino program, click the Serial Monitor icon (top right of the toolbar). A new window will open and continuously update itself with the latest battery level value.

6

At this point, however, the Arduino's voltmeter isn't actually measuring a battery. The board is still connected to your PC, so it's reading the voltage that your computer is supplying over USB. Unplug the USB cable and get your battery pack. Connect the battery to the Uno's DC socket and, if it's a fresh battery, all three LEDs will illuminate. But as power drains below the values in the `if...else` statements we saw in step 4, the LEDs will switch off one by one until only the red one is lit. You can test this without wasting power by swapping your fresh battery for one that's been partially drained.

USE A SWITCH TO TURN AN LED ON AND OFF

Create a pushbutton project to learn more about open and closed circuits, digital inputs and more

WHAT YOU'LL NEED

- An Arduino Uno board
- A USB cable
- A computer
- 7 x jumper wires
- 1 x LED
- 1 x button
- 2 x 220 Ω resistor
- 1 x 10k Ω resistor
- A breadboard

We won't actually be using any buttons or switches on our finished Magbot, but building a button project can help to illustrate a number of important concepts. First, it will help us understand about open and closed circuits. We'll also use this project to demonstrate how the Arduino's digital inputs work, as we'll be using these a lot in the next chapter. And we'll be explaining more about the function of resistors, too.

As we mentioned earlier, resistors let you control the current where necessary. They can lower the current and protect your components from accidental damage. And, as we'll see, you can use them to help fix other problems, too. There's a surprising amount going on here for such a simple project, so don't worry if some of it feels a little advanced compared to previous projects – it's all just useful practice at this stage.

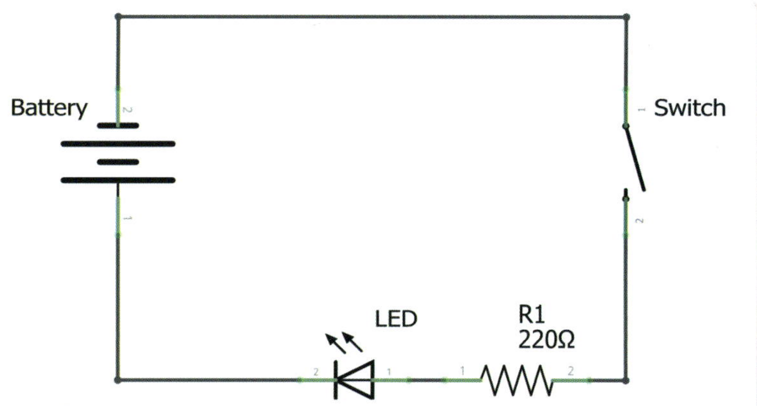

1

2

3

4

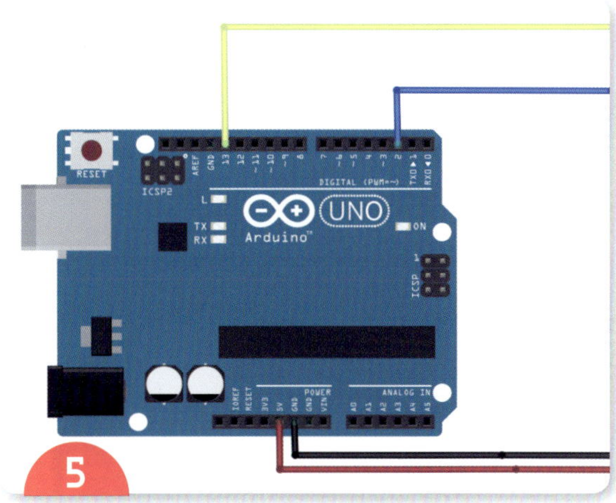

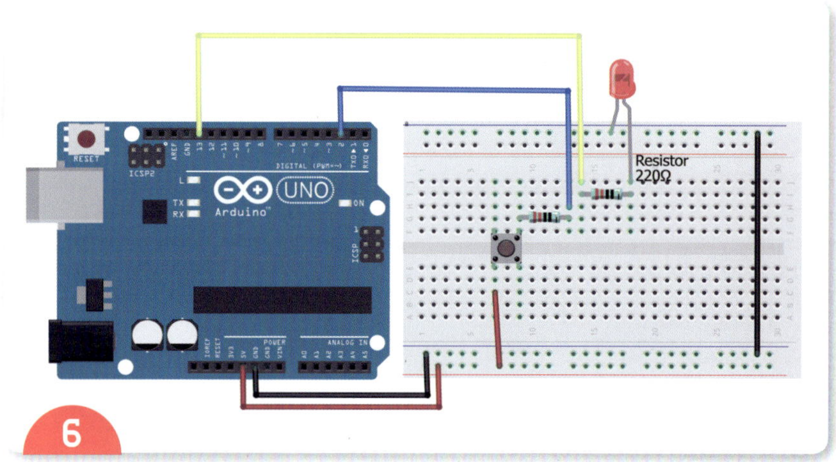

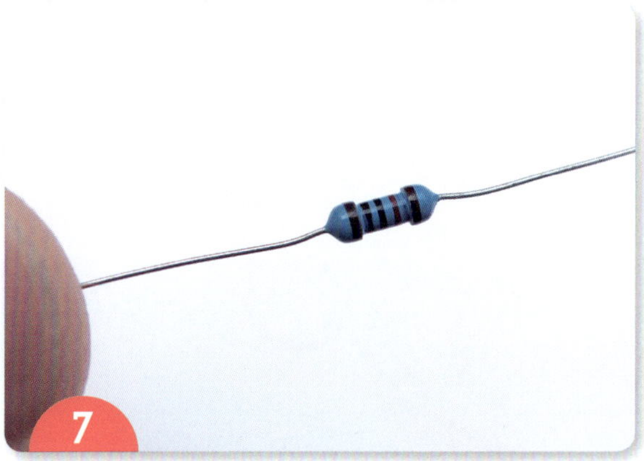

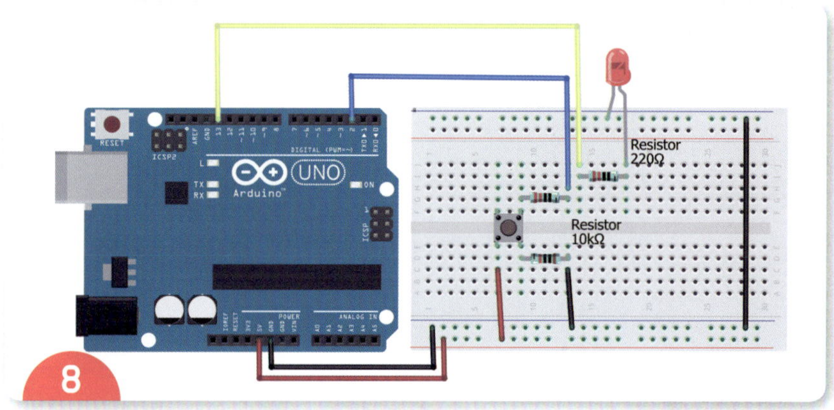

1

A switch is a component that opens or closes a circuit. Have a look at the circuit diagram opposite. In this theoretical example, we've added a basic on/off switch to a circuit with a battery powering an LED. The switch is represented by a symbol that looks like an open door. With the door open, the circuit is also open, which means that current can't flow and the LED won't emit any light – it's effectively 'switched off'. If you flip the switch and close the door, however, this closes the circuit, which allows current to flow and the LED will illuminate – now it's 'switched on'.

2

We could build a real switch like the one in the circuit diagram above, but we're going to do something slightly different; we're going to use a 6mm pushbutton switch like the one shown and connect it to a pin on our Arduino Uno as an input device. So far, we've only used outputs – when we blinked the LED, for example, we set pin 13 as an output and programmed the Uno to write the values High (on) and Low (off) continuously. An input is where the Uno reads a value instead of writing one – in this case, we'll be programming it to read whether the button is High (on) or Low (off).

3

Hold the button so that two legs are on its top edge and the other two are along the bottom. Imagine that inside are two wires – one on the left and one on the right. When you press the button, the wire on one side is connected to the other and the circuit is closed. Release the button to disconnect the wires and open the circuit. Insert the button into your breadboard so that it straddles the centreline, with two legs in sockets E7 and F7, and the other two in E9 and F9. The button is connected across its upper and lower legs, so this has the effect of connecting the rows above and below the centreline.

4

Assemble the components on the breadboard, as shown. First, connect socket C7 to the power (+) rail socket directly below it with a red wire. Then, use another black wire to connect the lower ground rail to the upper one. Insert the positive (anode) leg of an LED into socket J18 and insert the negative (cathode) leg into the corresponding socket on the ground rail above. Insert one 220 Ω resistor into sockets I14 and I18 – this will limit the current to the LED. Insert another 220 Ω resistor into G9 and G13 – this is there to protect your Arduino in case you accidentally create a short circuit.

5

Get your Arduino Uno and make sure it isn't attached to your PC or any other power source. Then, take a red jumper wire and attach it to the 5V pin on your Uno – you'll find this among the power pins on the lower edge. Now, take a black wire and attach it to the GND connector next to the 5V pin. Grab a couple more wires – we've used yellow and blue in this workshop (and throughout the book) but feel free to use any colour you have available. Attach the yellow wire to pin 13 and the blue one to pin 2 on the upper (digital) set of pins.

3 Fun with LEDs

TIP

To see precisely what the pull-down resistor is doing, try taking the 10k Ω resistor out of your breadboard and running the 'button' program. When the button is released, you'll see the effect of the 'floating' input for yourself – the LED will blink on and off randomly.

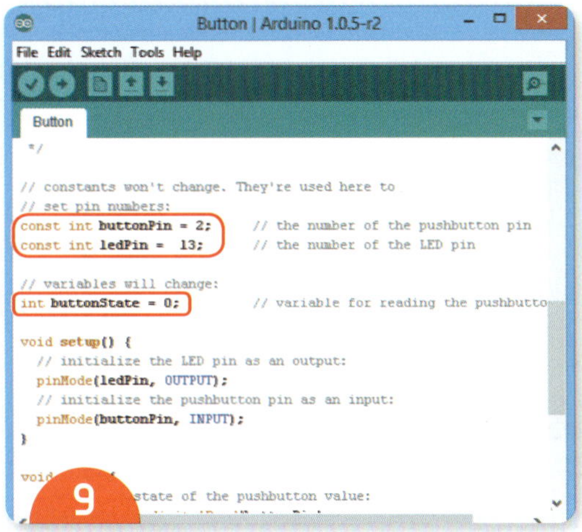

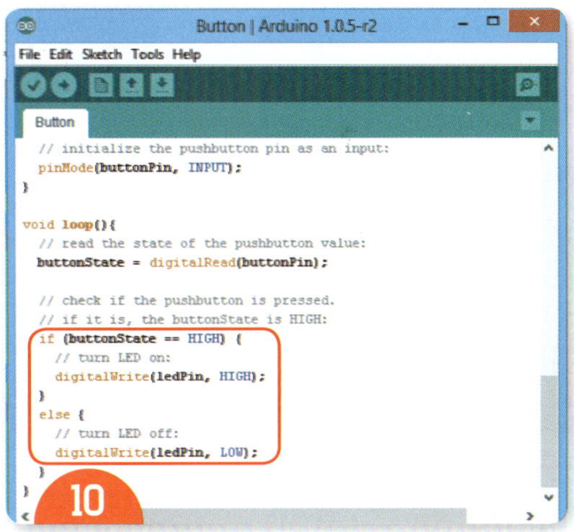

6

Connect the black wire from the ground pin on the Arduino to the first socket on the breadboard's lower ground rail (usually marked with a minus '-' sign). Likewise, connect the red wire from the 5V pin to the first or second socket on the lower power rail (usually marked with a positive '+' sign). Next, take the yellow wire from pin 13 and plug it into socket J14 on the breadboard so that it's in line with the left leg of the resistor in I14. Plug the blue wire from pin 2 into socket H13 so that it's in line with right leg of the resistor in G13.

7

We could upload our 'button' program to the Uno now, but the button wouldn't work correctly yet. If the button was pressed, pin 2 on the Uno would connect to a valid input, which it would read as a High value. But if the button was released, pin 2 wouldn't be connected to anything, which means it wouldn't be sure whether to read a High or a Low value – this is an undefined or 'floating' input. To fix this, we'll use a 'pull-down' resistor. Use a multimeter or online calculator to identify a 10 kilo ohm (10,000 Ω) resistor. Ours has five stripes – brown, black, black, red and brown.

8

Insert the resistor's legs into sockets D9 and D13 on your breadboard so that the left leg is lined up with the lower leg of the button in E9. Then ,connect socket C13 to the ground rail (-) socket directly below it with a black wire. Remember that current always takes the easiest path through a circuit. When the button is pressed, the current has a choice of paths, and the 5V path is easier than the 10k Ω resistor. Whenever the button is released, the resistor is the only choice. This will pull the power down to ground (zero), which ensures that pin 2 reads the input value as Low (off).

9

Plug your Uno into your PC via USB and open the Arduino software. Click File, Examples, then 02 Digital and select Button. Let's take a quick look at the code. Scroll past the comments and you'll see that this sketch includes some constants – things than won't change. The `const int buttonPin = 2;` bit sets the number of the pushbutton pin and `const int ledPin = 13;` sets the LED pin. The `int buttonState = 0;` establishes a 'button status' variable. The setup function below initialises the LED pin (13) as an output and the button pin (2) as an input.

10

If you look at the loop function, you'll see a new type of statement beginning `if`. Basically, this means that whenever `buttonstate` is read, if the `buttonstate` is High (in other words, pressed), the LED pin (13) will be set to High (on). But if the `buttonstate` is Low (in other words, released), the LED pin (13) will be set to Low (off). Click the Upload icon to transfer the sketch to your board. Now, try pressing the pushbutton. If you've connected everything correctly, the LED should stay lit for as long as you press the button. When you release the button, the LED should turn off.

IN THIS CHAPTER

HOW TO BUILD A ROBOT

SENSORS & INPUT

Real robots don't just carry on blindly repeating the same tasks – they can carry out different functions by automatically adjusting to different circumstances and environments. To do that, they need sensors. In this chapter, we'll be explaining all about sensors – what they are, how they work and how you can use them. We'll carry out some simple tests using light and temperature sensors, then move onto projects that explore the sensors we'll use on our robot.

ARDUINO
UNO
MADE IN ITALY
POWER
ANALOG IN
A0 A1 A2 A3 A4 A5

SENSORS AND INPUT EXPLAINED

Find out what sensors are, how they work and why almost every self-respecting robot needs them

WHAT YOU'LL LEARN

- What sensors are and why they're important
- How sensors can provide data to computer systems
- How we can make our robot smarter with sensors

Human beings are incredibly lucky without really knowing it. We take it for granted that we can experience the world around us in so many different ways. We can see, hear, smell, touch and taste it, and our senses provide us with valuable information about what we need to do next. If you saw a grand piano falling from the sky above you, for example, you could move safely out of the way.

Sadly, most desktop computers aren't as fortunate. They're able to sense which keys you've pressed on the keyboard or where you've moved your mouse cursor to, but that's about it. However, it is possible to provide machines with the means to increase their awareness of the real world. We can even provide them with programming so that they know what to do next when they sense something specific. We might have our senses, but machines have sensors.

▲ GPS devices use sensors to pinpoint your location on the planet.

WHAT IS A SENSOR?

A sensor is a type of component that can take something from the real world and convert it into data that can be processed by a computer. The simplest example might be a switch, like the pushbutton we looked at in the previous chapter. In this case, there were only two things to sense – whether the switch was being pressed or whether it had been released. But switches and buttons are only the beginning. There are dozens of different types of sensor that work in wildly different ways to measure all kinds of things, including many things that human beings themselves aren't able to gauge with their relatively basic set of five senses.

▼ Breathalysers have a sensor that uses electrochemical reaction.

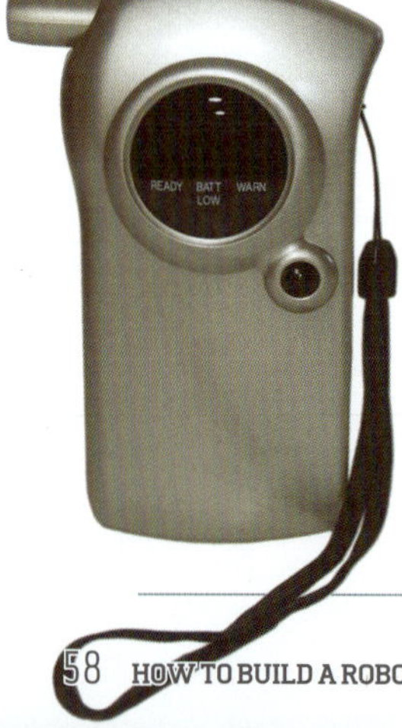

Sensors can be used to measure anything from temperature, pressure or moisture to how fast something is travelling or how much carbon monoxide is in the air. Modern cars are full of sensors. And if you use a GPS device, you're basically employing electronic sensors to pinpoint your position on the planet in relation to signals from satellites orbiting the earth.

HOW DO SENSORS WORK?

When we see, hear, smell, touch or taste something, it sends a signal to our brain, which we're then able to interpret in various ways. The overall function of an electronic sensor is similar. It takes what it's 'sensed' and sends it as a signal through a circuit to a computer or a chip, where the signal can be interpreted by programming logic. But, like our own senses, there's no hard and fast rule for how the sensors do their sensing.

A sensor somehow needs to generate an electronic signal. Our button experiment demonstrated this neatly. When the button was pressed, the circuit was closed and an electronic

▲ Cars are full of sensors, such as parking assist and the fuel gauge.

▲ Carbon monoxide alarms have sensors.

current flowed to our microcontroller, but when the button was released the circuit was opened again and the current flow stopped.

That's a really simple example, though. What if you need to measure something where there are loads of different possible states – not just on and off – such as how much light there is? Well, there are many ways this can be done, as we'll be seeing in some of our upcoming projects. Some sensors are made of special materials that react to environmental changes in ways that can vary the current in a circuit. Others use mechanical ways of reacting to something in the real world. But that's just the start – there are many other types of sensor, including magnetic, optical and even chemical varieties. Many breathalysers, for example, work using a clever electrochemical reaction, where the oxidisation of ethanol on someone's breath produces an electronic current that the device's microcontroller uses to calculate a measurement of the amount of alcohol in the person's bloodstream.

SMARTYPANTS

Often when a machine has lots of sensors and powerful programming to process all its inputs, we refer to it as 'smart'. A good example of this is a smartphone. The latest mobile handsets have lots of sensors built into them – screens that can 'feel' our touch gestures, cameras that respond to different light levels and alter display levels accordingly, gyroscopes that rotate the phone's display when we change its orientation, accelerometers that know how fast we're travelling and, in some cases, full GPS capabilities. Many phones even come with built-in temperature and humidity sensors, and can respond intelligently to our spoken commands. Thanks to sensors, smartphones are likely to carry on getting even smarter, too. Many scientists predict that smartphones will soon be capable of taking detailed measurements of the state of our health and fitness levels. And some seismologists can even foresee a time where sensors in smartphones could help to predict earthquakes. Other devices around our homes are likely to get smarter, too. Some people already use sensor-based home automation devices, but soon everyone's lighting and heating systems could be able to sense when and how they need to function.

There are dozens of different types of sensor that work in wildly different ways to measure all kinds of things

HOW DOES A ROBOT UNDERSTAND ITS SENSORS?

As the breathalyser example illustrates, a microcontroller or computer needs to have a way of receiving and interpreting the signals it receives from sensors that are attached to it. In the case of our robot, this is achieved by attaching the sensor to one of the pins on the Arduino Uno and running a sketch that reads the signals sent to that pin by the sensor.

With our button project, the sensor was only sending two types of signal – on or off, which can easily be understood by a binary system, such as a microcontroller or a PC. As we saw in chapter 1, the Uno's digital output pins also work as input pins, meaning the board can easily receive on/off signals like these as well as send them. Some sensors are able to send pulses of digital information, too – a coded series of multiple on/off signals that can be interpreted by a program that understands what these coded pulses mean. We'll see this in action later when we look at infrared remote control.

But the Uno also has six dedicated analog input pins, and these can be used for receiving signals that aren't just on or off, but instead need to be measured as a wide range of constantly changing values. The Uno then uses its onboard analog-to-digital converter (ADC) to translate analog values into binary data. This ability is crucial for robots that are designed to interact with the real world, because most of the world and the things in it are analog by their nature.

▲ The Arduino Uno has six analog inputs.

MAKE A LIGHT DETECTOR

Create a device that can measure light using a photocell and an analog input on your Arduino

WHAT YOU'LL NEED

- An Arduino Uno board
- A USB cable
- A computer
- 1 x light dependent resistor (photocell)
- 1 x LED
- 1 x 220 Ω resistor
- 1 x 10k Ω resistor
- 6 x jumper wires
- A breadboard

As we saw in the previous pages, sensors are components that allow machines to see, hear, feel and measure the world around them. Using a sensor in conjunction with the analog input sockets on our Arduino Uno and a spot of programming, we can make a device such as a robot carry out specific functions, depending on how much or how little of something is being detected by the sensor.

Here, we're going to show you how this works in practice. In this easy project, we're going to create and program a light detector that will increase or decrease the brightness of an LED, based on the amount of light detected by a light-sensitive sensor. We won't be using a light detector on our final robot – this is just for practice – but Magbot will feature several other similar sensors, as we'll demonstrate a little later on.

1

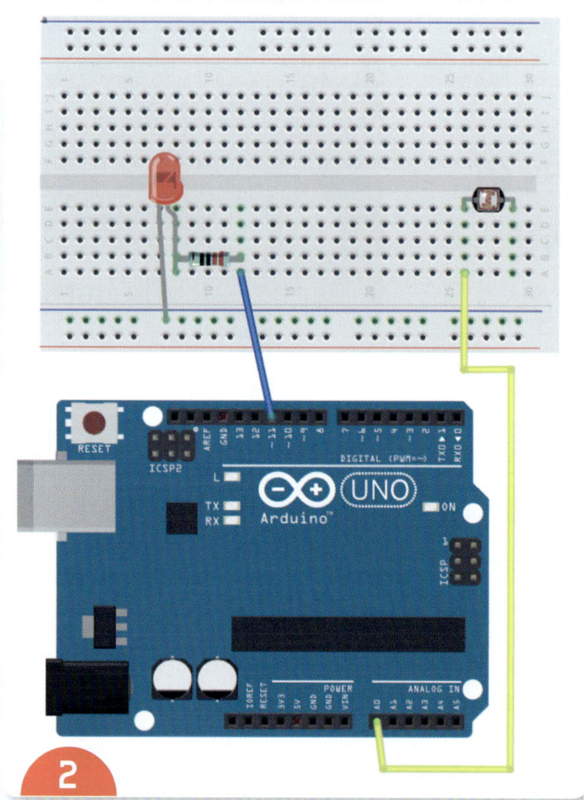

2

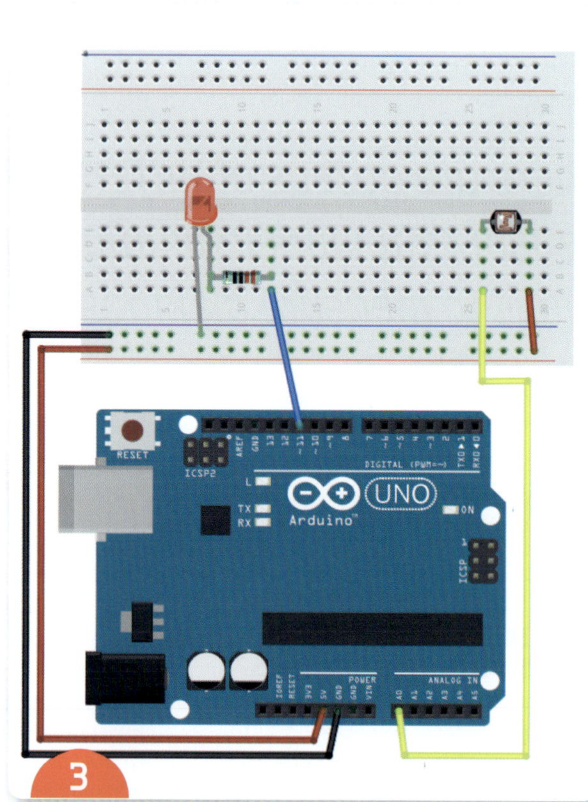

3

TIP

You'll see lines beginning `Serial` again in this sketch – this means you can use the Arduino's serial monitor to view the amount of light being measured by the photocell. With the Uno plugged into your PC, click the Serial Monitor button in the Arduino program.

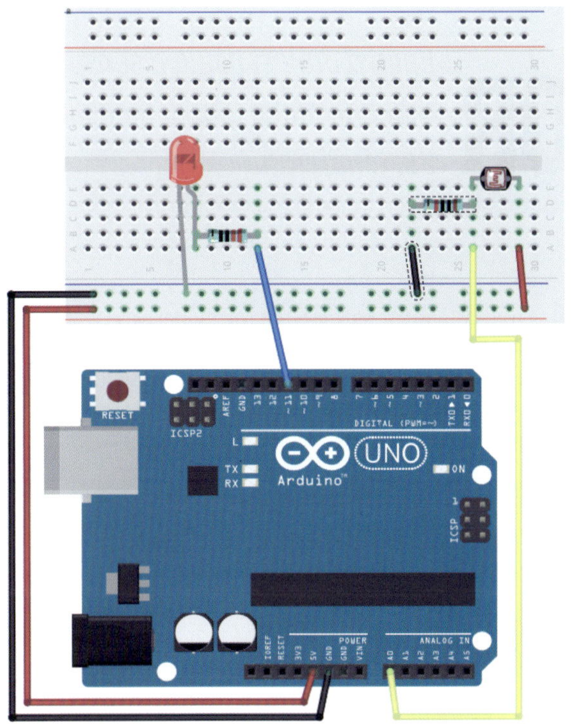

4

5

6

1

The key component in our light detector is the photocell. It's actually a type of resistor, and is often referred to as a light dependent resistor (LDR). But, unlike the resistors we've met so far, which all have a fixed resistance value, the photocell has a variable resistance governed by the amount of ambient light available. Its surface is made of a material that becomes more electrically conductive in the presence of light. With little or no light, resistance is high. But the more light you shine on it, the more the resistance falls, allowing current to flow more freely.

2

Insert the photocell into your breadboard, with one leg in socket E26 and the other in E29. Connect a coloured wire (we've used yellow) from pin A0 on your Uno to socket A26 so that the pin is lined up with the left leg of the photocell. Insert the anode (positive leg) of an LED into socket A8 and insert the cathode (negative leg) into the ground rail below. Get a 220 Ω resistor and insert it into sockets B8 and B12, then connect another coloured wire (we've used blue) from pin 11 on the Uno to socket A12, so that it's lined up with the right leg of the resistor.

3

Next, we'll connect the power and ground. Take one red wire and one black wire, and connect the red one from the 5V pin on the lower edge of the Uno to the first socket on the lower power rail on the breadboard. Then, connect the black wire from the first socket on the lower ground rail of the breadboard to the GND pin (the one next to the 5V pin) on the Uno. Now, use another red wire to connect the far right socket on the power rail to socket A29, so that it's lined up with the right leg of the photocell.

4

As things stand, current will flow to pin A0 when enough light is detected by the photocell. But if little or no light is detected, the photocell will resist the current flow, which would result in pin A0 reading an undefined or 'floating' input. So, as we did with the pushbutton project on p48, we'll use a resistor to prevent this happening. Insert a 10k Ω resistor into sockets D22 and D26 so that the right leg is lined up with the left leg of the photocell, then connect the left leg of the resistor to the ground rail below with a black wire.

5

Open a web browser on your PC and go to **www.snipca.com/12797**. Click and drag to select the code in the middle of the page, then right-click your selection and select Copy. Open the Arduino software, click in the blank sketch, then press Ctrl+V to paste the code and save your sketch as LightDetector. Have a look through the code before you upload it. The variable `int lightPin = 0;` sets the analog input A0 as the pin for the photocell, while `int ledPin=11;` sets pin 11 as the pin for the LED. In the setup function, pin 11 is defined as an output.

6

In the loop, `analogWrite(ledPin, analogRead(lightPin)/4);` tells the Uno to take the value it reads from the photocell pin, divide it by 4 and write the resulting value to the LED pin. Pin 11 is a PWM pin, which means the LED attached to it can fade, not just switch on and off, so the amount of light emitted by the LED will be directly proportional to the amount of light being measured by the sensor. Click Upload, then grab a torch. Shine it on your sensor and the LED should get brighter. Cover the sensor with your thumb and the LED should dim.

EXPERIMENT WITH A TEMPERATURE SENSOR

Build a project using a sensor that will allow you to measure the temperature

WHAT YOU'LL NEED

- An Arduino Uno board
- A USB cable
- A computer
- A temperature sensor (LM35)
- 5 x jumper wires
- A breadboard

Sensors can be used for a wide variety of purposes. Over the course of the remaining projects in this chapter, for instance, we'll be building some sensor-based parts that will allow Magbot to not only see and feel his way around, but also provide him with a way to recognise some basic remote commands. Before we get onto that, though, we're going to show you another practice project based around a temperature sensor. We'll create a very simple circuit to show how the sensor works and then explain how to view the results using the Arduino's serial monitor. The model we're using is designed for measuring temperature in Celsius/Centigrade, but we'll show you how, by adding a few lines of programming code, you can hack the sketch to show the temperature in Fahrenheit as well.

1

2

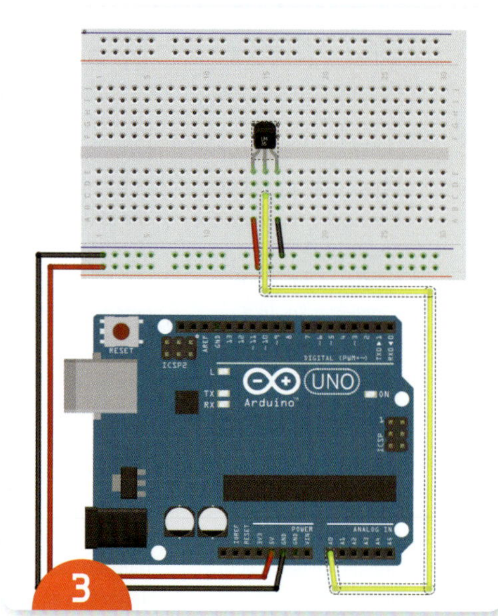

3

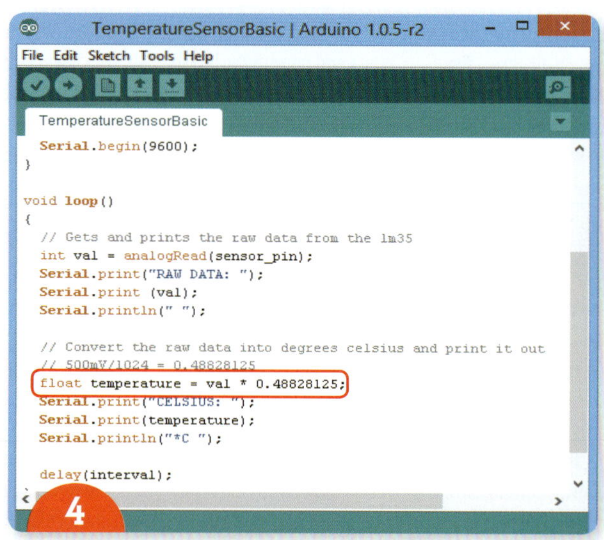

4

TIP

A good way to practise your coding skills would be to try hacking the 'basic' sketch to add the code for the Fahrenheit conversion yourself – you can use the 'full' sketch as your reference and copy or type the additional lines of code needed.

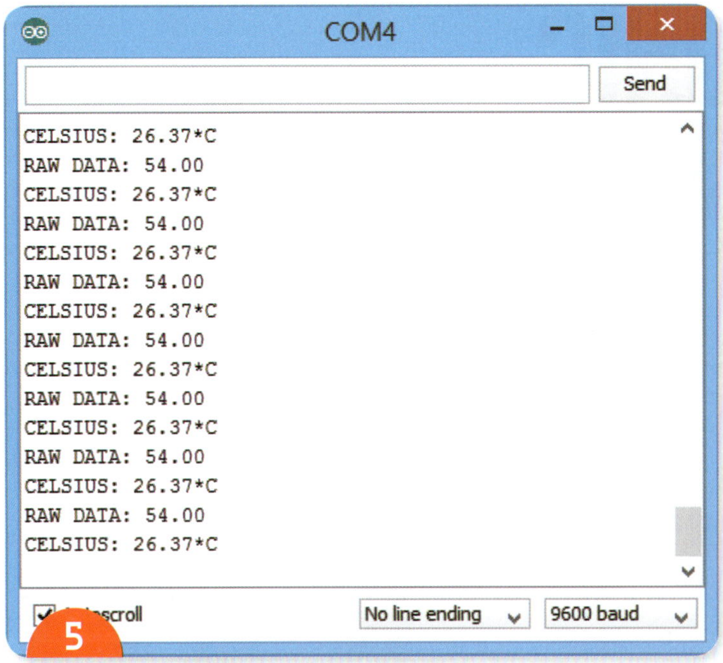

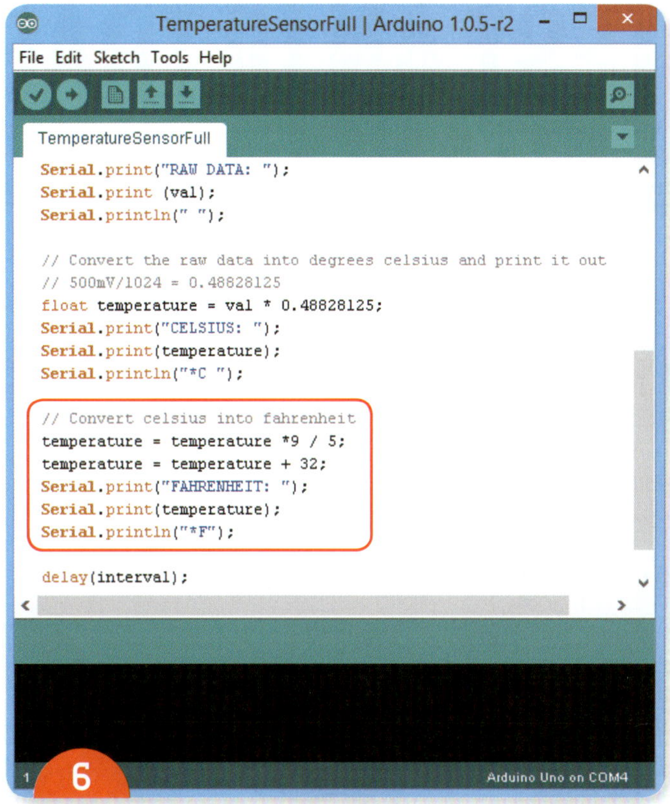

1

The temperature sensor we're using came with our components kit. The part number is LM35 and looks like the one shown here. The sensor is different to traditional temperature measurement devices – it doesn't use mechanical strips or coils or mercury. Nor does it act like a resistor in the same way as the photocell we experimented with in the previous project. Instead, it uses the fact that an increase or decrease in temperature results in a proportional increase or decrease in voltage. And, by using a basic formula, you can convert the voltage reading into a temperature measurement.

2

The circuit for our electronic temperature gauge is very simple. First, we'll hook up power. Connect a red (power) wire from the 5V pin on the lower edge of the Uno to the first socket on the left-hand side of the breadboard's lower power rail. Then, connect the black (ground) wire from the GND pin (the one next to the 5V pin) on the Uno to the first socket on the breadboard's lower ground rail. Use another red wire to connect socket A14 to the power rail underneath, and use another black wire to connect socket A16 to the ground rail below.

3

Next, use a yellow or other coloured wire to connect pin A0 on your Arduino to socket C15 on the breadboard. The only part that can be a little tricky is inserting the temperature sensor itself – it has three legs and, like LEDs, it needs to be connected the right way around; otherwise, it won't work properly. Hold the sensor so that the flat side is facing you. The right-hand leg is ground, the left-hand leg is power and the middle leg is analog voltage out, or 'V out'. Gently bend the sensor's left and right legs outward slightly so that you can slot the component into sockets E14, E15 and E16.

4

We included two sketches, TemperatureSensorBasic & TemperatureSensorFull, in our Magbot ZIP, so if you installed this as per our instructions in the battery indicator project, you'll be able to open your Arduino program, click on File, Sketchbook, Magbot and select TemperatureSensorBasic. The code defines pin 0 as an analog input pin and tells the pin to take a reading every second. Scroll down to the loop section and you'll see the line `float temperature = val * 0.48828125;` This formula takes the voltage reading from the sensor and converts it into a temperature value.

5

Upload the sketch to your Uno and click the Serial Monitor icon. In the monitor window, you'll see a set of two values, refreshed every second: 'Raw Data' and 'Celsius'. The raw data is the sensor's analog voltage reading and the Celsius value is the temperature. Since the Uno uses a 10-bit analog-to-digital converter, you first need to divide the number of millivolts (500) by 1024, which gives you 0.48828125. So, if you multiply the raw value in each case by 0.48828125, you'll get the Celsius value, which is precisely what the formula in the loop is doing for you.

6

Test the sensor by placing a heat source on or near it. Put your thumb over it, and the temperature shown in the serial monitor will increase. To display the temperature in Fahrenheit as well, click on File, Sketchbook, Magbot and select TemperatureSensorFull. This is the same as the previous sketch but with some lines in the loop (after the `//converts celsius into fahrenheit` comment) that use another formula to make an on-the-fly conversion to Fahrenheit and tell the serial monitor to print the results with the Celsius and raw values. Upload the sketch and open the serial monitor.

TEST AN ULTRASONIC DISTANCE SENSOR

Carry out some experiments to learn how your robot will sense the world around him

WHAT YOU'LL NEED

- An Arduino Uno board
- A USB cable
- A computer
- An ultrasonic module (HC-SR04)
- 4 x jumper wires
- A breadboard

In this project, we'll be making possibly our most recognisably robot-like part yet. We'll be building a circuit designed to test the ultrasonic module that our finished robot will eventually be using to help him navigate. As you'll see below, the unit looks just like a pair of robotic eyes but, in fact, Magbot with be more or less blind – he'll only be able to 'see' infrared, as we'll find out in our next project. Instead, like bats, dolphins and submarines, Magbot will use sonar in order to measure distances and help him move around his environment without clumsily bumping into every single obstacle in his path. Over the following steps, we'll explain how the ping/echo sensor works and show you how to test your component before you finally start putting Magbot together for real (in chapter 7).

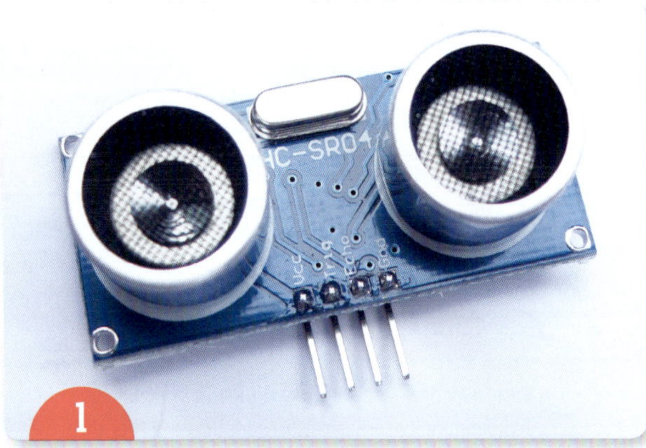

1

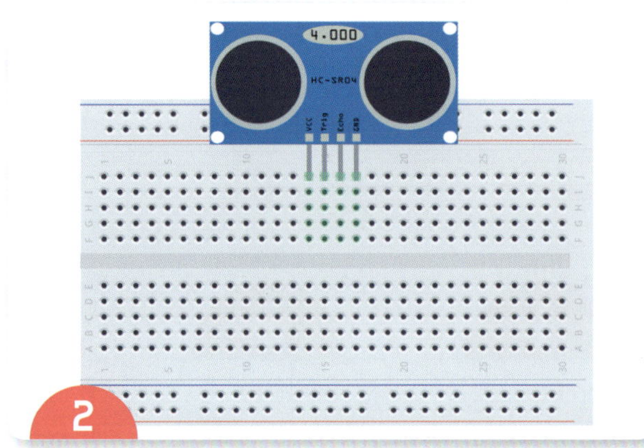

2

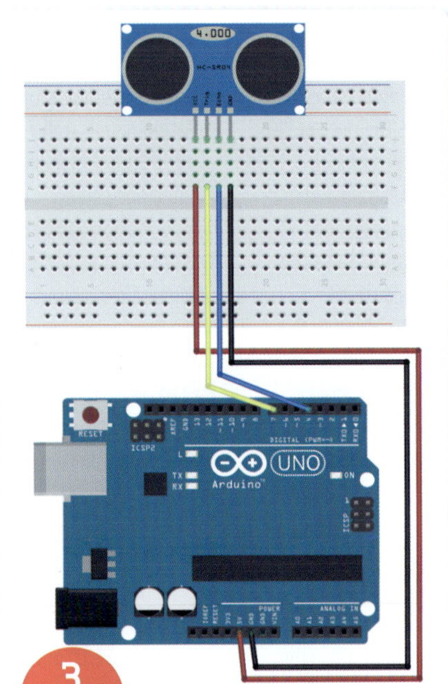

3

4

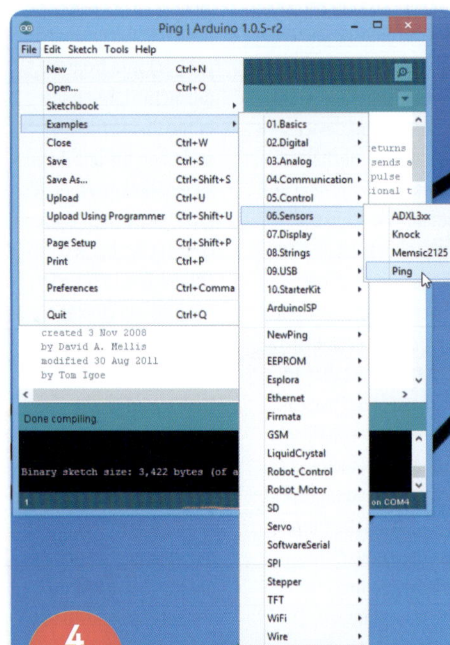

4

TIP

To test the accuracy of the distance sensor, grab a ruler and lay it flat on your work surface so that the sensor is in line with 0cm. Then, move your hand to 14cm – the serial window should read 14cm, too.

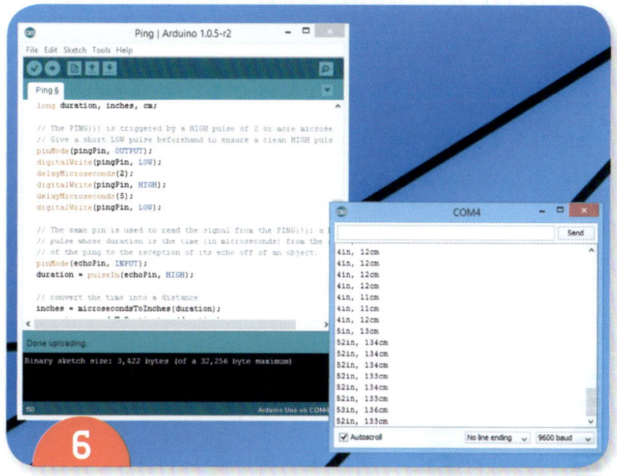

1

Here's what the ultrasonic distance sensor module looks like. Sensors like these are also sometimes referred to as rangefinders or ping modules. This particular model is a pretty common example (the precise part number is HC-SR04) and it's rated to detect distances of up to 500cm with fairly good accuracy. The two 'eyes' can, in fact, be thought of as more like a speaker and a microphone. The speaker outputs an inaudible ultrasonic sound wave (ping), which will keep travelling forward until it hits something, at which point it will bounce back and be heard by the microphone (echo). With some programming, this can be used to calculate distances.

2

There are four legs on the underside of the ultrasonic distance sensor module, and you'll need to wire these up correctly; otherwise, the sensor won't work. Hold the component with its 'eyes' looking at you – you should see that the legs are labelled. The leg on the far left, labelled 'VCC', is for power, and the leg on the far right, labelled 'GND', is for ground. Of the middle two legs, the one on the left is labelled 'Trig' for trigger (ping) and the one on the right is labelled 'Echo'. Insert the sensor into your breadboard so that the VCC leg slots into socket J14, with the remaining legs in J15, J16 and J17.

3

Now it's time to make your connections to and from the Arduino Uno. Connect a red (power) wire from the 5V pin on the Uno to socket F14 on the breadboard, so that it lines up with the VCC leg of the sensor. Use a black (ground) wire to connect the Uno's GND pin (the one next to the 5V pin) to socket F17, so that it's lined up with the sensor's 'GND' leg. Use a coloured wire (shown as yellow here) to connect pin 7 on the Uno to socket F15, in line with the 'Trig' leg, and another colour (shown as blue here) to connect pin 4 to socket F16, so that it's in line with the 'Echo' leg.

4

Hook your Uno up to your PC and start the Arduino software. There's a distance detection sketch included as one of the examples, so click File, Examples, 06 Sensors and select Ping. Click the Upload button to write the sketch to your Uno board. Now, click the Serial Monitor button to view the sensor's readings and you should see… nothing! The serial monitor should just produce a long series of zero values. This is because the Ping sample sketch was written for a slightly different sensor module – one with only three legs. Look through the sketch and you'll see that it uses the same pin to read and write signals to and from the sensor.

5

We'll be using purpose-built code for our distance sensor when we incorporate it into Magbot but, for this test, we're going to hack the example sketch to get it working. This will demonstrate how simple the code actually is. Scroll down to the line `const int pingPin = 7;` – this defines the ping pin as 7. We're going to add a second constant for pin 4 and call it echoPin, so click just after the semi-colon and press Enter, then type `const int echoPin = 4;`. Scroll down to the loop and look for the two lines `pinMode (pingPin, INPUT);` and `duration = pulseIn(pingPin, HIGH);` – in both lines change `pingPin` to `echoPin`.

6

That's it – you've officially hacked the code! If you like, you can click File, then Save As to save your work under a new name (the IDE software won't let you overwrite any of the sample sketches). When you're done saving, click the Upload again and, once the modified sketch has been written to your board, click the Serial Monitor button. This time, you should be greeted by a series of different distance values in inches and centimetres. You can now test the sensor by putting your hand in front of it and moving it nearer or further away – the values in the serial window should change accordingly.

SET UP REMOTE CONTROL

Discover how you'll be able to send wireless commands to your robot via an infrared sensor

WHAT YOU'LL NEED

- An Arduino Uno board
- A USB cable
- A computer
- 1 x infrared sensor
- 1 x IR remote handset
- 1 x 220 Ω resistor
- 1 x LED
- 7 x jumper wires
- A breadboard
- A TV or DVD remote

Infrared is far from a new technology. Most of us have been using it in our homes to wirelessly transmit data to our appliances for more than 30 years without really giving it much of a second thought. But, just as you use an infrared remote to control your TV, we're going to show you how to send wireless commands to Magbot.

In the first part of this project, we're going to build a simple circuit to test that the infrared sensor is receiving a signal. For this, you can use any IR remote control handset you have handy – the one for your TV or DVD player will work fine. In the second part, we're going to program our Uno to interpret different infrared signals and show you how to monitor them yourself.

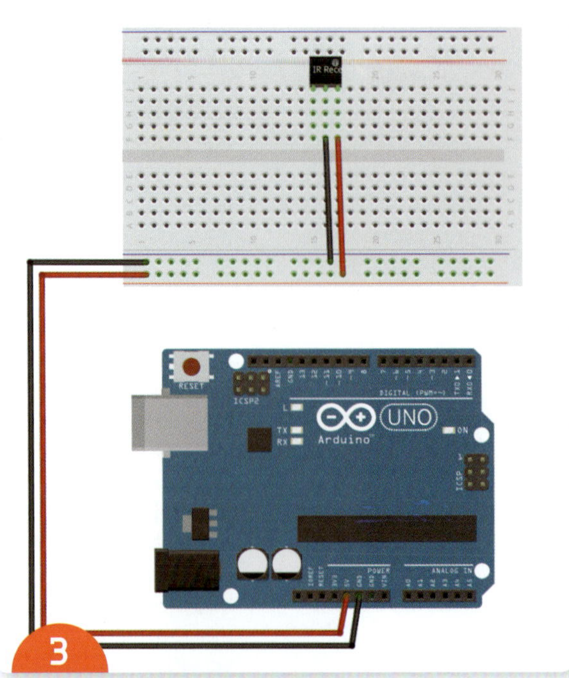

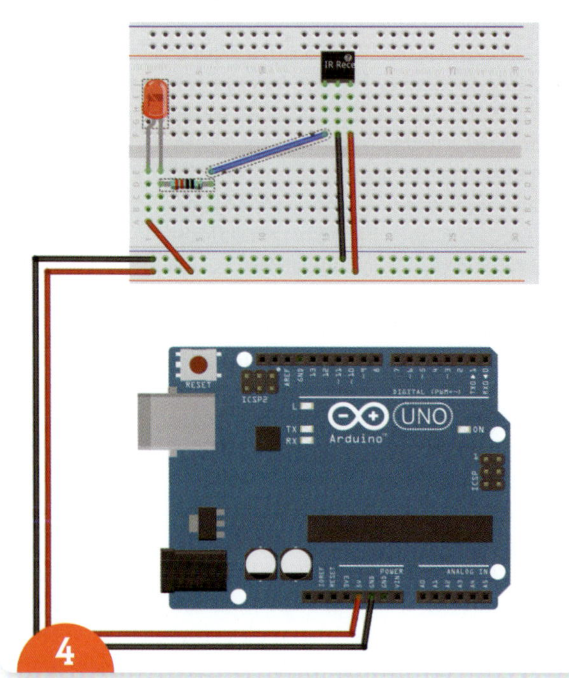

TIP

You can use the same trick we described in step 8 with your TV remote or any other handset that you suspect might be broken, using a camera to see if it's transmitting. Some cameras – those with IR filters, including the iPhone 4 and 5 – won't work, however.

5

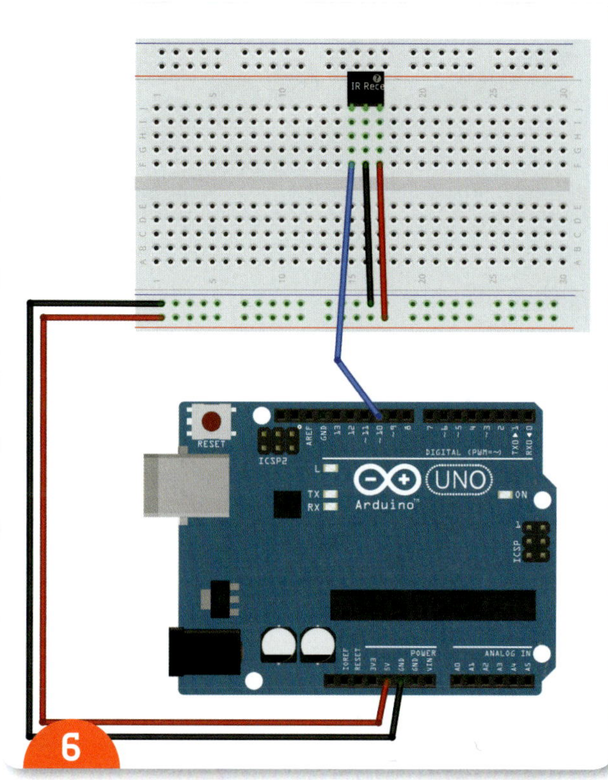

6

1

Our IR sensor is a fairly typical component – part number VS1838b. It's a type of light sensor, but it works in a very different way to the photocell we tested earlier, which was effectively a resistor that responded to normal light. The IR sensor senses infrared light waves that are invisible to the naked eye and turns these into a voltage signal. Remote control handsets, like the one for your TV, send out a series of different infrared pulses, depending on which button you press. When these pulses are received by an IR sensor, they are sent to a microcontroller as electronic signals, which are then interpreted as different commands.

2

Hold the sensor so that the black bit at the top with the metal 'X' on it is facing you – this is the infrared receiver itself. Each of the three legs serves a different purpose, so they need to be connected correctly. On our sensor, the leg on the far right is for power, the middle leg is for ground and the left leg is the 'V out' connection – this is the one that sends the signals to the microcontroller. Start by inserting the sensor into your breadboard, so that the 'V out' pin goes into socket J15 and the other two slot into sockets J16 and J17.

3

Next, we're going to connect our Arduino Uno. As it happens, for the first part of the test, we won't be using the microcontroller at all – we'll just be using the board to power our circuit. You could use a battery instead, but the Uno provides a conveniently steady 5V supply, so we'll use that. Connect red (power) and black (ground) wires from the 5V and GND pins to the first sockets on the lower power and ground rails respectively. Then, hook up the power rail to socket F17 with another red wire so that it's in line with the sensor's power leg. Now, connect socket F16 to the ground rail.

4

As a simple way to demonstrate that the sensor is receiving a signal, we're going to include an LED in our circuit, which should react whenever a signal is detected. Grab an LED, then insert the positive (anode) leg into socket E1 on your breadboard and the negative (cathode) leg into socket E2. Connect a red wire from socket A1 to the power rail below, then attach a coloured wire (blue in ours) from socket F15 (in line with the 'V out' leg of the sensor) to socket E6. Now, pop a 220 Ω resistor into sockets D2 and D6 to bridge the gap between the blue 'V out' wire and the LED.

5

With your circuit complete, connect the Arduino Uno to your PC via USB. Remember, at this stage, we're not using the Uno's microcontroller in any way and we're not connecting to our PC to upload any code just yet – we're just using the Arduino (and the PC) as a power supply for our circuit. If everything is wired up correctly, the LED should remain switched off at first. Now, point your TV remote at the infrared receiver and press any button. Did the LED flicker when you held down the button on your remote? If so, then you've just proved that your infrared sensor is working fine.

4 Sensors & input

7

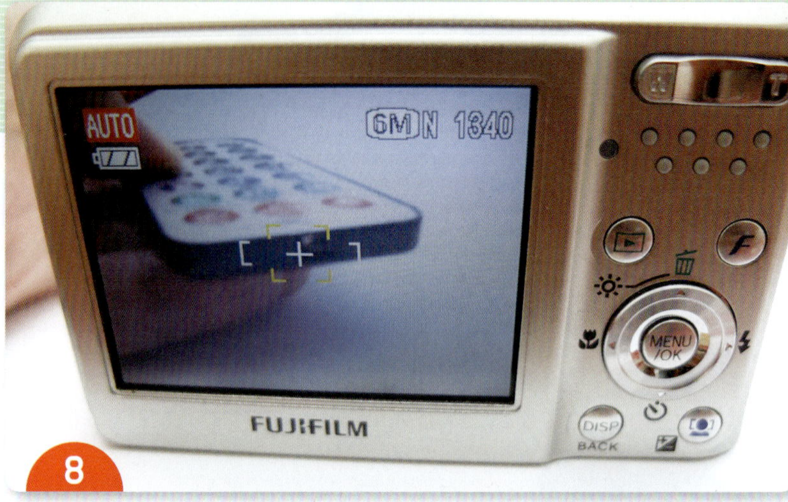

8

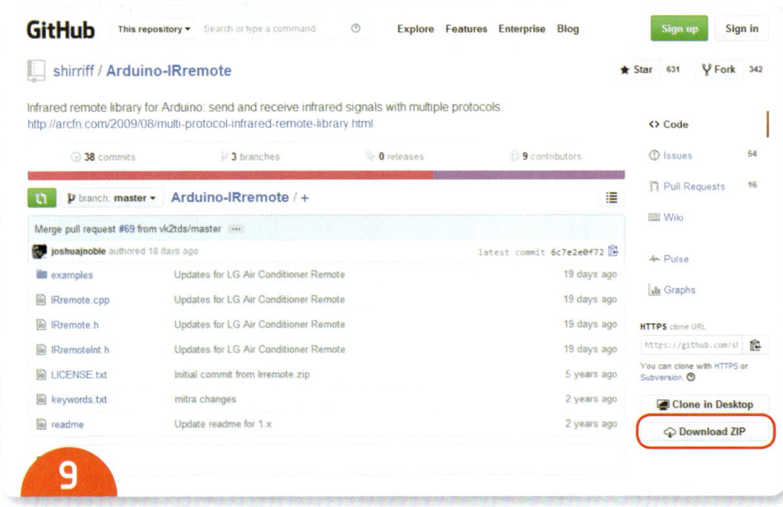

9

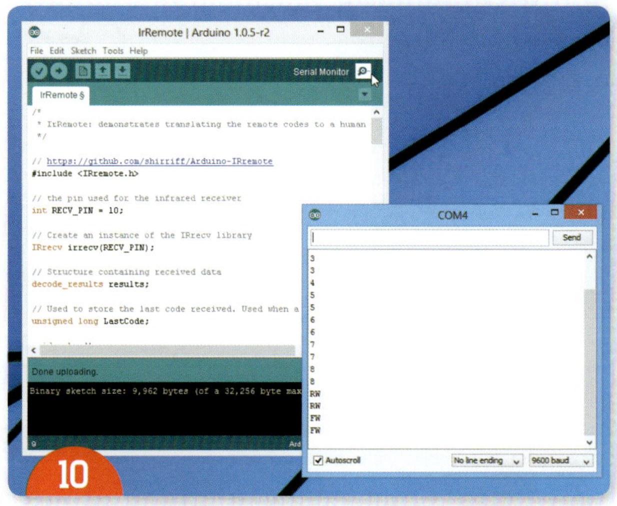

10

6

Now, we're going to incorporate the Arduino Uno properly into the circuit. We'll connect the sensor to an input pin on the Uno and upload some code that will allow the microcontroller to interpret the signals it's being sent. Luckily, you can leave most of your breadboard exactly as it is, with a few minor changes. Unplug your Uno from the PC, then pull one end of the blue wire out of socket E6 on the breadboard and plug it into pin 10 on the Uno. We won't need the LED, so you can pull that out, along with the resistor and the red wire running from socket A1 to the power rail.

7

Your component kit should have come with a mini remote control handset like the one shown. You can also buy similar remote handsets and IR sensors on their own for a couple of pounds. The handset itself is battery powered and should come provided with the battery required – usually a CR2025 lithium ion button cell. In most cases, you should find a piece of clear protective plastic sticking out from just below the battery cover. This is just there to stop the battery from running down by providing a barrier to the battery compartment's contacts, so you'll need to pull it out in order to use the handset.

8

There's a quick and easy way to see whether the remote handset is working properly. If you look at the end, you'll see a small LED – this is called the blaster and it's the part that sends the infrared signal to the sensor. If you press a button on the remote, you won't see anything happen, because the human eye can't see the light waves it's producing. But most digital cameras can see them. Grab a camera and turn it on. Point the blaster at the lens, then press any button. Did you see a blue-ish flicker from the remote's LED via the camera's rear screen? If so, the handset is working fine.

9

We've included the sketch you need along with the other code for Magbot. If you haven't already, go to **www.pcpro.co.uk/links/robot** and download the magbot.zip file. Extract the ZIP to the Arduino program's sketch folder. Launch the Arduino IDE program and click File, Sketchbook, then Magbot and select IrRemote from the list. You'll also need to download the library for this sketch. Click or copy and paste the URL towards the top of the sketch into a browser and, in the page that opens, click the Download Zip button. Unzip the file and rename the folder IRremote. Copy the IRremote folder to C:\Users\Yourusername\Documents\Arduino\libraries.

10

Restart the Arduino program and connect your Uno to your PC. Open the IrRemote sketch again, then click Upload to transfer the code and its libraries to your board. To test everything's working, click the Serial Monitor button in the Arduino program window and an empty window will open. Now, point your remote handset at the infrared receiver and press the '1' button. You should see the number '1' appear in the monitor. Test out some more buttons – the numbers you press should correspond with the numbers that appear in the monitor window. Press rewind and you should see 'RW'; press fast forward and you should see 'FF' and so on.

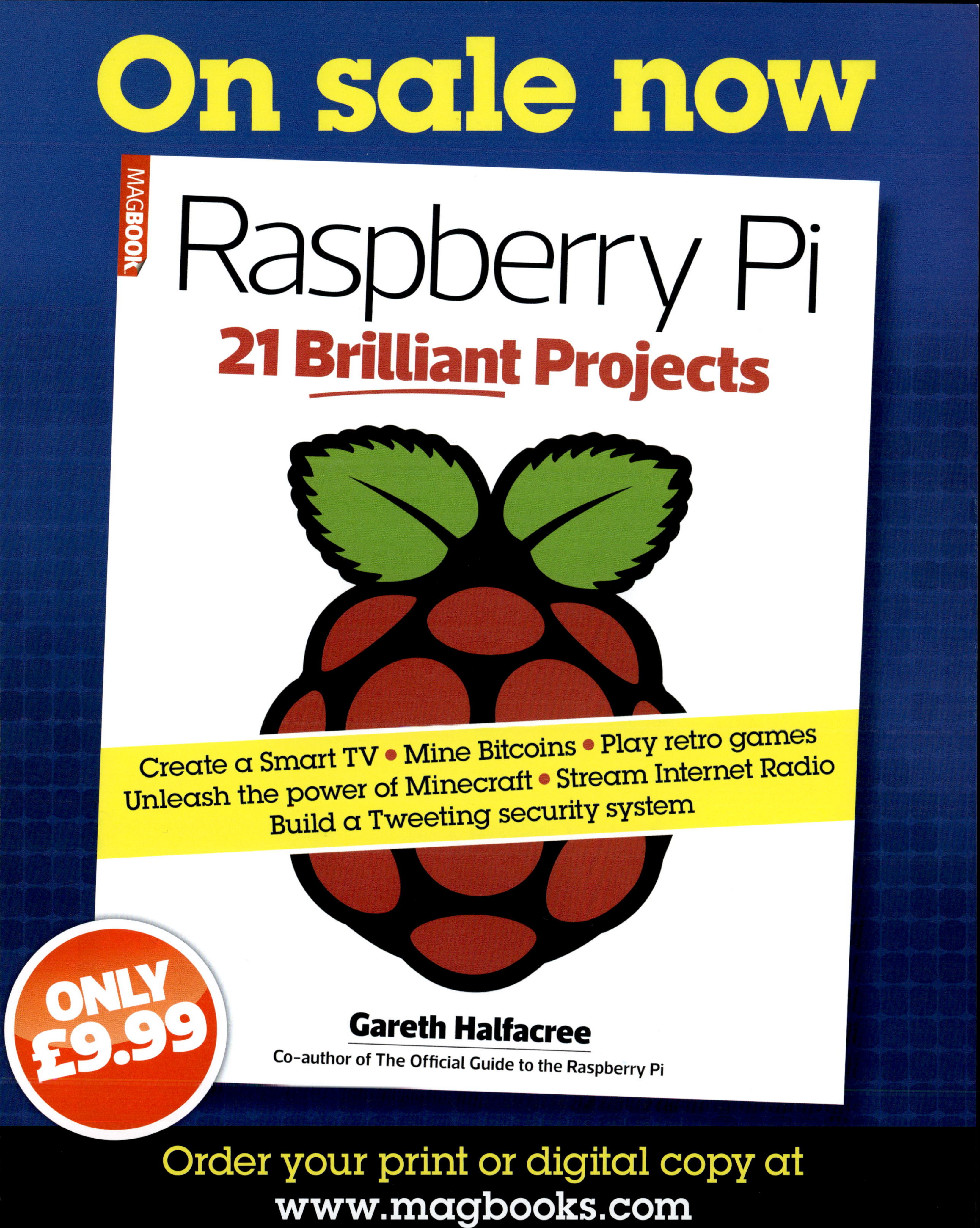
On sale now
MAGBOOK
Raspberry Pi
21 Brilliant Projects
Create a Smart TV • Mine Bitcoins • Play retro games
Unleash the power of Minecraft • Stream Internet Radio
Build a Tweeting security system
Gareth Halfacree
Co-author of The Official Guide to the Raspberry Pi
ONLY £9.99
Order your print or digital copy at
www.magbooks.com

MAKE A 'NOSE' FOR YOUR ROBOT

Find out why we're going to give our Magbot whiskers and how they're going to work

WHAT YOU'LL NEED

- An Arduino Uno board
- A USB cable
- A computer
- 1 x analog joystick
- A set of male-to-female jumper wires

Our final sensor project might sound a little curious at first. We're going to demonstrate how to use a joystick from a games controller as the 'nose' for our robot. Before you say anything – no, Magbot won't be able to smell. Instead, we're giving him a nose so that we can attach whiskers to aid with his navigation. We're doing this because the robot will have blind spots either side of him where his forward-facing ping/echo sensor (see our earlier project) is ineffective. In our tests, we found that early Magbot prototypes would manoeuvre happily around objects directly in front of them, but would sometimes get caught on obstacles that weren't in their 'eyeline'. The whiskers will work in a similar way to those of a cat – Magbot will be able to feel his way around nearby obstacles and navigate out of tight corners.

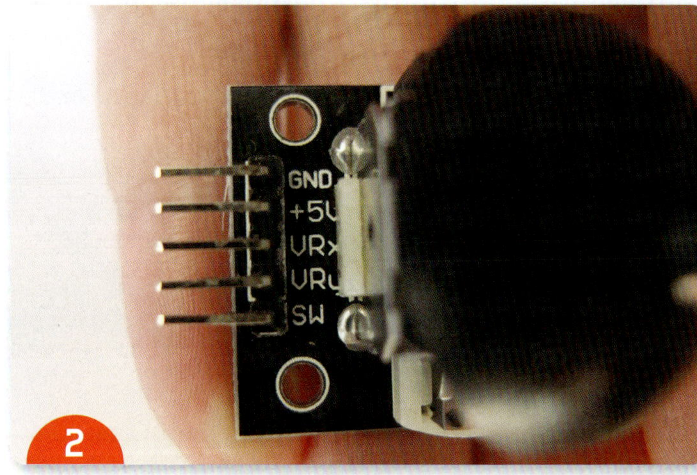

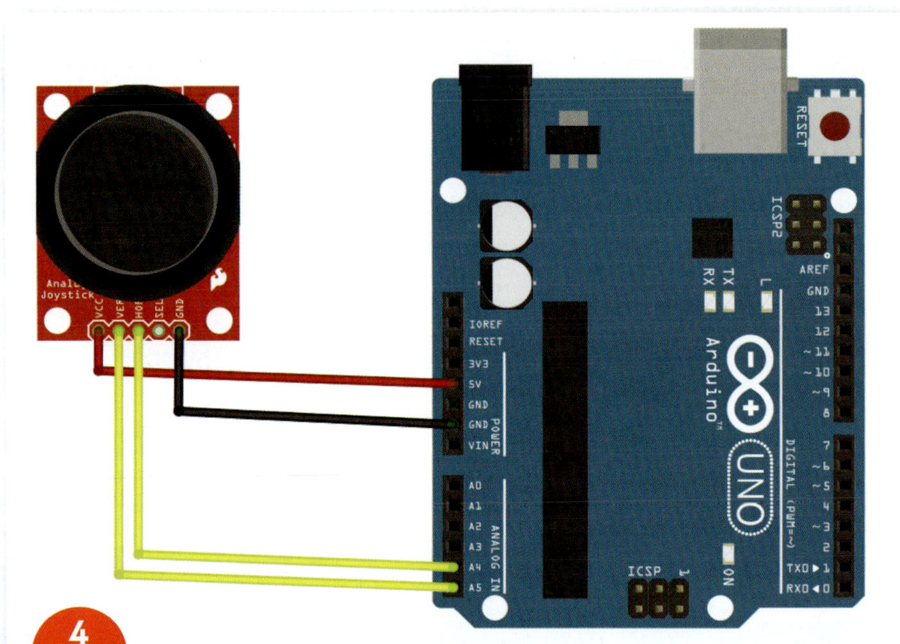

TIP

If you're finding the whiskers are too sensitive, look for the line `const byte whiskers_threshold = 5;`, which defines the sensitivity by stating how much the reading is allowed to fluctuate from the calibrated value. Change the value 5 to a higher number and test again.

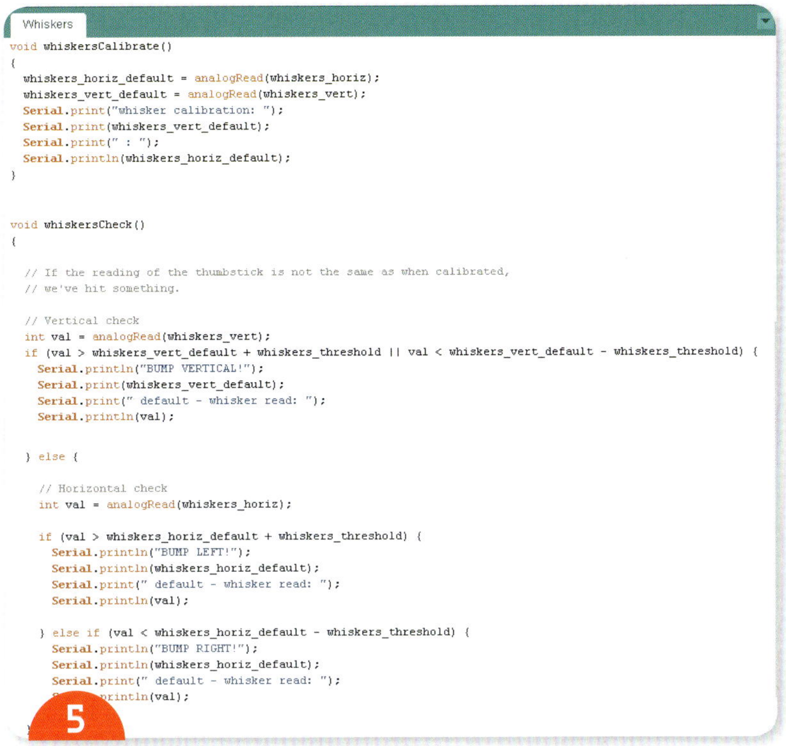

5

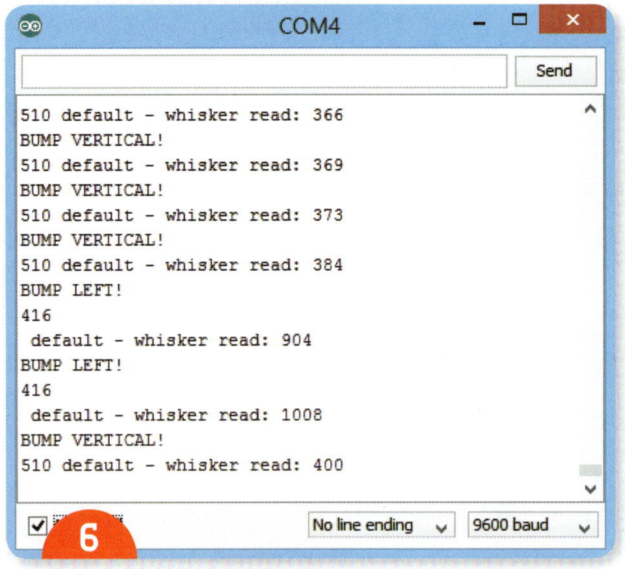

6

1

Here's our robot's nose – you may know it better as an analog joystick. It's exactly the same as the one you'll find on your PlayStation or Xbox game controller. It works by using a sensor called a potentiometer – two of them, in fact. There's one on each of the joystick's axes: the X axis (left to right) and the Y axis (up and down). Like the photocell at the beginning of this chapter, a potentiometer is a type of variable resistor. By varying the current depending on the direction of movement and using the laws of geometry to interpret the resulting signals, it's possible to calculate the position of the joystick's X-Y co-ordinates.

2

We're going to connect our joystick to our Arduino and upload some code to test that it's all working before we build it into our robot. This will help demonstrate how the whiskers are going to work. If you look at the joystick, you'll see five legs along one edge. They might be labelled differently depending on the manufacturer, but one will be for ground (GND), another will be for power (labelled either VCC or +5V), one is for the X axis (often labelled HOR or VRX), one is for the Y axis (VER or VRY) and one will be for a switch (labelled SW or SEL).

3

You can put your breadboard to one side for now. We're not going to use one for this test, as we don't need to connect any other components – just the joystick and the Arduino. So, instead, we're going to use some male-to-female jumper wires. These usually come in the form of a ribbon cable with multiple different coloured wires all stuck together. Each individual wire can make its own connection. The female end of each wire allows you to insert a male connection, such as the legs of our joystick. The other end of each wire can plug into the Uno's I/O pins as normal.

4

It's easier to start connecting the wires from one end of the ribbon cable, so use the last two from one end to connect the GND and power (VCC) legs on the joystick to the GND and 5V pins on your Uno respectively. Using the next two wires along, connect the horizontal (X axis) leg to pin A4 on the Uno and the vertical (Y axis) leg to pin A5. We're not going to use the joystick's switch function for our robot, so don't bother connecting this pin. You can tear the five wires you're using off the ribbon; otherwise, the remaining wires will be hanging off unused.

5

Connect the Arduino board to your PC and start the IDE program. Click File, Sketchbook, then Magbot and select Whiskers. Have a look through the sketch – this is basically a small section of the finished code we'll be using for Magbot himself! Constants and variables towards the top define the input pins, how often to check them and so on. Scroll down to the main part of the program and you'll see it has two functions – first, it will be calibrating the 'normal' centred position of the joystick, and then in the loop it will continuously check the position of the joystick.

6

Later, when we put all the bits for Magbot together, we'll connect stiff wires to either side of the joystick for his whiskers. If any of the wires come into contact with an object, this will nudge the joystick. Magbot will notice from his checks that the value is different to the calibrated value and realise he has bumped into something. To demonstrate this, open the serial monitor and move the joystick with your thumb. Nudge the stick on its X axis and you'll see a message saying either 'BUMP LEFT!' or 'BUMP RIGHT!' depending on which direction you press. Move the joystick on its Y axis and you'll see 'BUMP VERTICAL!'

IN THIS CHAPTER

HOW TO BUILD A ROBOT

MOTORS & MOVEMENT

Some robots walk on two legs, others walk on four. Some move around on tank treads, others fly through the air. Some don't get to travel much at all but still have moving parts, such as arms. Our robot will use good, old-fashioned wheels to get around. And, as with most other types of robotic movement, Magbot's wheels will be powered by motors. In this chapter, we're going to be exploring many of the concepts surrounding motion, and we'll be carrying out several practical tests, including a project that will see you building a simplified version of your finished robot.

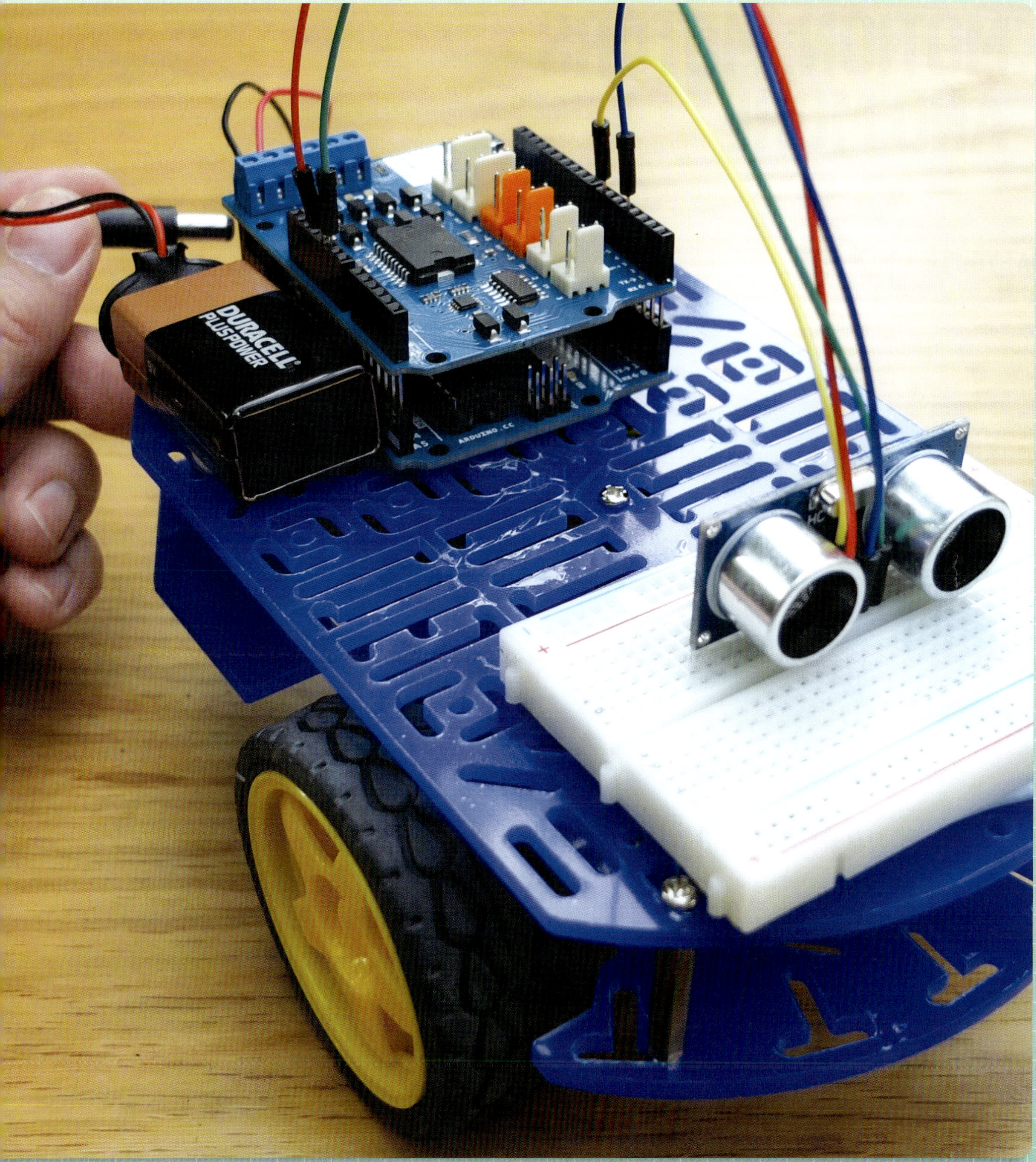
DURACELL
PLUSPOWER
ARDUINO.CC

MOTION, MOTORS AND MORE

It's time to get Magbot moving – we look at all the different options for making our robot mobile

WHAT YOU'LL LEARN

- What different types of robotic movement there are
- Why we'll be using a motor shield
- How the motors will make your robot move

We've carried out a wide variety of projects so far, from blinking LEDs to measuring distances. But all our projects up to this point have one crucial factor in common – they've all been stationary. Now, it's time to introduce a little bit of movement to the situation. And that means learning about motors – how they work, what they do and how we'll be using them in our own robot.

In the rest of this chapter, we'll be carrying out some practical experiments to test motors out for ourselves. Better still, we'll be taking the opportunity to build a simplified version of Magbot so we can see precisely how our robot's movement will work. Before we dive in, though, let's learn more about some of the technologies we'll be introducing.

HOW TO ACHIEVE MOVEMENT

In many people's view, a robot wouldn't be a robot if it couldn't move in one way or another. Movement is a very quick way to tell that a machine is working autonomously and 'thinking' for itself. With Magbot, for example, the idea is to build a robot that will be able to trundle around his world at will, avoiding any obstacles he finds in his path. But first we're going to need to find a way to make him mobile.

Thankfully, the basic principles behind getting a machine to move are fairly similar to those we've already employed whilst working with other components in our previous projects. Just as we programmed our microcontroller to output a signal to an LED to make it blink, it's also possible for our Arduino to output a signal to a motor to tell it to move. Attach that motor to something such as a wheel and– bingo! – you have movement.

There are several types of motor available, and some are more suited to specific types of project than others. So let's have a quick look at the main varieties.

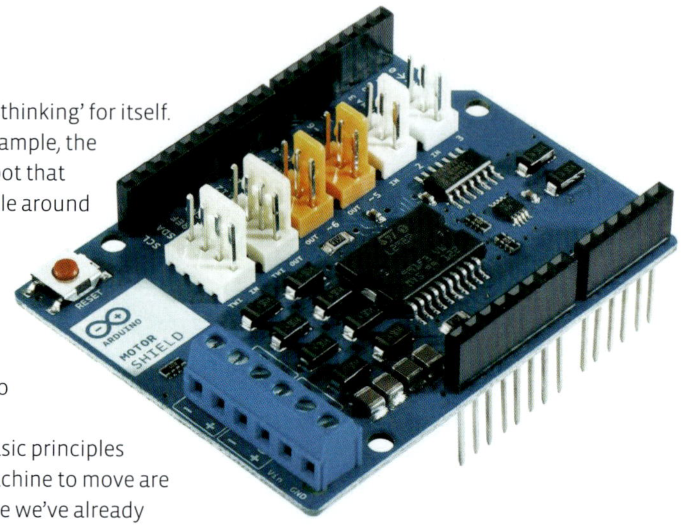

▲ Arduino's official motor shield.

DC motor

DC motors work using the science of electromagnetism to rotate an axle continuously. In simple terms, inside the motor is a rotating electromagnet, which is placed between two poles of a fixed magnet. When the electromagnet is powered, its north pole is attracted to the south pole of the fixed magnet (and repelled by the north pole), and this causes the rotor to turn. Just as the magnets poles are about to be aligned, the polarity is flipped, and this repeats the process, causing the rotation to continue. DC motors are also sometimes called 'brushed' motors, because they use carbon brushes to conduct the current to the motor's rotating parts. They're not very accurate, but they can often be very fast. And by using the Arduino's PWM output – the same ability we made use of to fade an LED back in chapter 3 – you can vary a DC motor's speed incrementally, as required. DC motors are often used to turn wheels.

HOW YOUR ROBOT WILL MOVE

Magbot will use a 2WD system, with two DC motors to get him moving and a third wheel – a non-powered caster – to provide balance and aid steering at the rear. The diagrams below show how the motors will drive Magbot forward, backwards left and right.

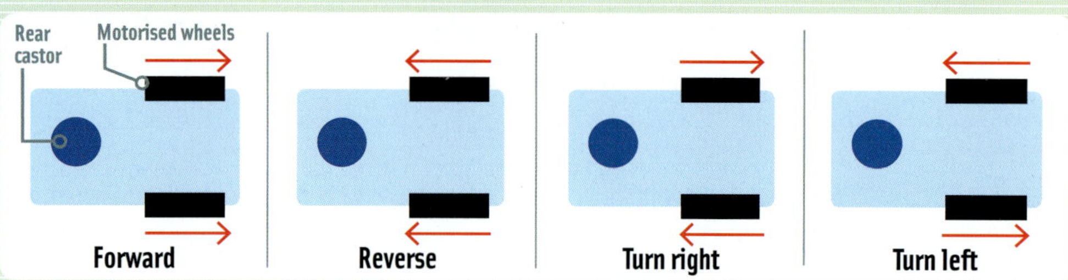

Stepper motor

A stepper motor works a little like a DC motor, except that it doesn't rotate continuously, but instead rotates in steps by a set number of degrees. Stepper motors also use electromagnets but in a different way. Here, a series of electromagnets are placed around a metal gear. When the electromagnets are powered in turn, this causes the gear to rotate one notch. A simple example of this would be the motor that moves the second hand on a battery-powered kitchen clock. When a PWM-capable microcontroller, such as your Arduino, is connected to a stepper motor, it can be programmed to output a series of pulses to the electromagnets, allowing you to turn the motor quickly. They're usually not as fast as DC motors, but stepper motors are used when accuracy is crucial.

OTHER TYPES OF SHIELD

Motor shields aren't the only type of shield available for use in your Arduino projects. You can get shields that add a whole grid of LEDs, shields that provide wired or wireless networking, LCD screens and more. Some even provide combinations of functions, such as buttons and LEDs. Shields can even be stacked, placing one on top of the next to add multiple functions at once, though you'll need to be careful, as not all shields will work together. We'll be looking at other types of shield in chapter 8.

In almost every case, it would be possible to manually build a circuit out of raw components yourself that achieves the same functions. As such, some people view shields as a bit of a 'cheat', but the truth is that they can cheaply and easily add a lot of useful functions without having to deal with a mass of wires and components. Early on in your electronics career, shields are indispensable.

Servo

Servos work very differently to other motors, as they use a combination of pre-assembled components, including a mini-DC motor, an integrated circuit and a series of gears. Servos aren't usually able to turn 360 degrees continuously – most only rotate on a 180-degree axis (though continuous-rotation servos do exist). By using PWM signals from a microcontroller, you can tell a servo to rotate to a specific angle on its axis very accurately. Servos are commonly used in robotics – often to provide joints for limbs. And, although Magbot himself won't actually be using one, we'll be showing you how they work in more detail later in this chapter.

Movement is a very quick way to tell that a machine is working autonomously

A DC motor uses electromagnetism.

A servo is a type of motor that combines pre-assembled components.

LEGS VS WHEELS

Motors can power all kinds of different robotic movement – servos are great for moving joints in arms and legs, for example, while DC motors are often used for rotating wheels. When it comes to choosing how a robot moves around, you first need to choose between wheels or legs. Then, you'll need to decide how many of each. Naturally, there are pros and cons to all of these options, but when you're starting out one of the chief concerns will be how straightforward each one is to achieve.

If you look at robots other people have made, they tend to come with two or four wheels, or two, four or six legs. Of these, the hardest to achieve is probably two legs. Though bipedal movement is the most familiar form of locomotion to us humans, it introduces all kinds of problems when trying to build a robot. You'll need to program at least four separate motors – usually servos – to work together as the equivalents of hip and knee joints. Stability is also a major concern for upright robots, particularly where it's going to be taking one foot off the ground with each step, like a person, shifting weight to one side of its body as it does so. This is a problem professional engineers have been wrestling with for decades, so it's unlikely to be something you'll want to attempt this early on in your electronics career.

Four- and six-legged robots are usually much more stable, since they tend to be horizontally orientated, rather than upright, and have at least three legs supporting them at any time. But you'll usually need to program even more motors to work in conjunction with each other and this can get complicated. We've seen some people cheat this by using less sophisticated programming to 'flail' multiple legs

▲ 2WD and 4WD robot chassis.

around in a somewhat random manner that can propel a robot forward, but this isn't particularly reliable. Nor is it very satisfying to achieve.

Wheels are usually the best bet for early robot projects. Wheeled motion is relatively simple to understand and program compared to legs, and – unless you're attempting to emulate the self-balancing two-wheeled MiP toy we mentioned earlier – there are fewer stability issues to worry about, since multiple wheels will be in contact with the ground at all times.

Like cars, robots can use either two-wheel drive (2WD) or four-wheel drive (4WD) systems. As you might imagine, a 4WD robot has four wheels, each of which is powered by its own motor, while a 2WD robot usually has three wheels – two that are driven by motors and one free-moving omni-wheel or caster, like those found on shopping trolleys, at either the front or the rear of the unit.

A 4WD system is more powerful and is a good choice if you're planning to let your robot roam over rugged terrain or if you're planning to use your robot to carry a heavier load. You can use a four (or more) motor system in conjunction with tank treads to make it even sturdier on rough ground. But the number of motors involved makes it slightly more complex for a first project and it will use more current, meaning battery life will be shorter.

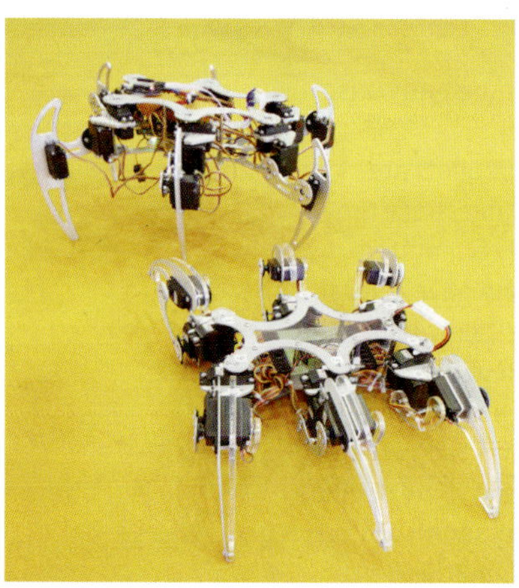

▼ Six-legged robots.

A 2WD system is usually more lightweight and simpler to construct and program for. Battery life is longer, since there are fewer motors to power, and they tend to be surprisingly manoeuvrable. On the downside, they're not so good on rough ground, as they lack power and casters work better on smooth surfaces.

We've opted for a 2WD system for Magbot, as it's by far the simplest and cheapest option, but it's also very satisfying to build and program for. You can buy motors on their own, but we've opted to buy them as part of a pack that comes with the chassis that will form Magbot's body, along with some wheels and all the accessories needed to put it all together.

SHIELDS EXPLAINED

The other key part we're going to introduce at this stage is a motor shield. This is an additional board that slots into the Arduino Uno and provides a layer of dedicated functions for driving your motors. In theory, it would be possible to connect the motors directly to the Arduino, but there are a number of key benefits to be gained by using a shield instead. Here are a few of them:

It's easier

The motor shield provides some convenient screw-block headers so you can wire your motors straight in without having to cobble together a hideous tangle of cables.

It provides more power

The 5V power supplied by the Uno on its own isn't enough to drive motors and supply power to all the other functions of your robot. But the motor shield allows you to connect a separate power supply of up to 12V, dedicated to powering your motors.

It's safer

By default, the shield shares its power supply with your Arduino Uno board, but it also provides a way to power both the Uno and the motors separately. The fact that the power supply for the motors is separate to the power supply of the Uno means the board is protected from any potential power spikes that can occur when driving motors.

It's adaptable

The shield provides six headers, allowing for the attachment of Tinkerkit inputs and outputs. We won't be using these in our projects, but it's an easy way to add an extra pre-built component to your projects, such as an accelerometer or a potentiometer. See **store.arduino.cc/category/16** for some ideas.

SHIELDS UP

The legs on the motor shield slot directly into the pins on your Arduino Uno. By default, the shield itself uses eight of your Uno's pins – pins A0, A1, 3, 8, 11, 12 and 13 – though we'll adapt our shield so that it only uses four of them when it comes to building Magbot, so that we can free up the pins for our robot's other functions. The remaining pins are all still accessible, but instead of plugging your wires into the headers on the Uno itself, as we've been doing up until now, we'll be plugging them into the corresponding pins on the shield. Have a look at the annotated image of the motor shield to familiarise yourself with the layout of the board before moving onto the practical projects. We'll be taking a brief look at servos over the page. After that, we'll be combining the motor shield with the chassis kit and the ping sensor we built in chapter 4 to make a very basic version of our finished robot.

THE MOTOR SHIELD

This is the motor shield we'll be using to handle Magbot's motion. We've used an official Arduino model, but most third-party equivalents will look and function in more or less the same way

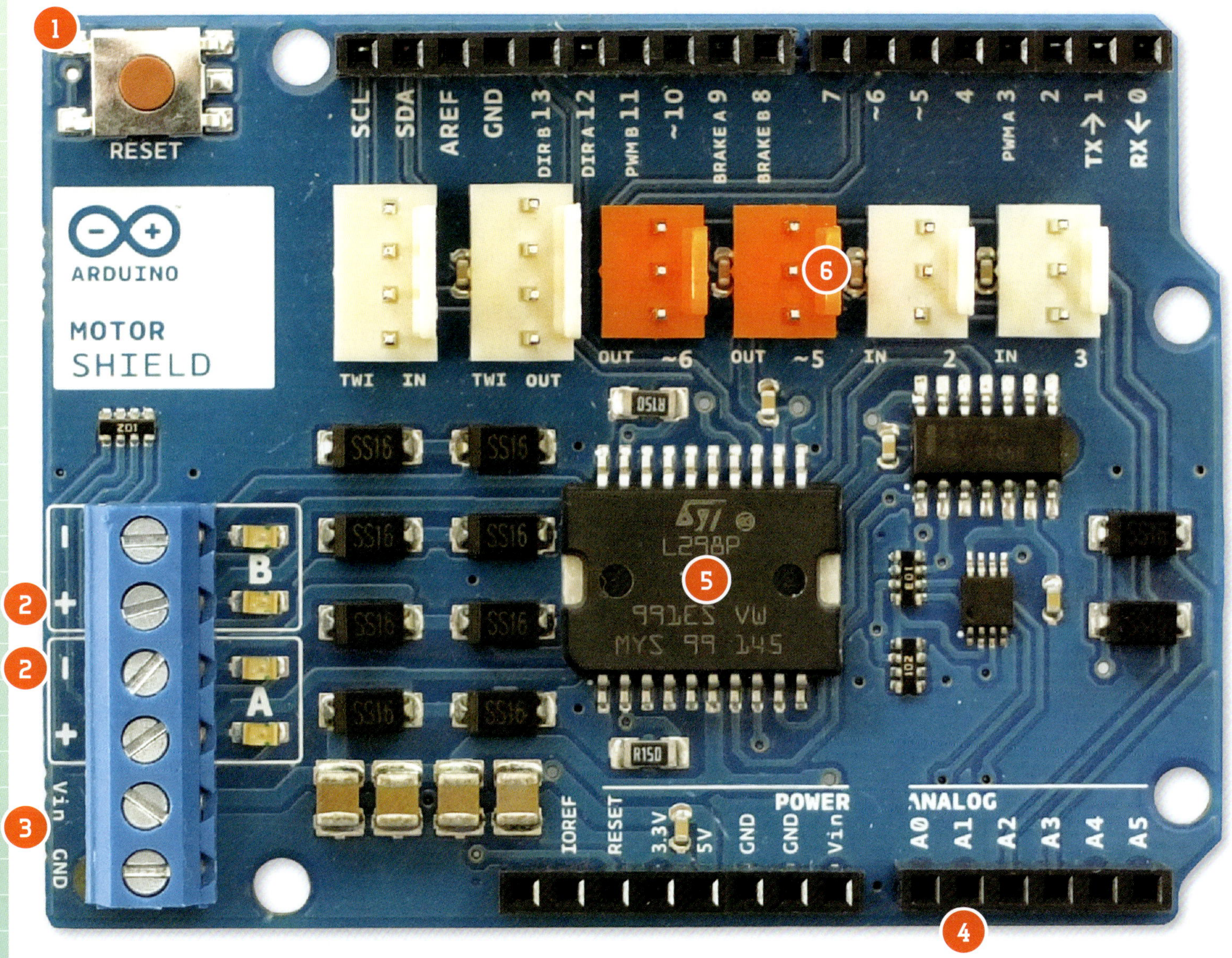

1 Reset button
This performs the same function as the one on the Uno board itself, effectively rebooting the board and restarting any code that's running.

2 Motor terminals
The top four screw block terminals here are actually two sets of + and - connections that allow you to connect two motors. The polarity defines the direction the motor will turn in.

3 Power terminals
The lower two screw block terminals are for connecting a separate power supply to the motor shield. The 'Vin' terminal is where you connect the power; GND is for the ground connection.

4 Arduino pin headers
When the shield is plugged into an Uno board, the headers on the shield provide access to the corresponding pins on the Arduino board itself.

5 The motor controller
This is the main integrated circuit of the board – it's an L298 dedicated motor bridge.

6 Tinkerkit connectors
The six connections here are for attaching external components. They're compatible with Tinkerkit components, but we won't be using them for Magbot.

EXPERIMENTING WITH SERVOS

Build a circuit to test and control the movement of a servo motor

WHAT YOU'LL NEED

- An Arduino Uno board
- A USB cable
- A computer
- 1 x micro servo module
- 1 x analog joystick
- 5 x jumper wires
- A set of male-to-female jumper wires
- A breadboard

We won't be using servos in our final robot, which is why we only included it as an optional item on our shopping list. That said, it's very useful to know how servos work, particularly if you're planning further robotic projects, as they have a wide variety of uses (see the tip opposite).

We're splitting this project into two parts. First, we'll build a simple circuit with just a servo and the Arduino board to show you how it works. Then, we'll add in a control device so that you can operate the servo yourself. In this case, we're going to borrow the joystick we used for Magbot's nose in the last chapter. Except this time, rather than seeing the results of your joystick movements in the serial monitor, you'll see them in real life by making the servo move.

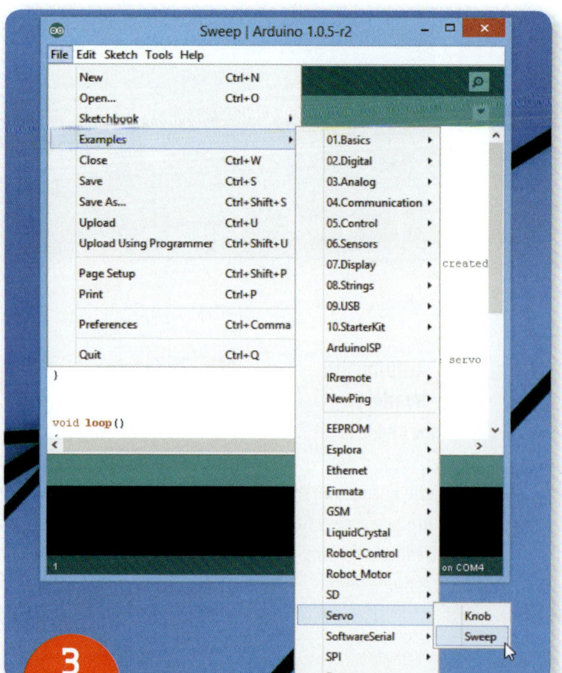

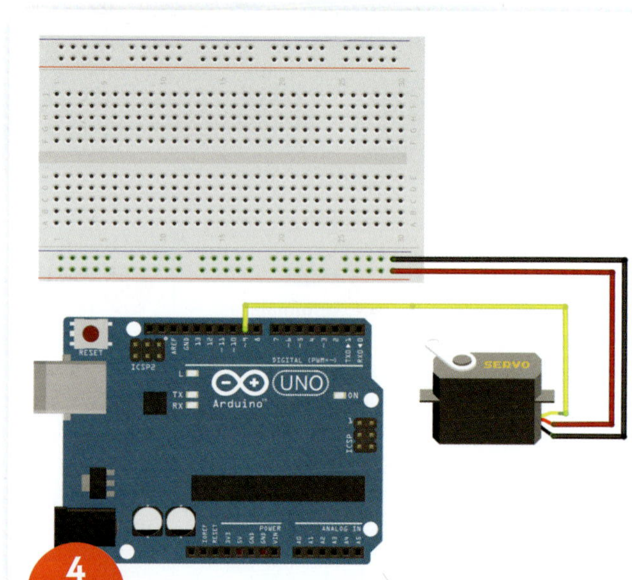

TIP

In 'the wild', servos are often used in radio-controlled airplanes and cars to control steering. They're also found in lifts. Robots can use them for walking or moving their arms. For example, industrial robots often use servos in the joints of their arms.

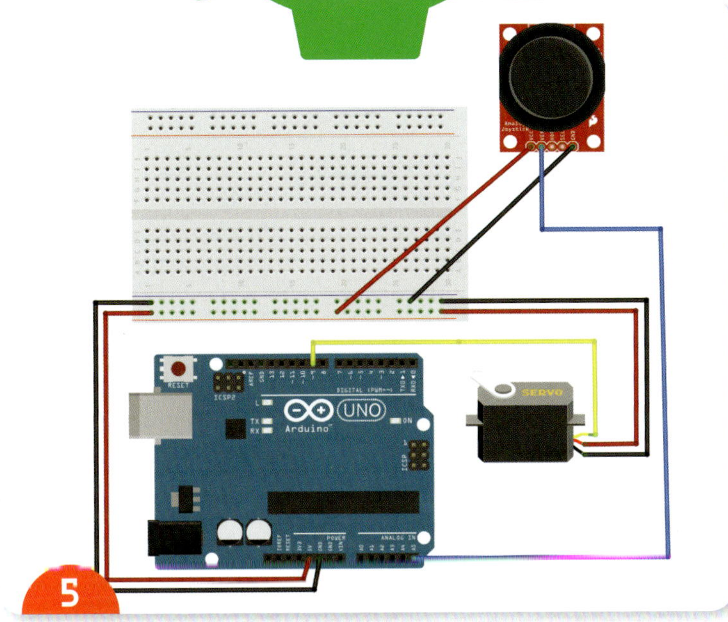

5

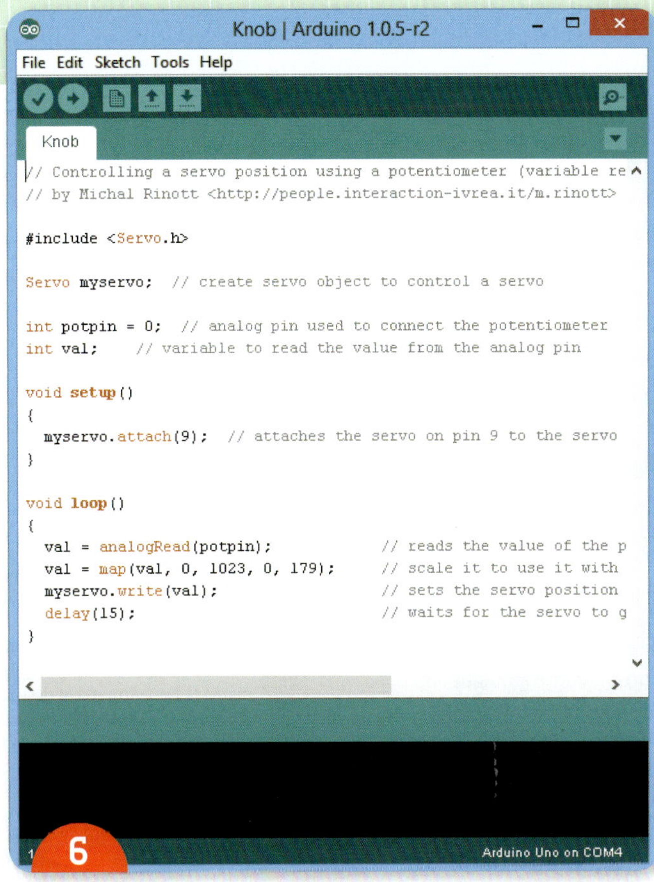

6

1

Here's the micro servo – it's the one from our shopping list in chapter 2. It might not look like much, but it's actually a pretty clever bit of design that combines lots of pre-assembled components, including a DC motor, integrated circuit and potentiometer. The motor drives some gears, and our one came in a see-through case, so you can see the gears yourself. Unlike the motors we're going to use for Magbot, this one doesn't turn continuously and only has 180 degrees of movement. By sending a variable pulse width modulation (PWM) signal to the servo, you can tell it precisely where to turn to on its axis.

2

You can put different types of attachment onto the output shaft of the servo, depending on the type of device you're building. Some servos are supplied with slotted discs that rotate. In our case, the unit came with a little packet of plastic servo arms. For this project, you can choose whichever one you like and slot it over the end of the shaft. There should be three wires attached to the servo. One is ground (black or, as in our case, brown), one is for power (usually red) and the other is for the input signal. In our case, this is orange, but it's sometimes yellow or white.

3

The wires may end in a female connector, which won't fit into the pins on the Arduino, so grab three wires and connect them to the three sockets in the connector. Try to match up the colours with those of the existing wires to make it easier to remember which wire is which. Then, plug the ground and power wires into the Uno's GND and 5V pins and connect the third wire to pin 9. Open the Arduino software and click File, Examples, then Servo and select Sweep. Read through and you'll see the sketch designed to rotate the servo arm by 180 degrees, then back again.

4

Connect the Uno and upload the sketch. The servo arm will whirr to its starting point (position '0' as defined by the sketch), then begin its loop of rotating back and forth. This is great, but all it really proves is that your servo is working (or not). So, now, let's build a more complex circuit to demonstrate how to get more control over the servo's movements. Unplug your Uno from your PC and leave the wire connecting the servo to pin 9, but disconnect the power and ground cables from the board, then wire them into the far right sockets on the power and ground rails on your breadboard.

5

Connect wires from the 5V and GND pins to the sockets on the far side of the same power and ground rails on the breadboard. Next, get the joystick module and the female-to-male jumper wire ribbon, then connect the ground and power legs of the joystick to the ground and power rails, as shown. Finally, connect the vertical axis (VRY) leg on the joystick to pin A0 on the Arduino. It might all look like a bit of a tangled mess of wires at this point, but don't worry. Hook the USB port up to your PC and, in the Arduino program, click File, Examples, then Servo and select Knob.

6

Have a browse through the sketch – you should have a pretty good grip on the principles of what's going on in a lot of the code by now. Click the Upload button to write this sketch to your board. Now, you can use the joystick to control the position of the servo arm. Nudge the joystick up and down, and the servo arm will move 90 degrees left or right accordingly. Because the Uno's input is analog and the output uses PWM, it's not just a simple left-right/on-off movement. Instead, the servo arm responds to the position, the intensity and the speed with which you press the joystick.

MAKE MAGBOT JUNIOR

Test out your motors and then see them in action by putting together a basic version of your finished robot

So now we're going to test out the motors for our robot. Seeing the motors whirr around on their own is one thing, but seeing them physically driving a robot around is something else. That's why we've used the latter half of this project to show you how to construct a simplified version of your final robot. If you'd prefer to wait until it's time to put it all together properly, skip steps 4 to 14. We'll be covering the construction of Magbot in full in chapter 7. However, we recommend building the basic bot first for a bit of practice, as well as for a gratifying glimpse of what's to come. In addition to the components listed opposite, you'll need a penknife, precision screwdriver set and a healthy supply of Blu-tak.

TIP

If all your robot does is spin on the spot, one of the motors could be wired to the motor shield the wrong way around. Try swapping the red cable for one of the motors to '+' and the black to '-' (or vice versa). See the troubleshooting section in chapter 9 for more motor tips.

WHAT YOU'LL NEED

- **An Arduino Uno board**
- **A USB cable**
- **A computer**
- **An Arduino Uno motor shield**
- **An ultrasonic module (HC-SR04)**
- **4 x jumper wires**
- **A robot car chassis kit (including motors)**
- **A breadboard**
- **A switched AA battery pack (optional)**
- **A 9V battery with power adaptor**
- **4 x AA batteries**

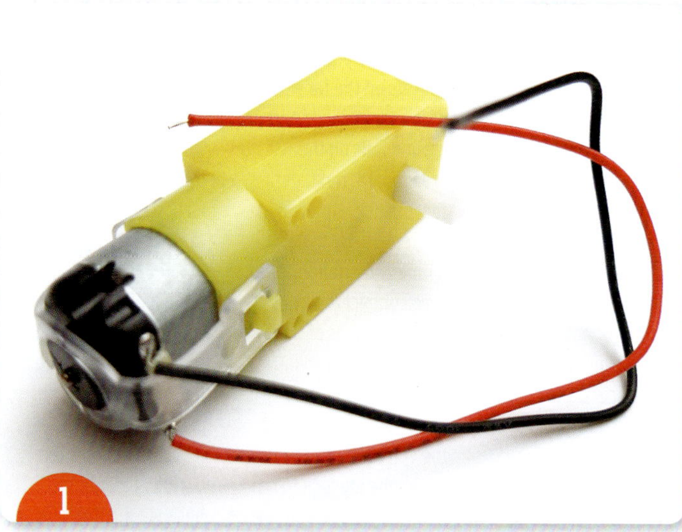

1

This is one of the motors that we'll be using to drive our robot. Magbot will be a two-wheel drive robot with two motors like this – one for each wheel. He'll also have a third caster wheel at the back. This won't be powered by a motor; instead, it will simply help him turn when he manoeuvres out of the way of obstacles, as we'll see when we build our prototype. The DC motors themselves aren't particularly special, but they came in a pack with the caster, the chassis and all the bits required to put them all together, making construction of the robot's body fairly straightforward.

2

There's a quick and easy way to test whether or not the motors are working. Get hold of the AA battery back that came with the chassis kit (or use the switched battery pack if you bought that from our list of optional items) and insert four fresh AA batteries. Grab a motor and you'll see two wires coming out of it – ours are black and red. Touch the bare end of one wire (it doesn't matter which) onto the bare end of the red wire from the battery pack, then touch the bare end of the other wire to the battery pack's black wire and the motor shaft should start rotating.

TIP

More adventurous robot builders might want to consider making their own chassis. If you have access to a jigsaw, you could buy a sheet of acrylic and cut it into shape yourself. Alternatively, you could recycle everyday materials – we've even seen robots made out of old CDs!

3

You can test the other motor in the same way to make sure they're both fine. And before we move on, we're going to try another quick test. Switch the wires on the motor so that the one that was touching the red wire is now touching the black one and vice versa. See what happens? The motor shaft will start rotating in the opposite direction to before. This important little nugget of information will help us a great deal later on when it comes to wiring up our motors and troubleshooting any problems that occur when we take our bot for its first spin.

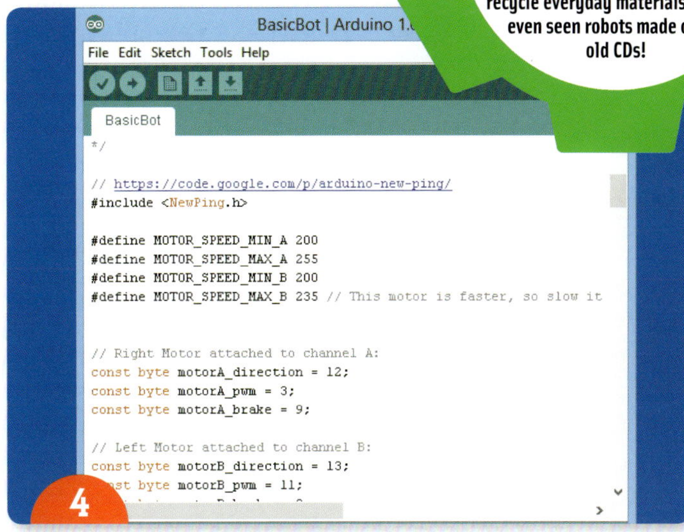

4

Before we go any further, we recommend uploading the programming code. Leave it until later and you'll need to disassemble some of the parts. Plug the Uno into your PC and go to File, Sketchbook, Magbot, then Sketches, and select BasicBot. Towards the top of the sketch, you'll see a line that reads `#include <NewPing.h>`. As we saw in our infrared project, this means we need a library. Libraries are additional code that needs to be uploaded to your Arduino along with the sketch to expand the functions of a sketch. You can think of them as a bit like real libraries – they contain reference material that can help make the sketches cleverer.

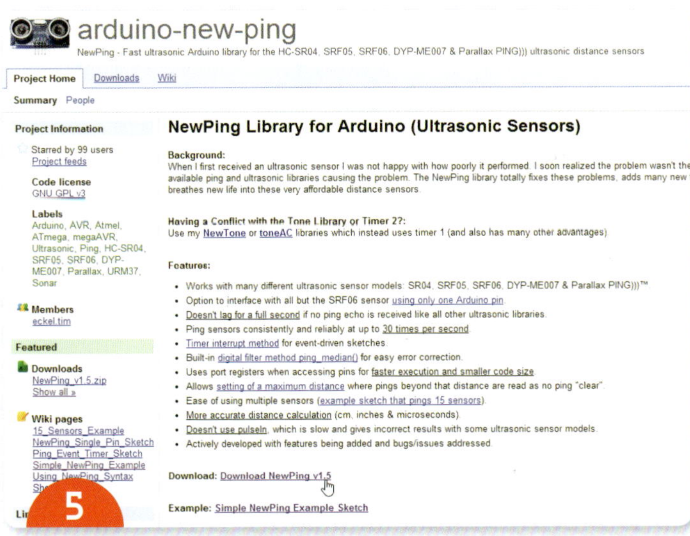

5

Just above, you'll see a URL in blue – programmers often insert URLs to show you where to get the library you need. Click the link (or copy and paste it into a web browser), then click 'Download NewPing v1.5'. Click the download icon and save the ZIP file to your desktop. Back in the Arduino program, click the Sketch menu, then Import Library, followed by Add Library. Now, browse to the location where you downloaded the NewPing v1.5.zip file and double-click on the ZIP file itself. The required files will automatically be installed. We'll be looking more at Magbot's code in later projects, so just click Upload for now, then unplug the USB cable.

6

Our next task is a slightly scary one – we're going to hack our motor shield in order to allow for the Arduino Uno and the motors to run off separate power supplies. Flip the motor shield module over so that all its legs are poking into the air and look for where it says Vin Connect. If you look up close, you'll see that this refers to two metal blobs that are connected across a vertical black line that runs down the middle by a very thin piece of metal. We need to physically cut this jumper, so grab a Stanley knife and very carefully cut down the black line in the direction shown.

To test that this has done the job, get your Arduino Uno and make absolutely certain it isn't connected to any other power supply – either your PC or another battery pack. This is a very important step, as otherwise you could damage your equipment. Carefully line up the legs from the motor shield with pins on the Uno, then push the two boards together. You'll need to be firm but careful when you do this. We accidentally bent two of the shield's legs on our first attempt. With the two boards together, get the AA battery pack that you used to test the motors.

On the motor shield, look for a set of six terminals along one edge – they're usually encased in blue plastic. With a flathead precision screwdriver, loosen the screws in the top of the Vin and GND terminals. Insert the bare end of the black cable from the AA battery pack into the GND terminal and the bare end of the red cable into the Vin terminal, then screw them both down. Now, check the Uno board – is its power LED lit? If not, everything's fine. But if it is lit, that means there's a power connection between the motor shield and the Uno, so you'll need to try cutting the Vin Connect jumper again.

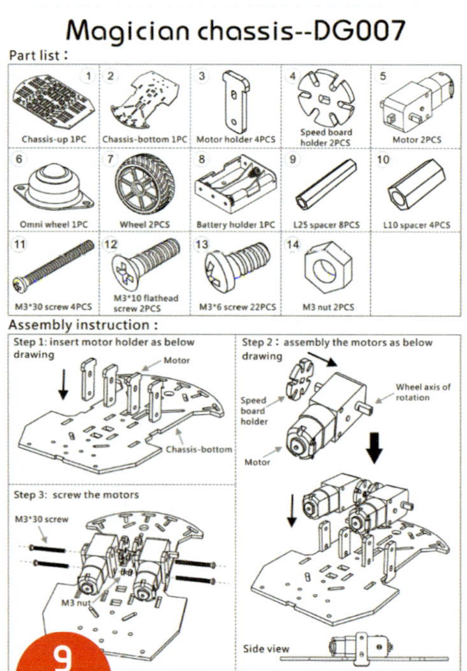

The Dagu Magician is a fairly typical chassis pack, in terms of both the equipment included and, unfortunately, the standard of the instructions that accompany them. You'll find a sheet that looks like the one shown. We discovered that not only were some of the parts different from those shown, but also the steps were incorrect on a couple of occasions and we had to improvise a little. As with flat-packed furniture, this is quite common at the cheaper end of the market. We're going to explain how to put some of the parts for our Dagu chassis together, but instructions will be similar for other similar products.

Add the motor supports, motors and wheels, as shown in the instructions. If you're using the same kit as us, you may find you need to start employing your liberal interpretation skills at about step 5. Instead of a caster wheel, the instructions refer to an 'omni-wheel' and suggested we only needed two screws to hold it in place. It also told us to use spacers, which aren't necessary with the caster. But we'll forgive it. If you bought the switched AA battery pack from our list of suggested optional items in chapter 2, ignore the part where the chassis instructions tell you to attach the supplied (non-switched) battery holder.

If you're using the AA battery pack that came with the chassis, however, we recommend inserting the batteries before you assemble the upper deck of the chassis; otherwise, you'll find you no longer have access to the battery holder once the remainder of the chassis has been added. Just make sure the bare ends of the black and red wires don't touch (use a blob of Blu-tak) or you'll get a short circuit. The alternative (and probably preferable) option is to simply ignore the part about screwing the battery pack into the base and use a less permanent way to hold it in place instead, such as Blu-tak or double-sided tape.

With the chassis complete, get your Arduino/motor shield stack. Use Blu-tak or sticky tape to fasten the Ardunio boards at the back of the chassis above the caster wheel. Now, get your breadboard, the ultrasonic sensor and your four jumper wires, and look at the diagram on the right. You should be getting pretty good at wiring these circuits up now, so we shouldn't need to specify the grid references for each individual breadboard socket anymore. Just remember – you're plugging your wires into pins 4, 7 GND and 5V on the motor shield now. The pins are directly linked to the Uno's pins below via the shield's legs.

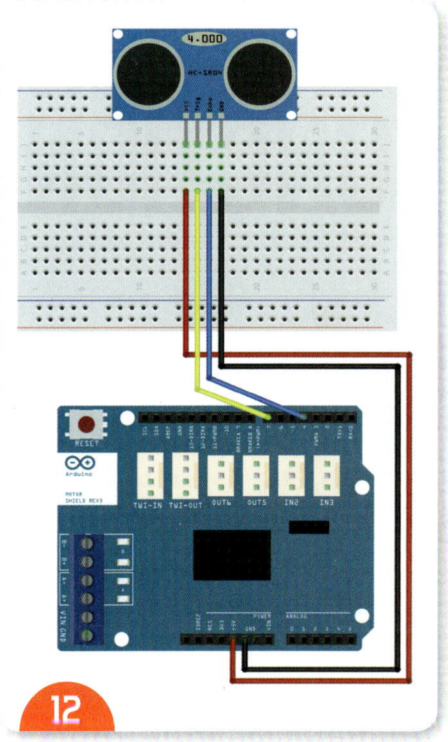

Mount the breadboard (using another bit of Blu-tak or tape) towards the front of your robot's chassis. Then, connect the wires from the motors up to the '+' and '-' terminals on the blue plastic connector using a precision screwdriver. This may take a little trial and error, but assuming you've installed both motors the same side up underneath, connect the red wire from the left-hand motor (from Magbot's point of view) to the first '-' terminal and the same motor's black wire to the '+' terminal next to it. For the right-hand motor, connect the black wire to the '-' terminal and the red wire to the '+' terminal.

Connect your AA battery pack to the blue Vin and GND terminals, as described in step 8. Finally, get a 9V battery and clip it to the power adaptor. Fix the battery to the chassis somewhere near the Arduino stack with Blu-tak, then plug the adaptor into the DC power socket on your Uno. After a second, Magbot Junior will spring to life! Pop him on the floor and watch him navigate around obstacles. Congratulations – you've made a robot! If all he does is spin in circles, see the tip on p80 for a solution. This incarnation of Magbot is still quite basic, and we're going to refine him over the coming projects.

REPLACING THE 'DELAY' FUNCTION

We explain why the delay function is bad and show you how to solve the problem

WHAT YOU'LL LEARN

- **Why the delay function can cause problems**
- **How to pause actions without stopping everything else**

So far, in pretty much all the sketches we've used – including the sketch we just uploaded to Magbot Junior in the previous project – have featured a function called `delay`. All the delay function does is pause the program for a specified amount of time (in milliseconds). Run the very basic Blink sketch we used back in chapter 3, for example, and the delay function there will tell the program how long to pause between blinks (see step 1 opposite).

Delay is fine when you're doing something as simple as turning an LED on and off, or for situations where there's only a single function being carried out, as with most of our practice projects up to this point. But when you're building something a little more complex, such as a robot, delay has an unfortunate side effect. This is because the delay function doesn't just pause the thing you want it to pause – it effectively pauses the entire program, including all the other actions that you want to continue. So if, for example, your robot has a blinking LED on it and you use delay, then while the delay is running your robot won't be able to read from its sensors or output sounds at the same time. In effect, the delay will bring almost all other activity to a halt.

Obviously, this isn't a great situation for a robot, where you want to be using sensors, motors, sounds, LEDs and more all working at once without interruption. So, from now, on we'll need to eliminate delay from our code, but we'll still need to pause various functions. So what's the solution? Well, there are a few different ways around the problem. One is to use something called `millis()` instead of delay. Unlike delay, millis doesn't actually pause anything; it just checks the number of milliseconds since the Arduino began running the current program. Another even better solution is to use a timer library. This lets you do things when you want them to happen without stopping everything, by calling functions it's been asked to call when it's time to do so.

At this point, don't worry about learning how to write this sort of code by yourself. We've included all the required timer libraries along with the sketches we're using for Magbot, so the timer function will work without you having to do anything. But working without the delay function is an important concept to wrap your head around if you want to take your understanding of projects like these further on your own. So without getting too technical, let's have a quick look at how all of this works in practice.

When building something a little more complex, delay has an unfortunate side effect

TIP

The SimpleTimer tabs automatically appear in the BasicBotWithoutDelay sketch because, from here on, we've bundled all the library files you'll need along with the sketches themselves. You won't need to manually install any of Magbot's libraries in the way we installed NewPing in the previous project.

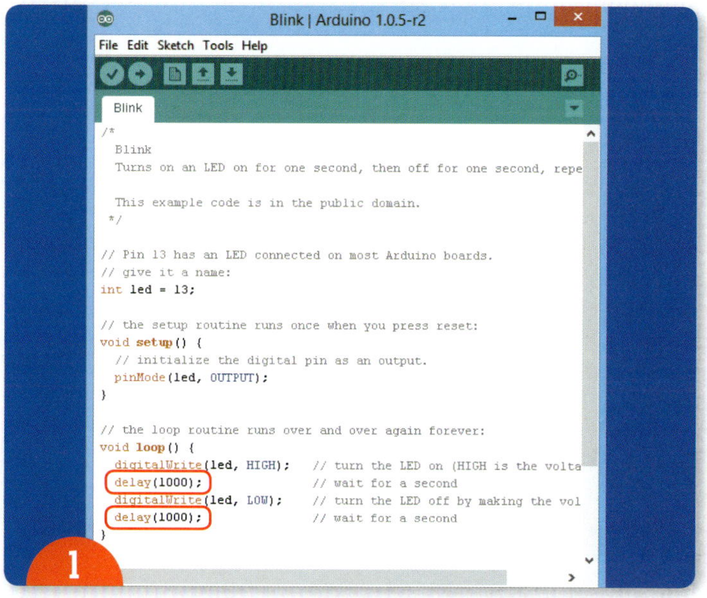

On your PC, open the Arduino program, click File, Examples, then 01 Basic and select Blink. Don't worry about building the circuit again – we're just going to check and compare the code with other sketches to see what's going on in each case. With Blink open, scroll down through the code and, towards the bottom, you'll see two lines that read **delay(1000);** – this is the delay function. All it's doing is telling the program to wait for 1000 milliseconds (in other words, one second) before doing the next thing. In this case, using delay is okay, since the code is only doing one thing – turning the LED on or off.

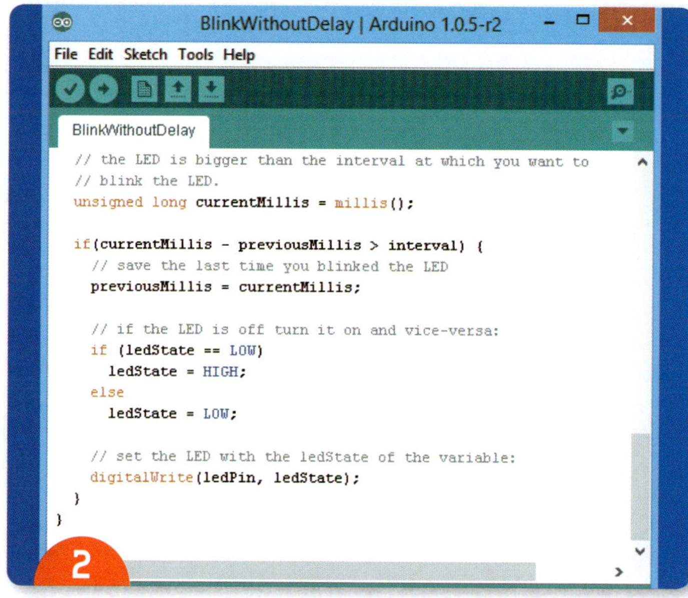

Now, click File, Examples, then 02 Digital and select BlinkWithoutDelay. Here, the sketch is using the **millis** function instead of delay. Scroll down to the variables and you'll see a line that reads **long previousMillis = 0;**. This tells the program to remember the last time the LED was turned on. Underneath, the variable **long interval = 1000;** sets the interval value at 1000 milliseconds (1 second). Now, scroll to the loop and read lines shown above. What this does is check the difference between the current time and the last time you blinked the LED; if it's bigger than the interval (1000 milliseconds), it will blink the LED.

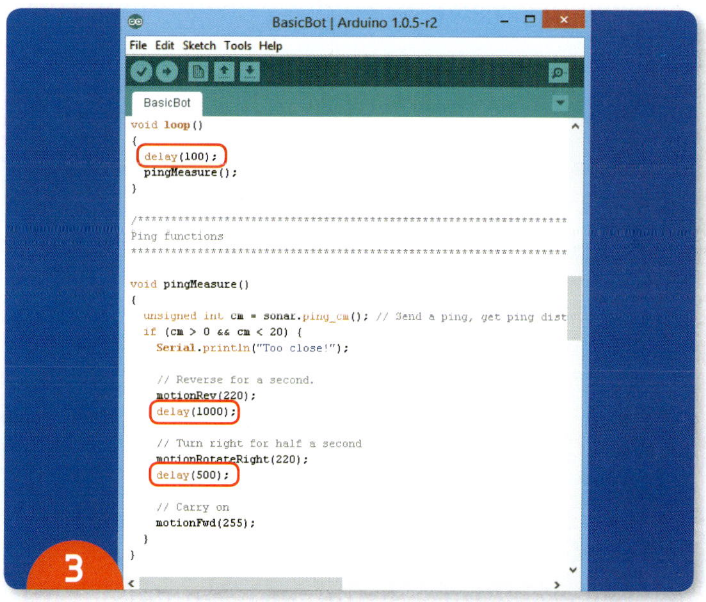

Close Blink and BlinkWithoutDelay, then click File, Sketchbook, Magbot, Sketches and finally BasicBot. If you followed the previous project, this is the same code that you just loaded on your Arduino. Scroll to the loop and you'll see three instances of delay. The first one **delay(100);** sets a delay of 100 milliseconds between ping measurements. The next one **delay(1000);** comes after the line **motionRev(220);**, telling the program to wait for 1000 milliseconds while reversing the motor before carrying out the next action. The third delay is similar – **delay(500);** refers to the line before it, telling the program to pause for 500 milliseconds while turning right.

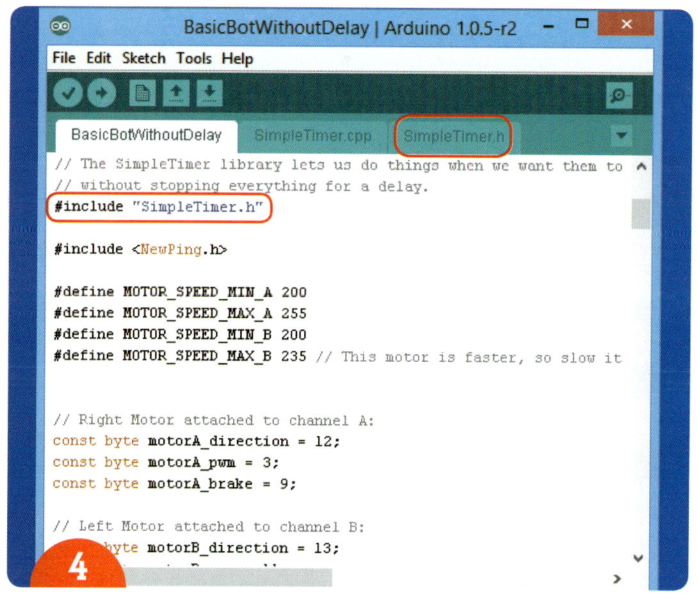

Now, click File, Sketchbook, Magbot, Sketches, then BasicBotWithoutDelay. Towards the top, you'll see the line **#include "SimpleTimer.h"**, which refers to the timer library the code will use. And if you look just above the code, you'll see tabs for SimpleTimer.cpp and SimpleTimer.h – these are the library files themselves. If you click the SimpleTimer.h tab and scroll through, you'll see it's built on the same principles as the **millis** function, but it allows us to do many different things at the same time. Click the main tab again and scroll down. You'll see references to **timer** throughout the loop, whenever it needs to pause an action.

IN THIS CHAPTER

HOW TO BUILD A ROBOT

SOUND

In this chapter, we're going to look at how electronic devices can be programmed to produce different types of sound. We're going to examine the theory behind this, explaining what you need to make sounds and how you can create them. Then, we're going to move onto some practical audio-based projects. We'll start off with some experiments involving sound, including an amazing project where you'll be able to control sounds using just hand gestures. Finally, we'll be examining what sounds your robot will make and find out how he'll make them.

MAKING SOUNDS AND MUSIC

Find out all about how to make and reproduce sounds and music electronically

WHAT YOU'LL LEARN

- How to make your own electronic music
- What MIDI and sequencing are
- How Magbot will produce his sounds

Almost every robot in science fiction – from R2-D2 to Wall-E – makes some kind of recognisable sound. Some movie robots can speak, others make a series of tones and bleeps to express themselves. In real life, things are somewhat different. Many 'real' robots, such as those on assembly lines, remain mute, as communication is often not necessary.

But for our Magbot, we've opted to include sounds – partly to provide him with a bit of personality and added functions, but also because exploring how electronic sounds and music work is a very enjoyable and worthwhile subject. If you know anything about music already, lots of what we're about to discuss will start falling into place quite quickly. But even if you have no prior musical experience, you'll find that most of the concepts are pretty simple.

▲ **Professional musicians have been using sequencing since the 1980s to create music digitally.**

PRODUCING SOUNDS ELECTRONICALLY

Just for a moment, let's define – in very simple terms – what sound actually is. Sounds are basically waves caused by vibrations in the air pressure. Sound waves have a number of important properties, including their amplitude, wavelength and frequency, all of which have an impact on our perception of the sound. We perceive differences in amplitude as differences in loudness, for example. Frequency, meanwhile, refers to how frequently – or how fast – the vibrations in air pressure are, and this is what affects the pitch of the sound. The higher the frequency of the vibration, the higher the pitch of the sound you'll hear. String a series of sounds with higher and lower pitches together and suddenly you're beginning to get something like music.

▼ **M-audio MIDI keyboard.**

To reproduce sounds or music, therefore, we need a mechanism that can take electronic signals from our robot and translate them into vibrations. The loudspeakers on iPod docks and TV sets do this using electromagnets, which respond to electrical signals sent to them by the audio circuitry, and this causes a flexible concave cone to vibrate at various speeds, or frequencies, producing sounds. In our projects, we'll be using a Piezo buzzer component instead of a traditional loudspeaker. As you'll see over the page, the buzzer doesn't use an electromagnet, but the principle is fairly similar – different pulses of electrical current cause a disc to vibrate of different frequencies, which in turn produces sounds of different pitches.

CREATING SOUNDS

So that's how we can reproduce sound electronically, but how do we generate the sounds in the first place? Well, the standard way of digitally creating a series of sounds at different pitches – in other words, musical notes – is by using a technique called sequencing. Basically, you tell a computer program to remember a sequence of different notes at various frequencies, which are then sent to the output device (the speaker).

Professional musicians have been using this technique since the 1980s to create music digitally. A system known as MIDI (short for Musical Instrument Digital Interface) allows a person to play an electronic instrument (usually a keyboard), and 'record' what's played as digital information using a device called a sequencer. But this isn't the same as recording the sounds as a digital music file, such as an MP3 or a WAV file. In fact, no sounds are recorded at all. Instead what's saved is a set of instructions that state which notes are being played, the order they're played in and how long each note is held, along with some other information, such as how hard the note was played and whether any other controls (pedals, and so on) were used.

For musicians, this has a number of major advantages. It means they can correct mistakes in what they've recorded without having to replay the entire sequence. And they can change the sound of the instrument after it's been recorded. So, even if you originally played the notes using a synthesised piano sound, you can swap this later for an organ, guitar or strings and so on.

MIDI files are also small and convenient, which is why they're often used in video games, mobile phone ringtones and many other music-producing electronic devices.

In the early days of MIDI, electronic sequencing equipment was expensive, but now cheap processing power means almost anyone can have a go. All you need is a PC and some sequencing software. Some professional sequencing programs are still quite expensive, but there are several good free ones, including LMMS (**lmms.sourceforge.net**), which is available for both Windows and Linux computers. If you're interested in making your own music, we definitely recommend giving it a go. Ideally, you should have a MIDI keyboard, too. Cheap keyboards are available, including M-Audio Keystation Mini (about £40 from Amazon). MIDI devices used to use their own special connections, but most modern MIDI keyboards and instruments just plug in via USB. If you don't have a keyboard or can't afford one, don't worry – you can use a virtual MIDI keyboard like the one we'll be using in our project on p92.

The standard way of digitally creating a series of sounds at different pitches is sequencing

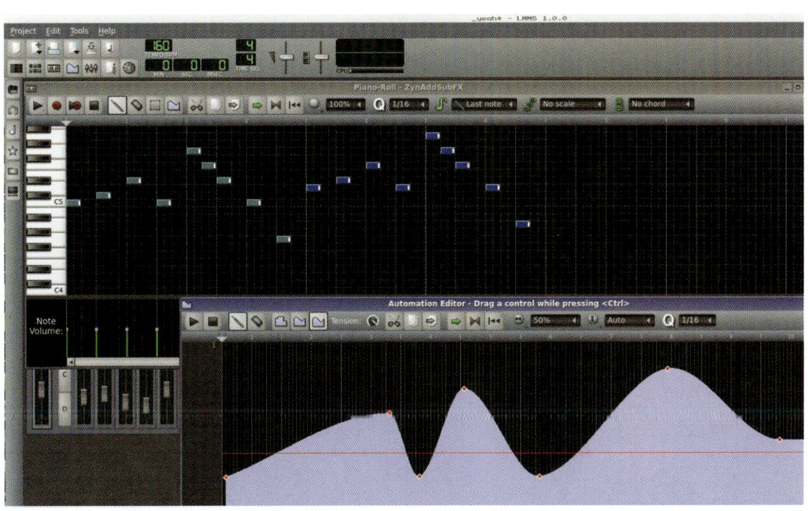

▲ **LMMS sequencer software is available for free.**

YOUR ROBOT'S SOUNDS

All of this is interesting, but how does it apply to the sounds we'll be making for Magbot? Well, we'll be using essentially the same technique when it comes to creating our robot's voice. As we'll see in the next two projects, Magbot will be able to communicate using a small selection of melodies – short bursts of musical notes that will let him tell you when something specific has happened, like when he's bumped into something.

Instead of using a keyboard and a sequencer, however, we're going to write the sequences of musical notes that Magbot will play directly into our code. Each note in the sequence will be sent from the Uno to the buzzer speaker as a series of electronic pulses. And it's the speed, or frequency, of these pulses that defines the frequency at which the speaker vibrates, which, in turn, defines the pitch of each sound. ○

AUDIO INPUT

With our robot, audio is going to be output digitally as a series of electronic 'on/off' pulses. But, thanks to its analog input pins, it's also possible for the Arduino Uno to receive audio input. By attaching a microphone and a storage device of some kind (such as a memory card), you could, for example, use the Uno as a recording device. Alternatively, you could carry out an experiment where LEDs respond to sounds. Sadly, we don't have the space to cover audio input in this book, but there are some great examples of projects you can try on the web. Have a look at www.snipca.com/13026 for some inspiration.

EXPERIMENTING WITH SOUNDS

We show you how to play a tune and turn your Arduino into an electronic musical instrument

WHAT YOU'LL NEED

- An Arduino Uno board
- A USB cable
- A computer
- 1 x speaker (Piezo buzzer)
- 1 x light dependent resistor (photocell)
- 1 x LED
- 1 x 220 Ω resistor
- 1 x 10k Ω resistor
- 7 x jumper wires
- 2 x female-to-male jumper wires
- A breadboard

Have you ever seen someone play a Theremin? It's a type of electronic musical instrument that people can play without making physical contact with it. Instead, you move your hands around two antennas, and how near or far your hands are to the antennas controls the pitch and volume of the sounds the instrument makes. It's quite amazing to watch, so have a look at some YouTube videos if you've never seen one being played. Even if you haven't seen one before, you've almost certainly heard one. The eerie music they produce is frequently used in the soundtracks for spooky movies. In this experiment, we're going to use our Arduino, a buzzer and light sensor to make a Theremin-like instrument that will make sounds that vary as we move our hands.

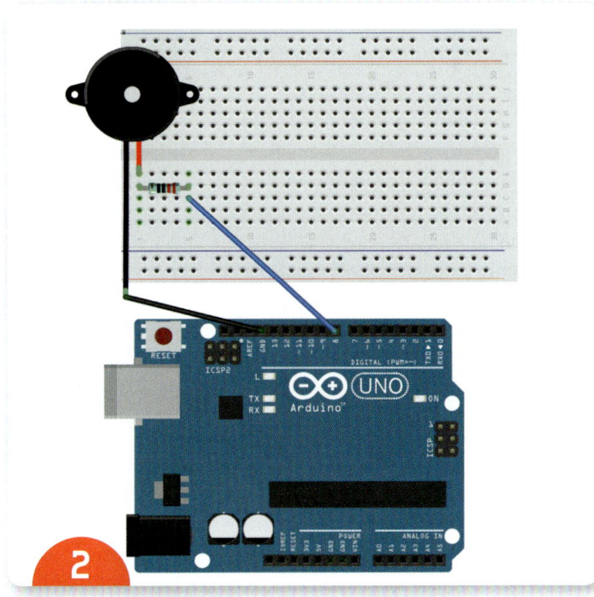

TIP

If you fancy experimenting a bit more, you could try changing the notes and durations in the variables section of the toneMelody example sketch. Check the library to see what notes are available, type them in and re-upload to hear the results. See over the page for more.

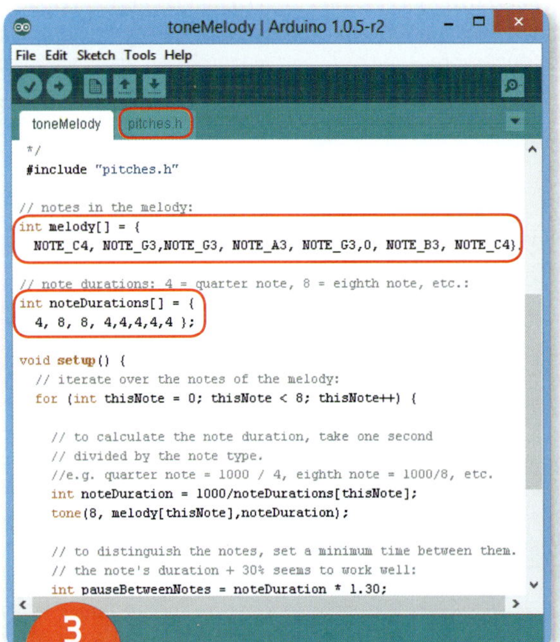

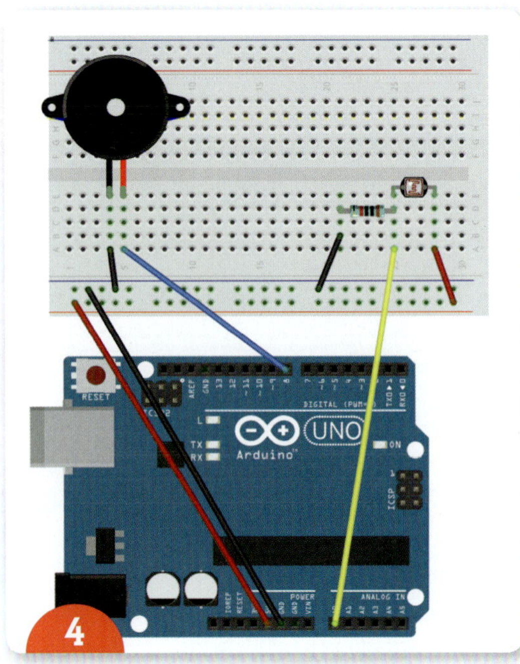

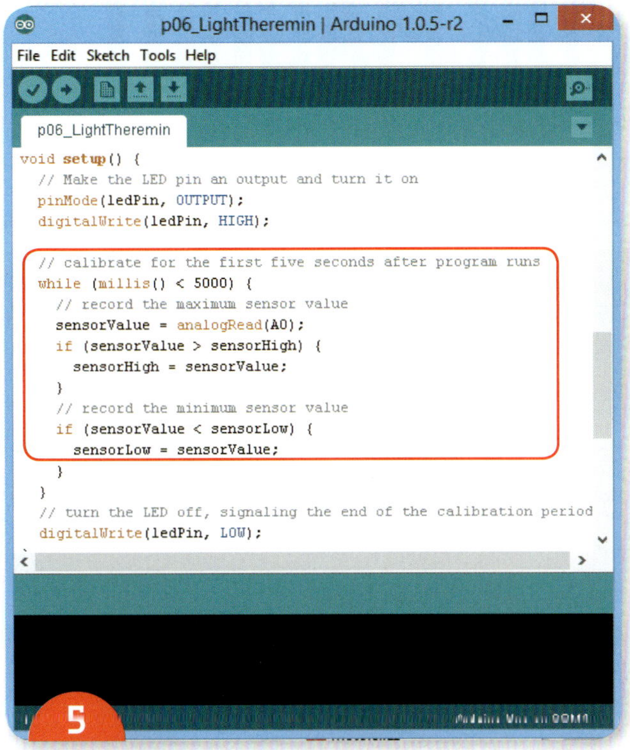

1

Our speaker is a Piezo buzzer – a clever little component that contains a disc made out of a special material. When electronic pulses of different frequencies are applied to it, the material contracts or expands in accordance with the frequency of the electronic signal. This produces vibrations in the air, resulting in sounds at different pitches. If you look down the hole in the middle of the speaker, you can see the disc. The hole helps to carry the sound it produces. The buzzer has power and ground connections – you should see a '+' sign on the top of the component to denote the power leg.

2

Before we build our faux-Theramin, let's carry out a very quick experiment to test that the buzzer is working. Tear off two female-to-male jumper wires from the end of your ribbon cable and connect them to the legs of the buzzer – make a note of which colour wire is connected to power (+) and which is connected to ground. Connect the other end of the ground wire directly to the GND pin on your Uno. Plug the power cable into socket E1 on your breadboard and insert a 220 Ω resistor across sockets D1-D5. Now, connect socket C5 to pin 8 on your Uno.

3

Plug the Uno into your PC and launch the Arduino IDE software. Click File, Examples, then 02 Digital and select the sketch called toneMelody. This is designed to play a very simple tune through your speaker. You'll see that the sketch comes with a library called 'pitches.h' (it should have its own tab). The sketches' variables state which notes the melody will play and the durations of each. If you click the Library tab, you'll see that the notes refer to specific frequencies. Upload the sketch to your board and the buzzer should play a tune you might recognise. Press the reset button to hear it again.

4

Disconnect from your computer and disassemble your circuit to build the Theremin. Connect the Uno's 5V and GND pins to the power and ground rails on the breadboard. Connect the buzzer to sockets E4 and E5. Use a wire to connect the ground row of the buzzer to the ground rail, then connect another wire from the buzzer's power to pin 8. On the other side of the breadboard, insert the light sensor into sockets E25 and E28. Connect row 28 to the power rail and row 25 to pin A0 on the Uno. Use a 10k Ω resistor across D25 to D20, then connect row 20 to the ground rail.

5

Plug the Uno back into your PC and fire up the Arduino IDE software again. This time, click on File, Examples, then 10 Starter Kit and select the sketch called 'p06_Light_Theremin'. This is a surprisingly simple sketch that reads the input from pin A0 (the amount of light detected by the light sensor) and maps the values to a range of pitches, which are then output via pin 8 to the speaker. Scroll through the code before you upload it to see what's happening. You'll see a section referring to calibration in the setup – this is to set the maximum and minimum values from the sensor.

6

Upload the sketch and start moving the flat of your hand steadily up and down over the light sensor. This will calibrate those minimum and maximum values. After five seconds, calibration will be complete and you'll hear a tone. Now, any hand movements you make over the sensor will result in a change in pitch of the sound coming from the buzzer. The further away you move your hand, the more light the sensor detects and the higher the pitch of the sound emitted by the buzzer. The closer you move your hand, the less light reaches the sensor and the result is a lower pitch sound.

CREATING SOUNDS FOR MAGBOT

Let's examine the sounds Magbot will be making to discover how they'll work

WHAT YOU'LL NEED

- An Arduino Uno board
- A USB cable
- A computer
- 1 x speaker (Piezo buzzer)
- 1 x 220 Ω resistor
- 2 x jumper wires
- 2 x female-to-male jumper wires
- A breadboard

When we build Magbot, he'll be able to communicate using sounds. We're going to include a Piezo buzzer in his circuitry and we're going to program him to produce certain combinations of sounds when he encounters specific situations or receives commands. In this way, he'll be able to tell you whether he's encountered an obstacle in his path using his ping sensor or whether he's hit his whiskers on something. He'll also play a little 'hello' melody when he wakes up and make affirmative sounds to let you know he's received commands you send him via your infrared remote control. We're going to give each sound its own distinctive melody, so that you'll quickly begin to recognise what Magbot is trying to tell you whenever he 'speaks'.

In this quick project, we're going to build a circuit and upload a sketch to our Arduino that will allow us to listen to Magbot's sounds and examine the code to see how they work. If you already have any musical abilities, you'll probably have a good understanding of some of the concepts we'll be using, but don't worry if not, as we'll make sure we keep things as simple as possible. We've already created the melodies and written them into Magbot's code, so you won't actually have to write any music – we'll just be showing you how the melodies work. To help illustrate this, we're going to use a piano keyboard. Again, don't worry if you don't have a real piano to hand. You can use a free virtual piano instead.

Don't worry if you don't have a real piano to hand. You can use a free virtual piano

While we've been working on the sounds for Magbot, we've been using a very good free, open source virtual MIDI piano keyboard called VMPK, and we recommend downloading it. It will come in very handy should you wish to compose further robotic melodies yourself. You can get VMPK from **vmpk.sourceforge.net**. It works on Windows PCs, and there are also versions available for Macs and Linux computers. Windows PCs usually come with a built-in driver for MIDI instruments (including virtual ones), but if you're using Linux you may also need to download a software synthesizer in order to hear the notes. Qsynth (**qsynth.sourceforge.net**) is a good option.

Before you start the next steps, download and install VMPK. Open the keyboard and click on a few keys to make sure it's producing sound (you can also use your computer's keyboard to play notes). We recommend enlarging the program window to make it easier to play. Also, if you're not familiar with the names of the notes, click the View menu and select Note Names – this will label each note on the keyboard.

TIP

In the `damage_notes` sequence of notes, you'll see two instances of `0`. These refer to a pause – a beat where you don't play a note. Each sequence has a list of `_durations`, which correspond to how long each note should be played, including the pauses.

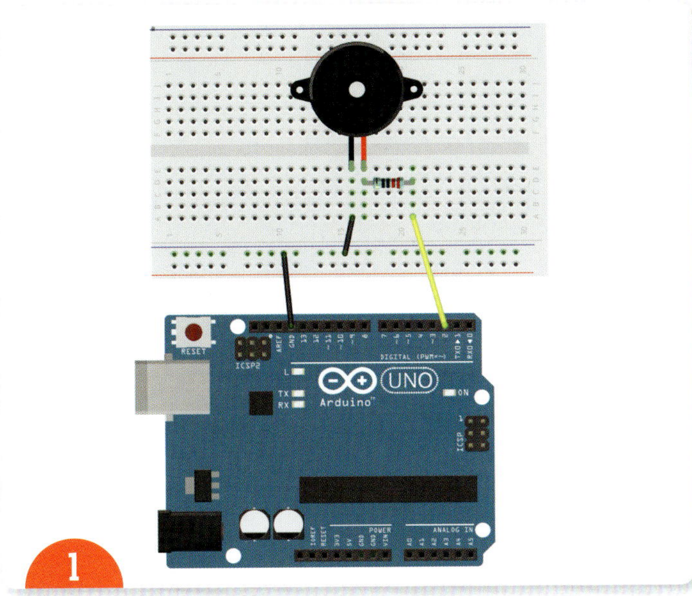

Let's start by building a very simple circuit that will allow us to test out Magbot's sounds. Get your Piezo buzzer and attach a pair of female-to-male jumper wires to the buzzer's power and ground legs. Plug the other end of the wires into your breadboard – ground into socket E16 and power into E17. Put a 220 Ω resistor across sockets D17 to D21, then attach a wire from socket A21 to pin 2 on your Arduino Uno. Plug a black wire from the Uno's GND pin to socket A16 so it's linked to the speaker's ground connection. Grab a USB cable and plug the Uno into your PC.

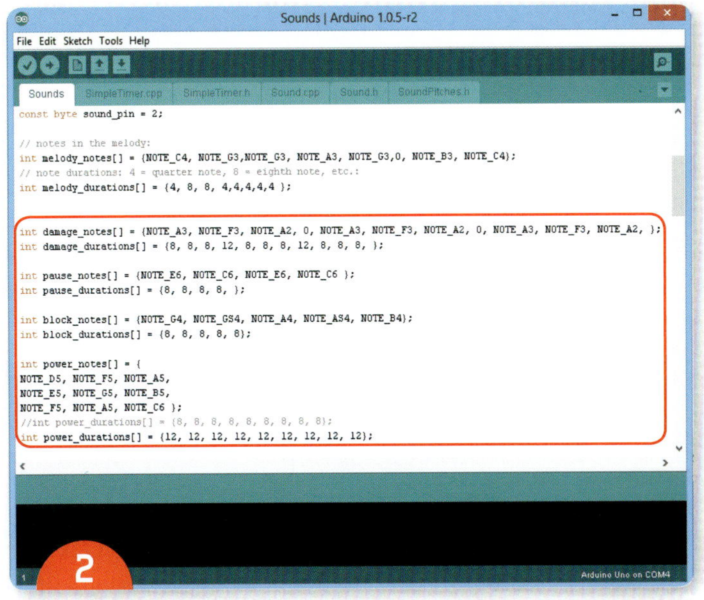

We'll assume you've already downloaded and installed Magbot's code (if not, refer back to the battery indicator project in chapter 3). On your computer, open the Arduino IDE software and click File, Sketchbook, Magbot, then Sketches and select Sounds. Upload the code to your Uno and it will start playing back as a series of four different melodies – in the code, these are called `damage_notes`, `pause_notes`, `block_notes` and `power_notes`. In the variables, you'll also find one called `melody_notes`, but we're not using this. The melodies will play once each in turn and then stop. To hear them again, press the Uno's reset button.

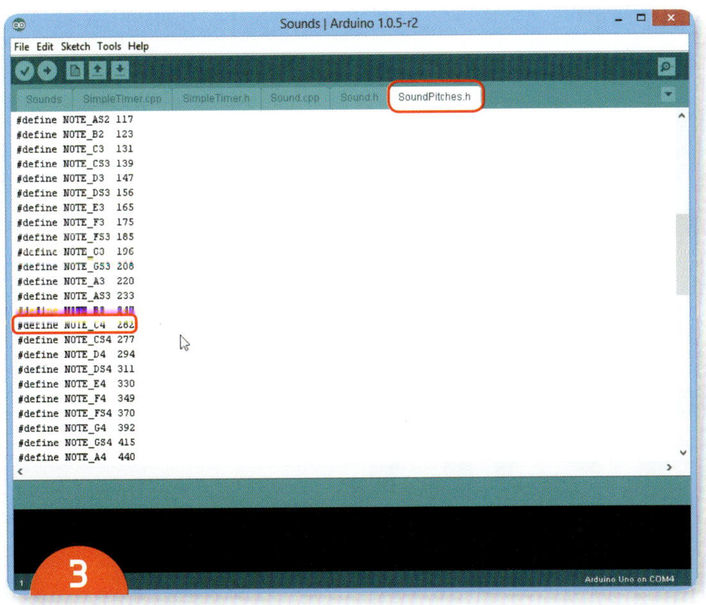

Look at the tabs above the code. Similar to the previous project, there's a pitches library (this one's called SoundPitches.h) and a separate Sound library. Also present is the SimpleTimer library, so that we can run our sound program without using delay – see chapter 5 for more on this. As we saw at the beginning of this chapter, each note has a frequency, and these are listed in the SoundPitches library. Scroll through and you'll see that C4 – middle C – has a frequency of 262Hz. Now, click on the Sounds tab, open the virtual MIDI piano and arrange the keyboard and Arduino windows so you can see them both.

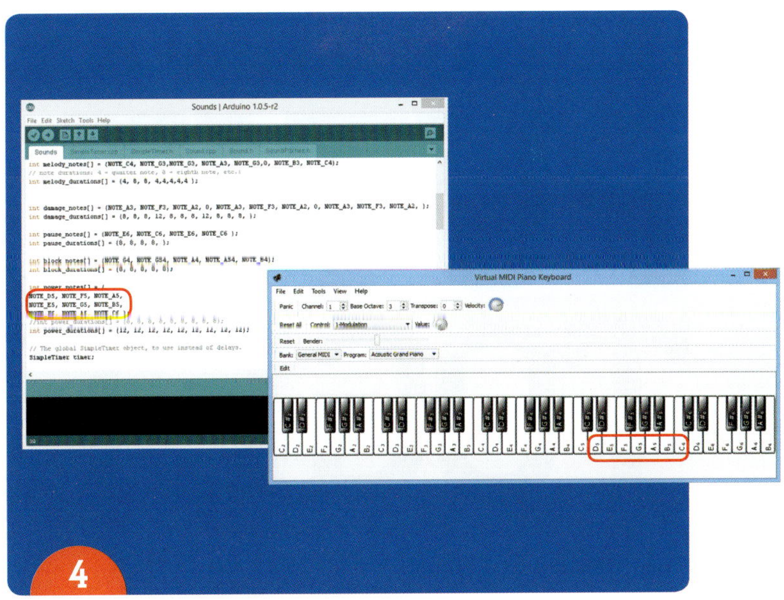

You'll notice that the notes listed in the sequences in the code correspond directly with the labels on the keys of the keyboard. Notes with an 'S' in the code are denoted by the '#' on the keyboard – in other words, `AS4` is the same as A#4. Look at the notes listed under the `power_notes` variable. Click the keys D5, F5, A5, E5, G5, B5, F5, A5, C6 as quickly as you can on your virtual keyboard, then press the reset button on your Arduino Uno. The tune you just played on the keyboard should be the same as the first of the four melodies produced by the Arduino.

IN THIS CHAPTER

HOW TO BUILD A ROBOT

PUT IT ALL TOGETHER

The time has come to take everything we've learned so far and combine it all to create our finished robot. Everything from the LEDs in our early projects to the sounds we created will be used to make Magbot. It might sound daunting, but if you've followed all the steps we've taken to get to this point, you'll have more than enough knowledge to tackle the task. In this chapter, we'll also take you on a guided tour of Magbot's code to see exactly how it works. And we'll make Budgetbot – the robot made from the components on our £18 shopping list.

PREPARE FOR YOUR PROJECT

When it comes to bigger projects, a little preparation can go a long way. Here, we get everything ready to make our robot

WHAT YOU'LL LEARN

- What components and accessories you'll need to make Magbot
- Useful tips for working efficiently and safely
- How to get Magbot's whiskers ready

If you've been working through this book methodically, you'll have already made many of the parts of your robot – the ping sensor, the battery level indicator, the motors and so on. But after building each one, you've pulled them apart to make something else. Well, now's the time to bring all of those various bits together and combine them to make our finished robot.

The process of making Magbot – or Budgetbot – is obviously going to be a little bit more involved than any of the practice projects, but don't worry. Everything you've learned so far will stand you in good stead for what's to come. That said, it pays to prepare for any big job, which is why we're going to take a brief moment to get ourselves ready for the project at hand. We'll also take the opportunity to pre-build one of Magbot's parts, so that it's ready for us when the time comes.

CLEAR THE DECKS

The first thing you'll want to do is clear some space. You're going to be using many more components for Magbot than you've done in any of the practice projects up until now, so your workspace is likely to get crowded. We've provided a complete list of all the components you'll need for the robot in the box opposite, so get all the bits and pieces ready and easily accessible so they're all within reach when needed.

Most component kits provide a selection of short, medium and long jumper wires. You may find it useful to sort these by length. When you build Magbot, you'll find that some of the wiring will need to stretch a little further than has been necessary up until now, since we're going to be arranging the breadboard and the Arduino boards on the top of the chassis. The breadboard needs to go right at the front so that the ping sensor is facing forward. But the Arduino Uno and motor shield need to go at the back so they can plug into the motors. By sorting your wires by length, this will save you having to wrestle with a great tangle of cables every time you need a longer wire. You can reserve all the shorter ones for connections that involve linking one socket to another on the breadboard.

It sounds silly, but sorting your wires by size can save a lot of pain.

Use a wooden tray underneath to catch screws you drop.

HELPFUL HINTS

We've used Blu-tak elsewhere, but you'll probably need a lot of it when it comes to making Magbot. It's not particularly elegant, but when you're trying things out, Blu-tak is a great mess-free way of sticking things together. It can also be very useful for preventing short circuits, particularly if you're using the AA battery pack that came with your chassis. Unlike the optional AA pack we recommended in chapter 2, the ones that come with chassis kits don't normally have an on/off switch on them, so once the batteries are inserted the current is

Mount your robot on a wooden block to stop him rolling away.

ready to go. If the bare ends of the loose wires touch, the batteries may overheat and melt or even explode, so you probably want to avoid this. If you connect both wires to the motor shield, on the other hand, power will drain – that's what the on/off switch on the switched pack is for. So, while you're working (and whenever Magbot is not in use), disconnect either the red or black wire from the motor shield to stop power draining, and use a large blob of Blu-tak to cover the bare end and stick it down safely on the upper deck of the chassis.

We've already recommended using a tray on the surface underneath you as you work, and this is particularly useful when it comes to anything that involves small screws. That way, when a screw or a component inevitably falls out of your fingers while you're working, the tray will catch it and you won't have to go scrabbling around on the floor.

Once the chassis has been built, it can be awkward working on something that's resting on wheels. Similarly, if you switch Magbot on to test him, you don't want him to suddenly drive off the edge of your workbench. So you may wish to consider mounting the chassis on a wooden block underneath so that the wheels are suspended. You could even use strips of Velcro to hold the robot in place on the block while you work.

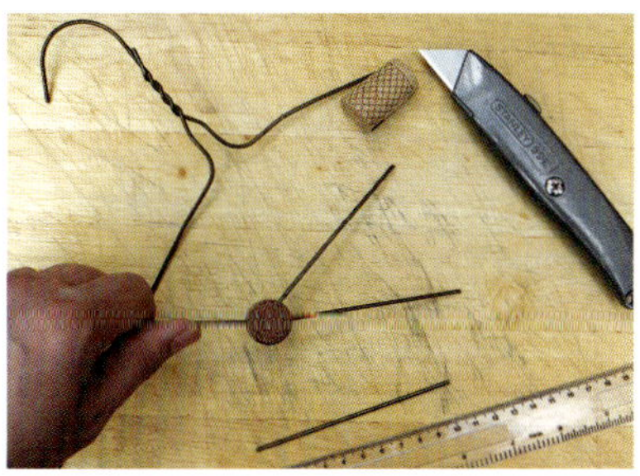

How to make Magbot's whiskers.

MAKE THE WHISKERS

Before we start, we're going to make Magbot's whiskers so that they're ready to go as soon as we need them. For this, you'll need the joystick module we tested in chapter 4, along with a wire coathanger, a wine bottle cork, some glue and a small screw. Using wire cutters, clip off four straight bits of wire from the coathanger. These should all be of equal length – about 10cm each. Next, cut off a slice of the cork – a little over 1cm in thickness. Now, get the four pieces of wire and stick them into the sides of the cork so they poke out at an angle, two on each side, as shown. Use some strong glue at the base of each whisker to hold them in place firmly. Place the cork on the top of the thumbstick and use the screw to fix it into place. The bare coathanger wire can be sharp, so stick some blobs of Blu-tak on the end of each to protect yourself while you work. We'll show you a more permanent way to cover the ends later on. You could also consider painting the cork so that it looks more 'nose'-like.

WHAT YOU'LL NEED

To save space, we've listed all the components you'll need to make Magbot here instead of in the project itself. If you're making Budgetbot instead, refer to the Budgetbot project directly to find out what you'll need.

- An Arduino Uno board
- A USB cable
- A computer
- An Arduino motor shield
- An Ultrasonic module HC-SR04
- 1 x chassis kit (including 2 x DC motors)
- 3 x LEDs (red, yellow, green)
- 1 x Piezo buzzer
- 1 x ultrasonic module (HC-SR04)
- 1 x infrared sensor
- 1 x IR remote handset
- 1 x analog joystick
- 6 x 220 Ω resistors
- 18 x jumper wires
- 6 x female-to-male jumper wires
- A breadboard
- A switched AA battery pack
- 4 x AA batteries
- 1 x 9V battery with clip connector

WHAT YOU'LL ALSO NEED

In addition to the components themselves and your usual accessories, there are a number of other items that you'll definitely need to hand before you start building Magbot.

- A Stanley knife
- A chopping board
- A precision screwdriver set
- Blu-tak (lots of it)
- Double-sided sticky tape
- A magnifying glass

BUILD MAGBOT

At last, it's time to explain how to put Magbot's hardware together, step by step

WHAT YOU'LL NEED

See the previous pages for the full list of components you'll need

So now the time has come for us to combine many of the components we've been using in our practice projects and use all the knowledge we've gained to build our finished robot. Mostly, it will work just like our previous projects – only bigger. One thing to note is that we won't be examining any of Magbot's code in this project. Instead, we'll be looking at Magbot's specially written sketch in a dedicated project following on from this one. Before then, we're just going to upload his program and physically put all of his hardware together. Remember that these steps are intended for those who bought the items from our 'official' shopping list in chapter 2. For those who went the bargain route, we'll be showing you how to build Budgetbot later in this chapter.

TIP

Now that you're building your actual robot, some of the wires need to stretch a fairly long way. If, like us, your components box didn't come with many longer wires, you can always extend the shorter wires by using a female-to-male wire on one end.

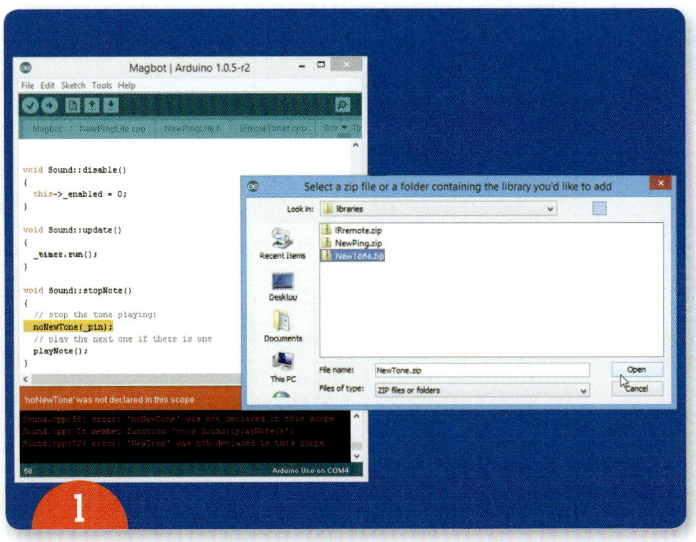

First of all, we need to double-check that you have all the software libraries you need installed. Open the Arduino IDE software and click File, Sketchbook, Magbot, then Sketches, and select Magbot. Before you attach your Uno and upload the code, click the Verify button (the tick icon on the toolbar). Do you see any error messages in the bottom portion of the window, in orange? You might see one referring to NewTone. If so, click Sketch, Import Library, then Add Library. Browse to the Arduino folder (C:\Users\Yourusername\Documents\Arduino in Windows), then open the Magbot\Libraries folder and double-click NewTone.zip.

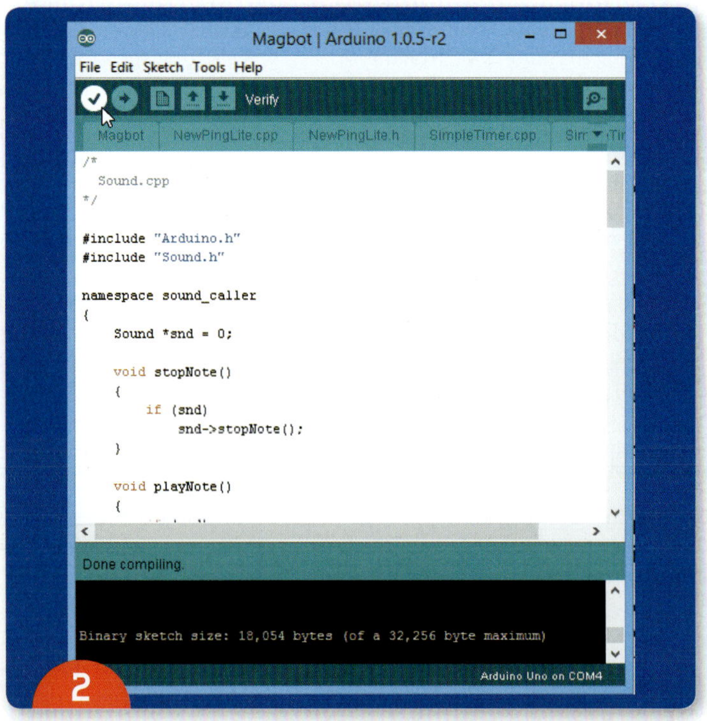

Close and restart the Arduino IDE program, open the Magbot sketch and try compiling the code again (click the Verify button). If you've followed all our other projects successfully so far, you shouldn't get any more errors, but, if you do, repeat the process outlined above twice more to install both the IRremote.zip and NewPing.zip libraries. Restart the IDE program again and try verifying the code once more. You shouldn't see any errors now. Uploading code to Magbot can be awkward once he has been assembled, so let's do it now. Plug your Arduino Uno into your PC and click the Upload button.

If you built Magbot Junior, you'll remember cutting the Vin Connect jumper on the motor shield. Well, now you need to do more of the same to free up some pins for other functions. Flip the motor shield module over so its legs are poking upwards and look for the jumpers labelled SNS0 and SNS1. Take a Stanley knife and very carefully run its blade down the black line between the two blobs of metal in the direction shown to cut the thin piece of metal between them. Do this for both jumpers. If you didn't make Magbot Junior earlier, you'll need to do the same for the Vin Connect jumper now, too.

For the next few steps, we're going to cover similar ground to some of the Magbot Junior steps, so if you worked through that project you may want to skip ahead to step 10. First, we're going to attach the motor shield to the Arduino Uno. Carefully line up the legs from the motor shield with pins on the Uno, then push the two boards together. You'll need to be firm but careful when you do this – we accidentally bent two of the shield's legs on our first attempt. Next, we need to test that the Vin Connect jumper has definitely been cut – this is very important; otherwise, you could damage your equipment.

Insert four AA batteries into your battery pack. On the motor shield, look for a set of six terminals along one edge – they're usually blue. With a flathead precision screwdriver, loosen the Vin and GND terminals. Insert the bare end of the battery pack's black cable into the GND terminal and the bare end of the red cable into the Vin terminal and screw them both down. Now, check the Uno board – is its power LED lit? If not, everything's fine. But if it is lit, there's a power connection between the shield and the Uno. You'll need to try cutting the Vin Connect jumper again. Disconnect the battery pack first.

The Dagu Magician is a fairly typical chassis pack in terms of both the parts included and, unfortunately, the standard of the instructions that accompany them. You'll find a sheet that looks like the one shown. We discovered that not only were some of the parts different from those shown, but also the steps were incorrect on a couple of occasions and we had to improvise a little. As with flat-packed furniture, this is quite common at the cheaper end of the market. We're going to explain how to put some of the parts for our Dagu chassis together, but instructions will be similar for other similar products.

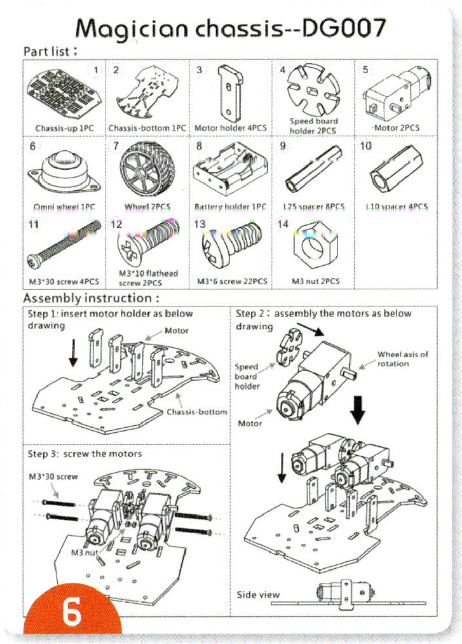

7 Put it all together

Add the motor supports, motors and wheels as shown in the instructions. If you're using the same kit as us, you may find you need to start employing your liberal interpretation skills at about step 5. Instead of caster wheel, the instructions refer to an 'omni-wheel' and suggested we only needed two screws to hold it in place. It also told us to use spacers, which aren't necessary with the caster. But we'll forgive it. If you bought the switched AA battery pack from our list of suggested optional items in chapter 2, ignore the part where the chassis instructions tell you to attach the supplied (non-switched) battery holder.

Whichever battery pack you're using, we recommend using Blu-tak or tape to hold it in place instead of screwing it down, as this will allow access to insert batteries whenever needed. Once the chassis is complete, you can slide the battery pack between the two decks towards the rear of the unit (just above the caster wheel) and stick it into place. With the switched pack, angle it so the switch is poking out at the back. With the non-switched battery pack, make sure the bare ends of the black and red wires don't touch (use another blob of Blu-tak) when batteries are inserted, or you'll get a short circuit.

Use Blu-tak (or tape) to fasten your Arduino/motor shield stack at the back of the chassis above the battery pack. Mount the breadboard (using another bit of Blu-tak) towards the front of the chassis with row J at the front. Then, connect the wires from the motors up to the A and B terminals on the blue plastic screw header. This may take some trial and error; start by connecting the red wire from the left-hand motor (from Magbot's point of view) to the B- terminal and the same motor's black wire to the B+ terminal. For the right-hand motor, connect the black wire to A- and the red wire to A+.

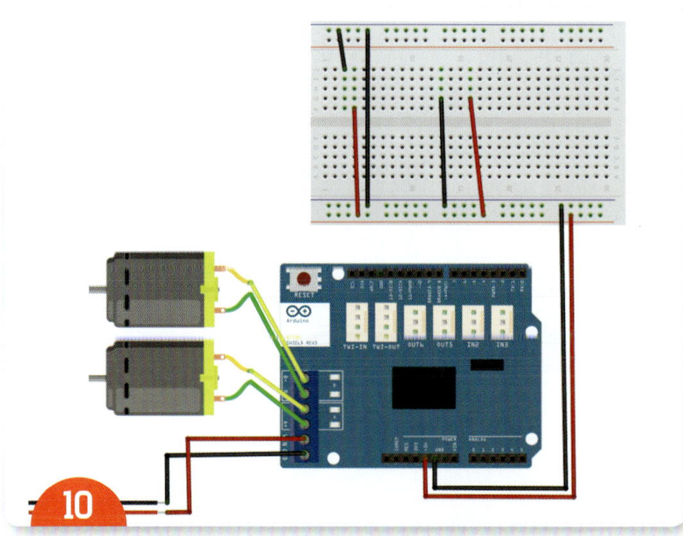

In the diagram above, the motors are already attached. Next, let's route the power around the breadboard. Connect the 5V and GND pins on the lower edge of the motor shield to the far-right block of sockets on the lower power and ground rails of your breadboard. Plug a red wire from the middle block of power rail sockets into socket G16 and plug a black wire from the ground rail into G13. Connect the socket in the lower far-left power rail block to socket F4 and connect the lower ground rail to the top one. Finally, connect a cable from the upper ground rail to socket J3.

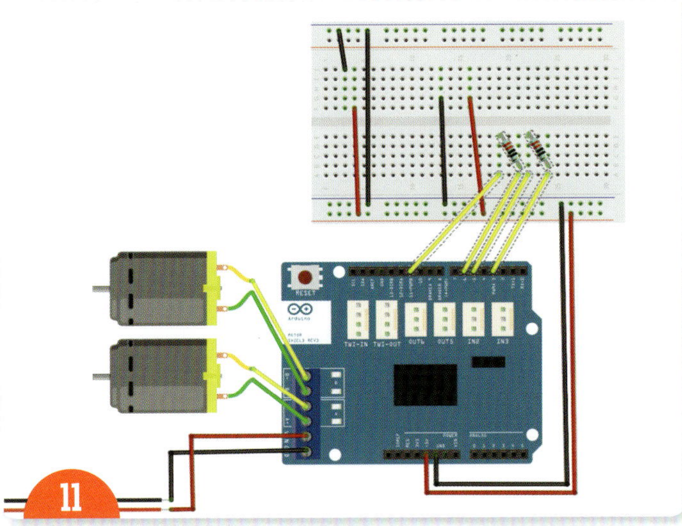

The next step might seem odd but it's an important one. We need to re-route pins 3 and 11 on the motor shield; otherwise, we won't be able to use the Arduino's timers for both sound and remote control. We're going to route pin 3 to pin 5 and pin 11 to pin 6, but we can't just plug these pins straight into each other without adding some safety, so we're going to go via the breadboard and use resistors. In the diagram, you'll see yellow wires going between pins 3, 5, 6 and 11 and the sockets in column A of the breadboard with two 220 Ω resistors bridging each pair. Wire yours the same.

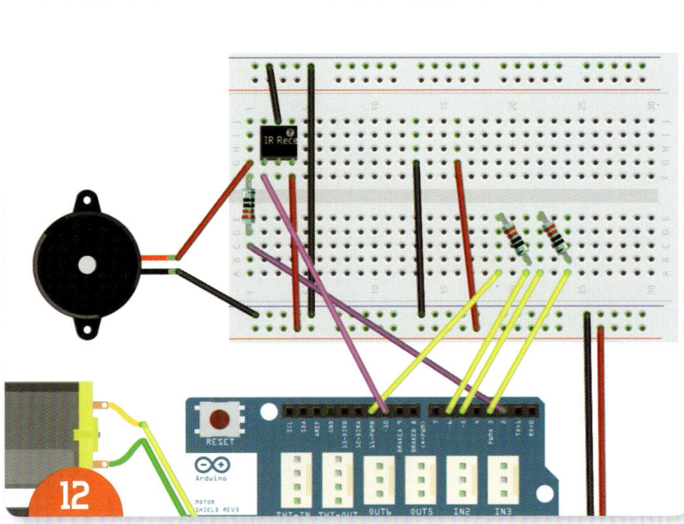

From here on, the wiring is going to get a bit complex – we've provided a larger, full-page version of the complete diagram on p103, which you can refer to if needs be. For now, let's add the buzzer and the IR remote. Plug the buzzer into a pair of female-to-male wires and insert the ground wire into the lower ground rail, then the power wire into G1. Pop a 220 Ω resistor across D1 to F1, then connect C1 to pin 2 on the motor shield. Insert the IR receiver with its 'V out' leg in socket G2 and the other legs in G3 and G4, then connect F2 to pin 10 on the motor shield.

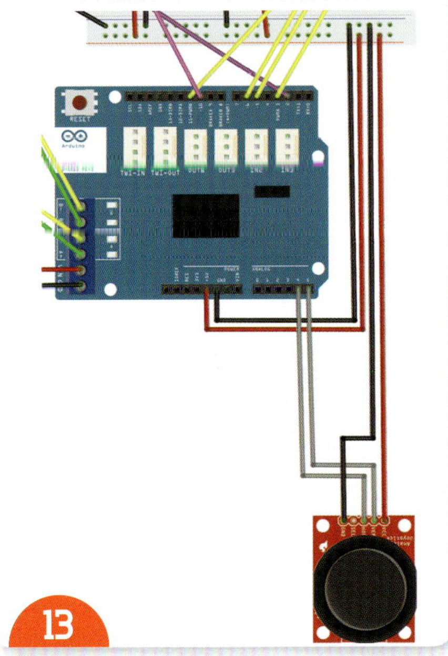

Get the whiskers module you put together at the beginning of this chapter and attach a strip of four female-to-male jumper wires to all the joystick's connectors except for the switch (the one labelled SW or SEL). Attach the wires from the VCC (power) and GND (ground) legs to sockets on the far right-hand block of the lower power and ground rails on the breadboard, as shown. Then, attach the wire from the X axis leg (the one usually labelled HOR or VRX) to pin A4 on the motor shield, and the wire from the Y axis (usually labelled VER or VRY) leg to pin A5 on the motor shield.

For the time being, you should be able to wedge the joystick's circuit board vertically between the upper and lower decks of the chassis with the 'nose' and whiskers pointing outward, as shown. This should hold the mechanism in place fairly firmly for the time being, though this isn't a particularly good permanent solution. Have a look at our 'finishing touches' later on in this chapter for more ideas. Also, you'll need to be a little careful of the sharp ends of the whisker wires themselves. Four big blobs of Blu-tak will do for now, but, again, we'll show you a better way later on.

7 Put it all together

For your battery indicator, attach wires from pins A0, A1 and A2 to sockets C26, B28, A30 respectively. Straddle three 220 Ω resistors across D26-F26, D28-F28 and D30-F30. Put the (positive) anodes of the green, yellow and red LEDs into J26, J28 and J30, inserting the (negative) cathodes of each into the ground rail above. Next, connect a wire from socket G14 to pin 4 on the motor shield and another wire from socket G15 to pin 7. Finally, insert the ping sensor into sockets I13, I14, I15 and I16 so that the sensors are facing outward and the VCC leg is in socket I16. Our diagram shows the rear of the sensor.

Reconnect the AA battery pack to the blue Vin and GND terminals on the motor shield, as described in step 5. If you're using the switched pack, flip the switch to 'On' at this point. Finally, get a 9V battery and clip it to the power adaptor. Fix the battery to the chassis somewhere near the Arduino/motor shield stack (with good old Blu-tak again), then plug the adaptor into the DC power socket on your Uno. After a second, Magbot should greet you with his 'hello' melody, and the three battery indicator LEDs should illuminate. Place Magbot on the floor – preferably a smooth (non-carpeted) surface.

Grab your infrared remote control handset – point it at Magbot and press the play/pause button. This should start the robot off on his little routine. He should move forward until he senses something in the way, either via his ping sensor or his whiskers. At which point, he'll alert you with a little sound and turn while reversing to steer away from the object. Press play/pause again and he'll stop. Magbot has a few extra actions. Buttons 2 and 3 on the remote will make him perform two different little 'dance' manoeuvres. Buttons 4 and 5 will make him perform simple 'happy' or 'sad' manoeuvres.

Don't worry too much if Magbot doesn't work as planned (or at all) straight away. He's pretty complicated, so the chances are you may just have mis-wired a connection or left out a component somewhere along the way. If he's not working at all, go through the steps again to check his wiring and refer to the full diagram opposite. If his motors or sensors are behaving oddly, check the troubleshooting section in chapter 9 for some advice about tweaking the code to fix problems. Remember to unplug the 9V battery and switch off the AA battery pack when you work on Magbot or when you're finished with him.

TIP

You'll notice in our photos that our wire colours in the photos don't match those in the diagram. This is because we were limited by the wires that came in our components box, as you're likely to be, too. The colours we're using in the diagrams are just for consistency.

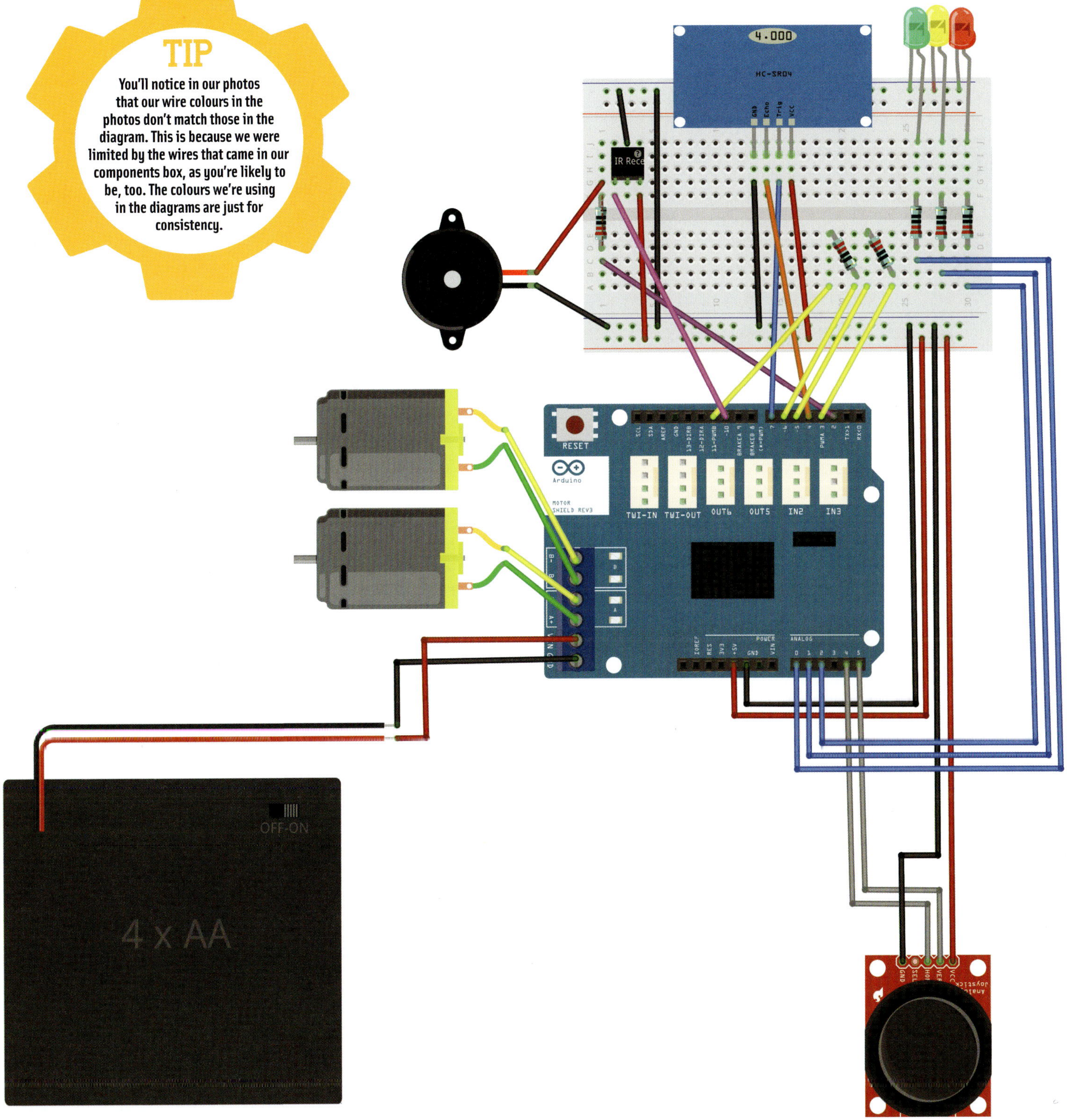

EXAMINING MAGBOT'S CODE

We run through the final sketch for Magbot to discover more about how he works

WHAT YOU'LL NEED

- A computer

Now that we've built Magbot, you might assume that's the end of the story. In fact, our hope is that building your first robot will just be the start, and that you'll put everything you've learned so far into brilliant future projects of your own devising. With this in mind, having dealt with the hardware side, we felt it was worth taking you step by step through the code we created for Magbot, to explain how some of its key features work. We don't have room to deconstruct everything, but you'll find out why Magbot is different to a lot of the simpler robots you'll find other people making online. You won't need to pull Magbot apart for this – just put him to one side for the time being, fire up your PC and open the Magbot sketch in the Arduino IDE software.

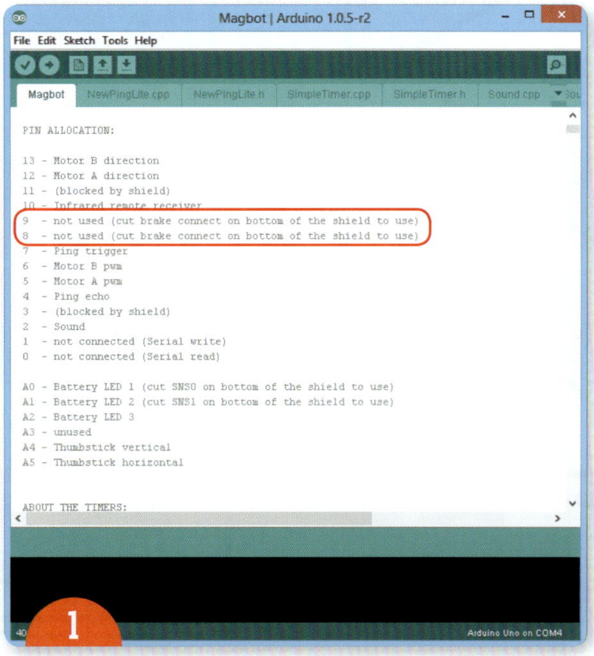

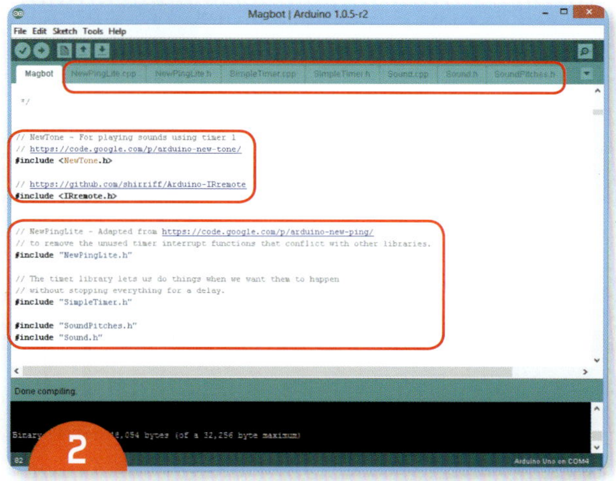

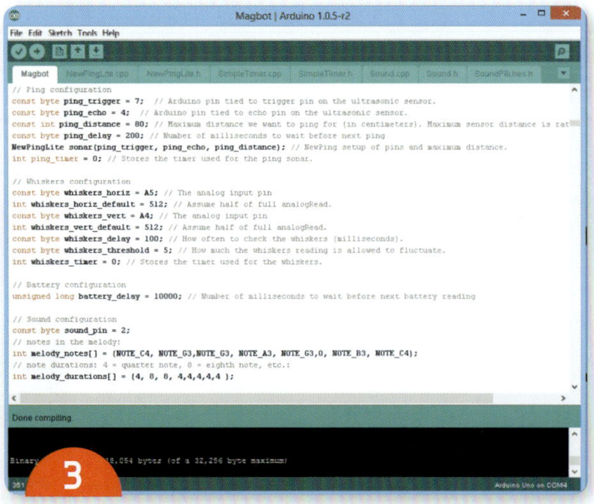

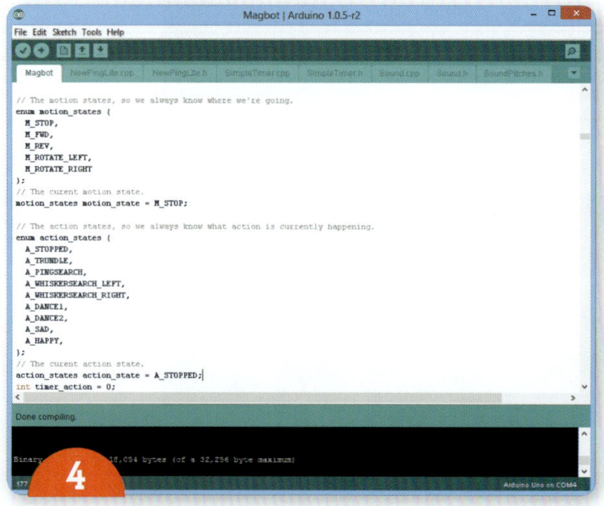

TIP

The code that we wrote for Magbot is there for you to use, adapt and build upon as you see fit. If you alter the code yourself, however, we suggest using the Save As option and saving the edited sketch under a different filename.

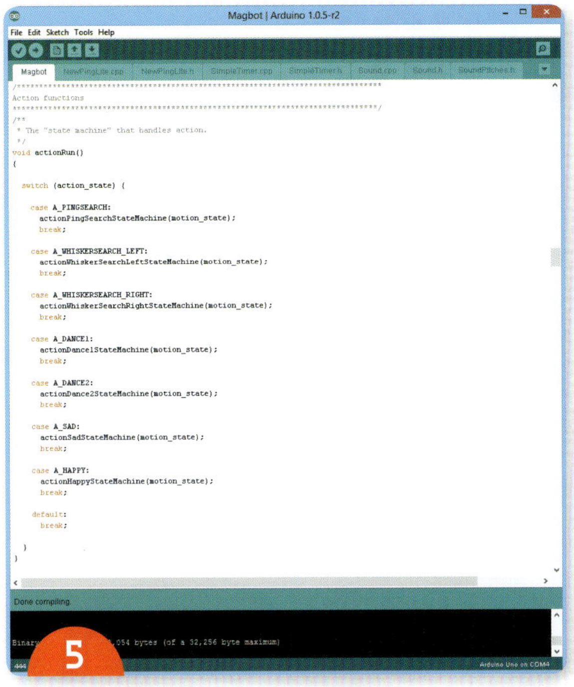

5

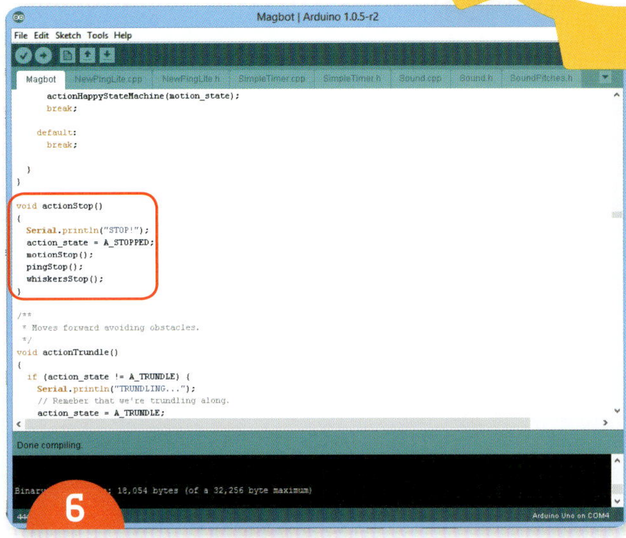

6

1

At the top of the code, you'll find some comments – we've listed exactly which pins are being used, for example, and by which function. You'll notice that some of the pins are blocked by the motor shield (3 and 11, for example). That means you aren't able to use these. There are a couple of pins, however, that you could use if you ever wanted to add an extra function or two. Pins 8 and 9 are used by the motor shield's brakes, but since we aren't using these you could cut the brake connect on the underside of the shield as we did with Vin connect and the two sensor jumpers when we built Magbot.

2

Scroll down past the comments and you'll see a section listing which libraries we're using. There are two slightly different sorts of library here. The top two (both with blue URLs) are libraries that need to be installed before the code will work properly – these are the libraries we checked for during the first couple of steps in our Magbot-building project. The bottom four (`NewPingLite.h`, `SimpleTimer.h`, `SoundPitches.h` and `Sound.h`) all refer to software that we've already included along with the Magbot sketch. Have a look at the tabs along the top of the program window and you'll see they correspond with these.

3

Scroll down a bit more and you'll find some configuration data, divided up by headings: 'Ping configuration', 'Whiskers configuration' and so on. These contain mostly the same constants and variables we saw in each of the relevant practical projects we worked on prior to making Magbot. For example, you'll find the melodies we tested out in the sound project in chapter 6. Towards the bottom of the configuration section, however, you'll find something new: state machines. There are two separate lists of these: motion states **M_STOP**, **M_FWD**, **M_REV** and so on, and action states **A_STOPPED**, **A_TRUNDLE**, **A_PINGSEARCH**, and so on.

4

State machines are basically a way of making sure that the robot knows what it's doing at all times. For example, Magbot only needs to use his ping sensor when he's travelling forward. So if he's backing up, he doesn't need to carry out his ping function. If Magbot knows that his current state is 'backing up' – or **M_REV** – he'll know he shouldn't carry out a ping until that state has changed. The motion and action states we've defined here in the configuration section will all be used by Magbot's various individual functions to check what he's doing at any given time.

5

In the setup, all the pins are set to the appropriate modes. Again, we've seen most of this before in the individual projects, but now they're all happening together. After the loop, you'll find all of Magbot's functions. Scroll down to the Action functions section – this tells Magbot what to do when he's in a particular action state and it's where he decides whether or not he should still be doing the action he's doing. The code here doesn't laboriously list everything he needs to do when he's in each state. Instead, it references something else in the code and says 'do what it says in this piece of code'.

6

Look at the section we've highlighted above. Here, let's say something else has called the action `actionStop();` – for instance, if button 1 on the remote was pressed. When that's called, the functions listed all happen and it sets the action state as **A_STOPPED;** so that all the other functions know that's the current state. If you look through the code for Magbot's other individual functions, you'll see that many of them use 'if... else' arguments that reference the machine states. And that's why Magbot is cleverer than many other robots – he's always aware what his current state is and knows what he should or shouldn't do next.

HOW TO MAKE BUDGETBOT

We explain how to put Magbot's less costly cousin together in a few easy-to-follow steps

WHAT YOU'LL NEED

- An Arduino-compatible Nano board
- A USB cable
- A computer
- 1 x L293D motor drive chip
- 1 x ultrasonic module HC-SR04
- 1 x chassis kit (including 2 x DC motors and AA battery pack)
- 19 x jumper wires (more for optional functions)
- A breadboard
- 4 x AA batteries
- 1 x 9V battery

Budgetbot is much cheaper than Magbot, but he's no less complex. The trade-off is that you'll have to do more work yourself. For example, instead of buying an expensive motor shield, we've gone for a raw motor drive chip, which we'll need to build into a circuit on our breadboard. We're also using an Arduino-compatible Nano instead of an official Uno, though the main difference here is just the smaller form factor. Budgetbot is designed to function in almost exactly the same ways as Magbot, but to keep costs low we've kept certain functions optional. To take advantage of them, you'll need to buy some of the extras we listed in chapter 2. For this project, you'll also need a cork, some wire ties, a screw, a precision screwdriver set and lots of Blu-tak or tape.

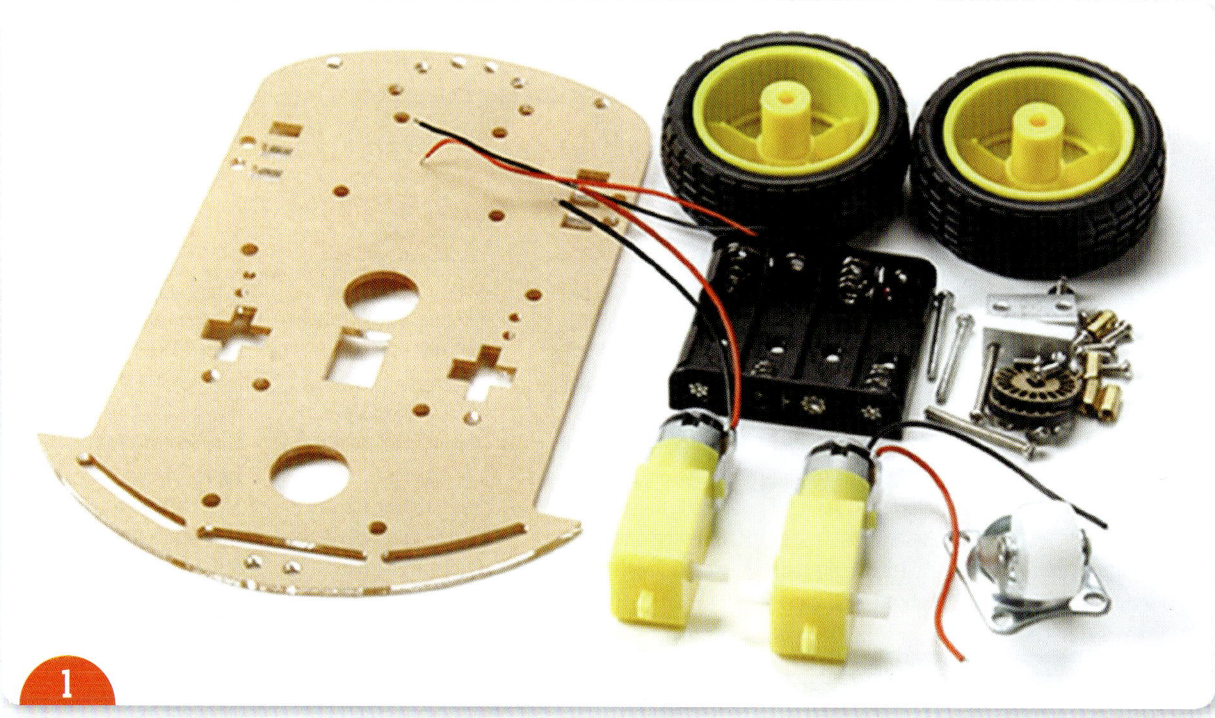

1

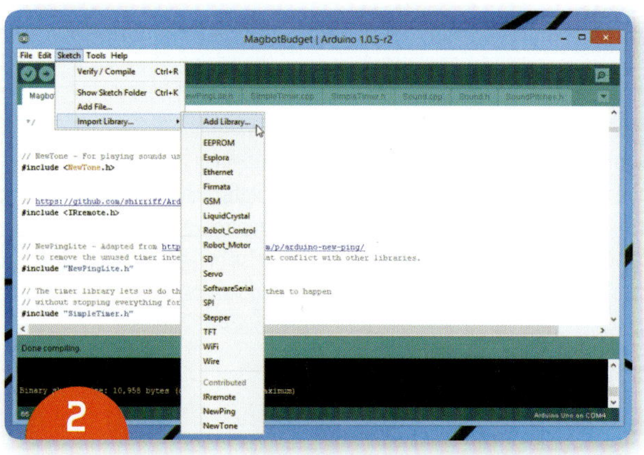

2

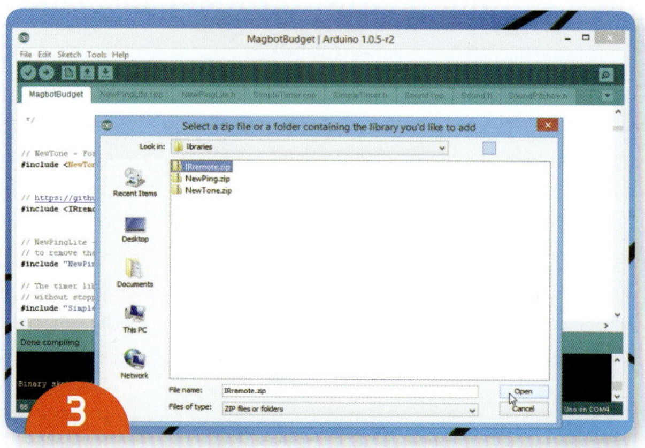

3

4

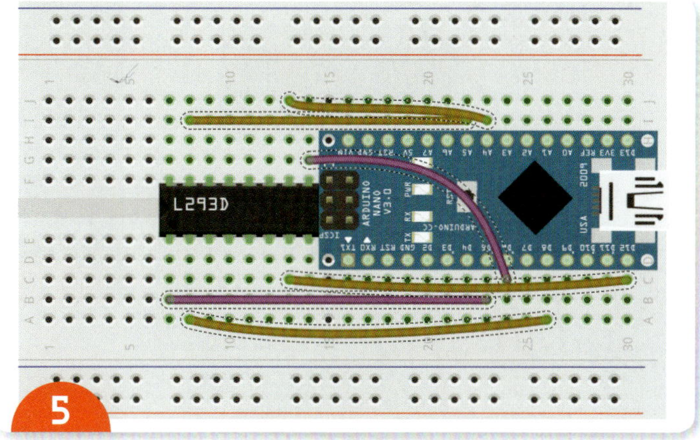

5

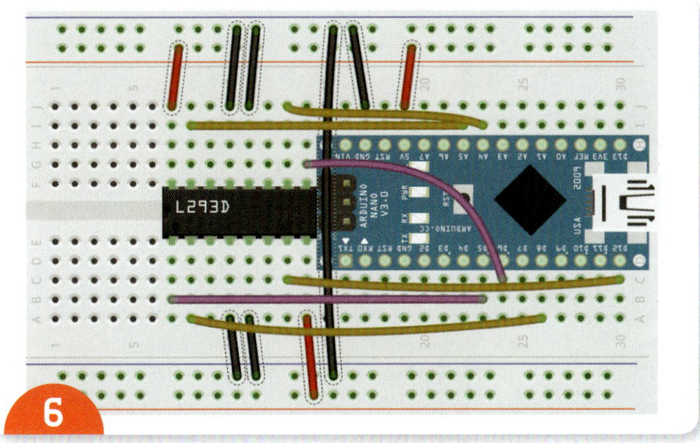

6

TIP

Budgetbot's code and functions are very similar to Magbot's, so even if you're only making Budgetbot we recommend reading through the previous two projects, as these will provide useful information about what your robot can do and how it works.

1

First, put together your chassis. We're not going to describe this in any great detail, as precise instructions will vary depending on the chassis kit you purchased. Most budget chassis kits only have a single deck of acrylic (unlike the double-deck chassis we used for Magbot), which makes them somewhat simpler to build. Your kit should have come with a selection of parts similar to those shown, including a pair of DC motors. Use the instruction sheet provided with the kit to build the chassis, but bear in mind that these can be somewhat unreliable, so be prepared for some anomalies and errors.

2

Now, we need to check that you have all the software libraries installed. Open the Arduino IDE software, click File, Sketchbook, Magbot, then Sketches, and select MagbotBudget. Before you attach your Nano and upload the code, click the Verify button (the tick icon on the toolbar). Do you see any error messages in the bottom portion of the window, in orange? You might see one referring to NewTone. If so, click Sketch, Import Library, then Add Library. Browse to the Arduino folder (C:\Users\Yourusername\Documents\Arduino in Windows), open the Magbot\Libraries folder and double-click NewTone.zip.

3

Close and restart the Arduino IDE program, re-open the MagbotBudget sketch and try compiling the code again (click Verify). If you've followed all our other projects successfully so far, you shouldn't get any more errors, but, if you do, repeat the process outlined above twice more to install both the IRremote.zip and NewPing.zip libraries. Restart the IDE program again and try verifying the code once more. You shouldn't see any errors now. Uploading code to the robot can be awkward once he's been assembled, so let's do it now. Plug your Arduino-compatible Nano into your PC via USB and click Upload.

4

Unplug the Nano from your PC, then get your breadboard and insert the Nano directly onto the board. The Nano will need to straddle the centreline – pin 12 will need to go into socket D30 on the breadboard and pin 13 will need to go into socket H30 with the USB port facing to the right, as shown. Next, insert the L293D motor drive chip into the breadboard – this will also need to straddle the centreline. The chip should have a small notch at one end – this end needs to go on the left, facing away from the Nano, as shown. The left-most pins need to go into sockets E7 and F7.

5

In the absence of a dedicated motor board, we'll need to wire the motor drive chip to the correct pins on the Nano manually. Along the top edge, connect pin A5 on the Nano to the same row at the second leg from the left on the motor chip. A4 on the Nano needs to be connected to the second leg from the right. Connect pins 5, 8 and 12 on the Nano to the same rows as the first, second and seventh legs respectively on the lower edge of the motor chip. Connect pin 6 on the Nano to the last leg on the right on the top of the motor chip.

7 Put it all together

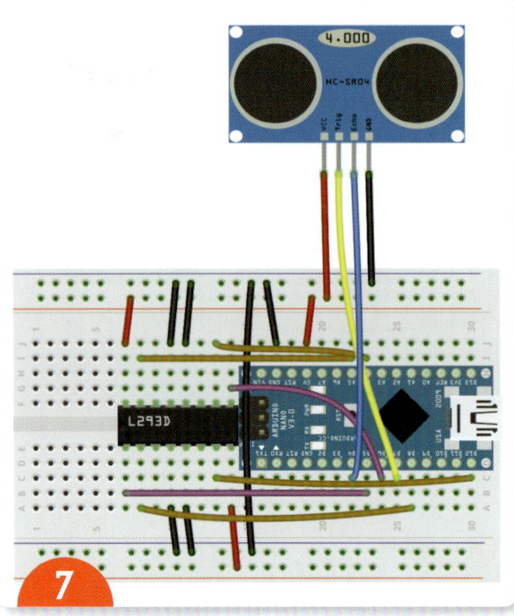

6

Now, we're going to route power around the board. We'll effectively be routing two lots of power, since the motors and the Nano are going to be using separate power supplies. For the time being, just insert two wires from the upper power rail – one to socket J7 and the other to J19. Connect four wires from the upper ground rail – one to J10, one to J11, one to J18 and one across the board to the lower ground rail. Connect two wires from the lower ground rail to sockets A10 and A11, and connect another wire from the lower power rail to socket A14.

7

Female-to-male jumper wires are optional items on our Budgetbot shopping list. If you've got some, connect a strip of four to the legs of the ping sensor. If you didn't buy any, see the tips section in chapter 9 for some ways to connect wires without soldering. Connect the wire attached to the Trig leg to the socket next to pin D7 on the Nano, and connect the wire from the Echo leg to the socket next to pin D4 on the Nano. Attach the wire from the VCC leg to the upper power rail, and the wire from the GND leg to the upper ground rail.

8

To keep costs down, sound, infrared remote control and whiskers are all optional. But Budgetbot's code supports all these functions, exactly as the full-price Magbot does. And if you want to include them, you can do so easily. Since they're optional, we're not going to go into too much detail about how to set up the hardware, but we've included them on the full diagram for Budgetbot, which you can see opposite. For our robot, we've scavenged a joystick from an old Xbox controller to make the whiskers. You'll find out more about making whiskers at the beginning of this chapter.

9

Get your AA battery pack and stick it to the base of the chassis with Blu-tak or double-sided tape. While you work, make sure the bare ends of the black and red wires from the battery pack don't touch or you'll get a short circuit. Stick one of the ends to the base with a blob of Blu-tak. Stick yet more Blu-tak on the top of the batteries and mount your breadboard on top of this with the Nano pointing backwards. You'll need something to mount the ping sensor on. Here, we've attached both the sensor and the whiskers to a cork – fix the cork to the chassis using a screw underneath.

10

Wire in the motors as shown opposite – the left motor (from Budgetbot's point of view) needs to go into sockets D9 and C12 on the breadboard; the right motor needs to plug into G9 and H12. Getting this right can involve a bit of trial and error, since connecting the wires incorrectly will make the wheels turn the wrong way. Connect the wires from the AA battery pack to the power (red) and ground (black) rails on Budgetbot's left. Finally, get a 9V battery (and a clip if you have one) and connect the positive terminal to socket J16 and the negative terminal into the right-hand ground rail.

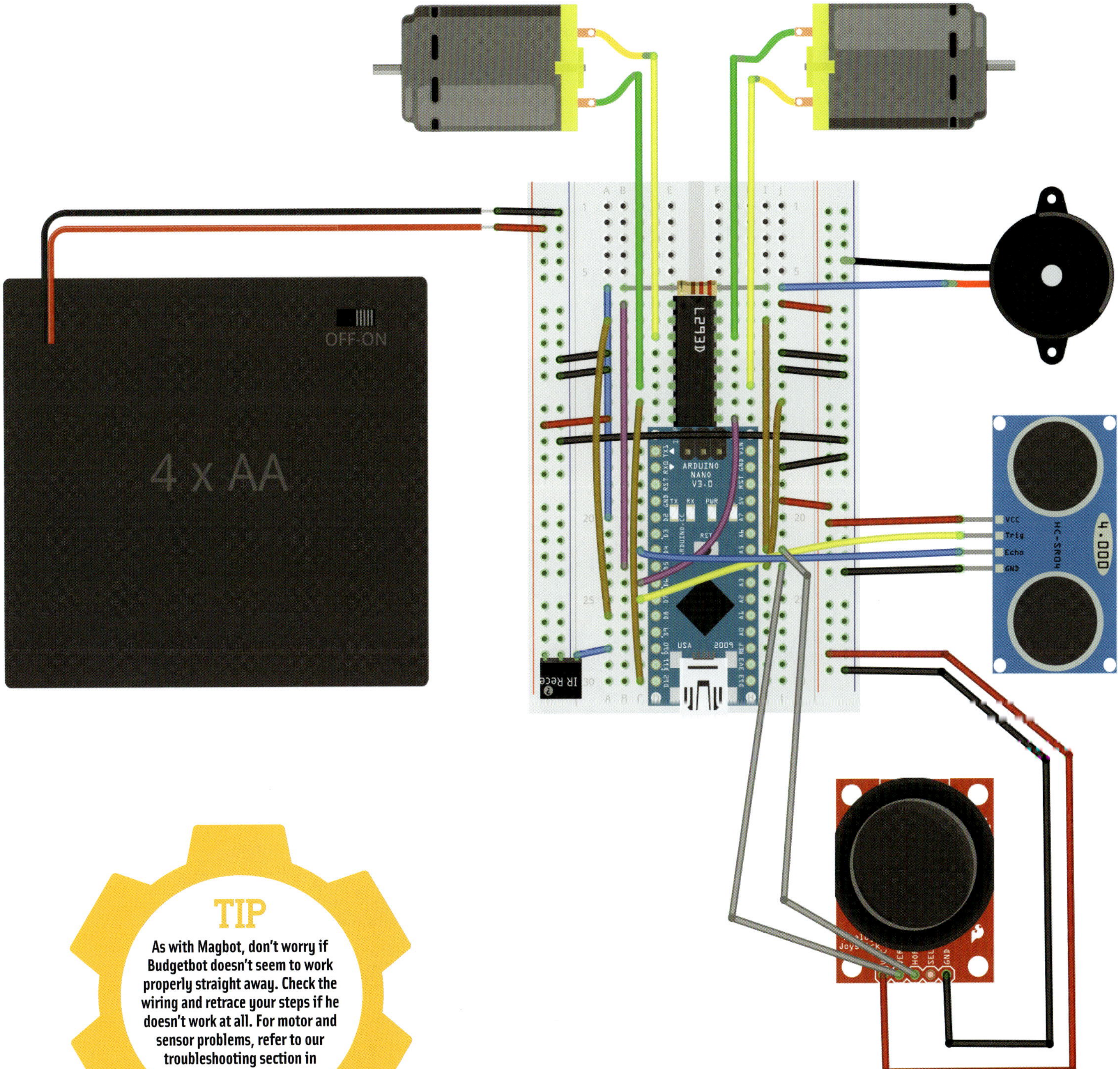

TIP

As with Magbot, don't worry if Budgetbot doesn't seem to work properly straight away. Check the wiring and retrace your steps if he doesn't work at all. For motor and sensor problems, refer to our troubleshooting section in chapter 9.

ADD SOME FINISHING TOUCHES

We suggest some design flourishes you can employ to personalise and smarten up your robot

WHAT YOU'LL NEED

- Magbot or Budgetbot
- A computer
- 2 x wine bottle corks
- Some wire
- Wire ties
- Stickers, glue or Blu-tak
- Lego
- A screwdriver and some small screws
- A Stanley knife
- Your imagination

Because our robots have been built entirely from scratch, you could be forgiven for thinking they look a little, well, 'functional' would probably be the polite way of saying it. And, if you search online, you'll find a number of bots other people have made that look very similar. But just like the electronic make-up of your robot and the programming code at work behind the scenes, its design and appearance are entirely customisable. You might want to tidy up your robot a bit; for example, customise its chassis or give it a whole new personality just by adding a few little touches. It's up to you how you personalise your robot, but in this project we're going to get you started with a few suggestions of our own.

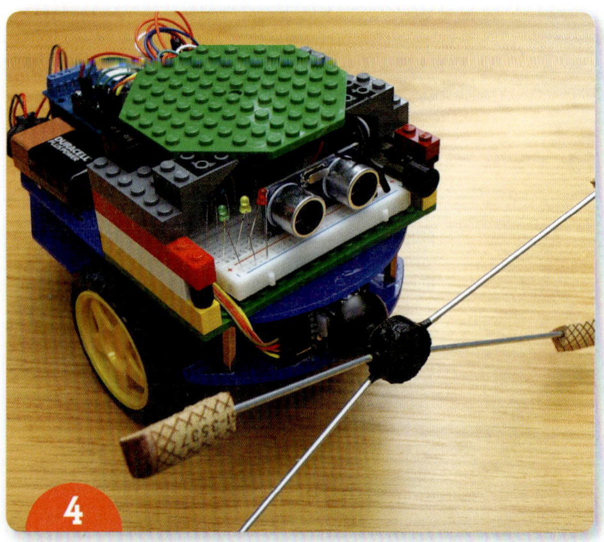

TIP

3D printers are still relatively rare, but if you know someone who's got one you could consider designing and printing your own plastic add-ons and parts for your robot, such as a 90-degree bracket for attaching the joystick to the front of the chassis.

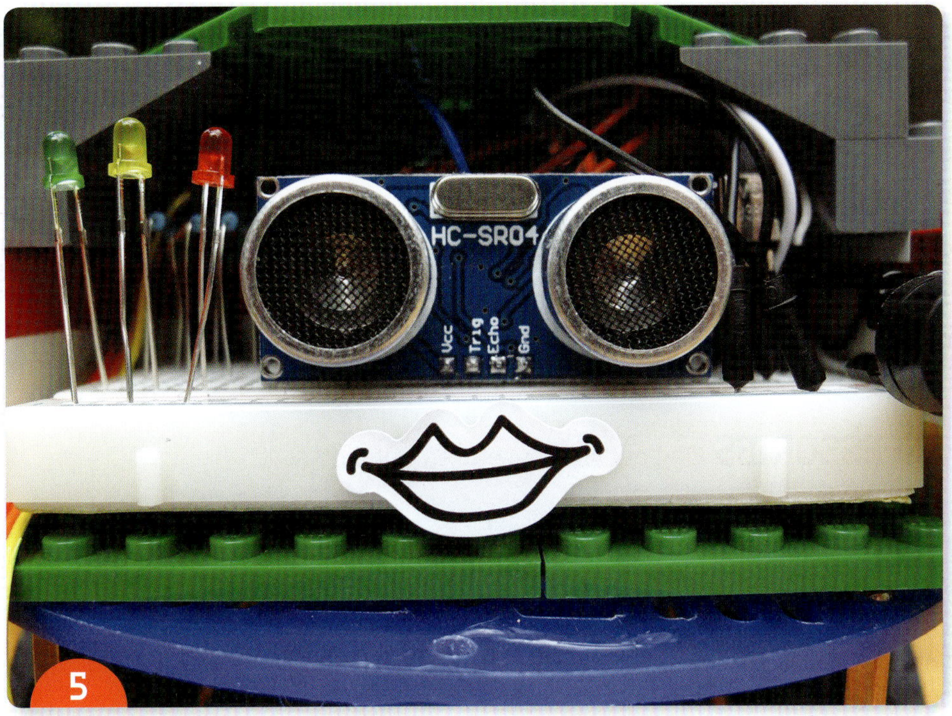

5

6

1

By the time you've finished putting together your robot, the likelihood is that he'll look like he has one big tangle of wires sprouting out of his top. If you're a fan of the messy look, then fine. But some people might prefer to do a bit of tidying up. The simplest way to neaten things up is to get some wire ties like the one shown and use them to clump the wires together. If you prefer (and if your wires are long enough), you could consider threading the wires out of sight through the middle part of the chassis – just make sure they don't go anywhere near the wheels.

2

When we made Magbot, we just stuck his ping sensor into the breadboard and wedged the joystick board between the upper and lower chassis. But as an alternative, you could consider mounting the whiskers and the ping sensor, as we did with Budgetbot. Here, we've attached both sensors to the cork with wire. You can then screw the cork to the top deck of the chassis from underneath. Alternatively, if you just wanted a firmer attachment for the whiskers module, you could screw a cork in horizontally between the decks of the chassis from underneath, then screw the joystick board into the front of it.

3

The coathanger wire we used for Magbot's whiskers is ideal because it's so strong. But the bare ends that we clipped off can be dangerously sharp. We recommended using large blobs of Blu-tak (or Plasticine) on the ends while making the robot, but it's not very permanent and the blobs can weigh down the whiskers. It's better to use cork. Take a cork from a wine bottle and carefully trim off about a quarter of the length with a Stanley knife. Then, take the longer part and slice it into quarters lengthways. Carefully twist the four pieces onto the ends of the whiskers, being careful not to poke the wire through the cork.

4

A great way to give your robot a makeover is to use Lego. If you have any Lego lying around the house, you can easily build on the basic chassis to create, for example, a cabin to protect your breadboard and its components. That's precisely what we've done in the image above. Our efforts are somewhat crude, but you get the idea. Just be careful not to overload your robot, as the more he has to carry, the slower he'll move. Avoid building anything too elaborate or delicate, either – remember your robot's going to be trundling around on the floor and occasionally bashing into things. You don't want it to keep falling apart.

5

Other ways to spruce up your bot include stickers or paints. Even something as simple as sticking a smiley face just underneath the ping sensor can instantly bring a little personality to your robot. If you don't have any suitable stickers at home, just do a Google image search for the image you want – 'cartoon smile', for example – then print the image on normal paper and stick it on with double-sided tape or glue. The bare cork on the ends of Magbot's whiskers is a good candidate for being painted. If you don't have paints, you could use dark felt-tip pens instead.

6

At this point, you should probably just let your imagination run riot. But if, after all your efforts, Magbot still looks and feels like a prototype, that's because he is one. Everything we've done so far in this book comes under the banner of prototyping. If you want to, it's possible to make some of the robot's circuitry permanent by soldering wires and components together. We aren't going to go into any detail here, but you can read more about soldering in general in the next chapter. In some ways, however, it's better to keep Magbot as a prototype – that way, you can alter or add to him as your knowledge and experience grow.

IN THIS CHAPTER

HOW TO BUILD A ROBOT

FURTHER PROJECTS

By now, you'll have worked on numerous projects and completed your robot, so what next? Well, what you do with your newfound skills is up to you, but in this chapter we'll give you some things to choose from. We'll look at the inspirational projects other electronics enthusiasts have created and explore the equipment available to help you take your skills further. We have a few more fun projects for you to try, too, including turning your robot into a roving wireless spy-camera.

Raspberry Pi Camera Rev 1.3
Campo Viejo
EDIMAX

IDEAS AND INSPIRATION

Don't stop making things now that you've finished your robot – we explore some of the amazing projects that you could work on next

WHAT YOU'LL LEARN

- **What brilliant electronic projects other people have made**
- **Where you could go next with your own projects**
- **How to keep all your batteries charged for free**

We're almost at the end of this book. You've built your robot and, if you're like us, you're probably already thinking about what electronic projects you could turn your talents to next.

So where do you start? What do you need? Well, the great thing is that by now you already have a lot of the stuff needed to take your experience further. The Arduino Uno at the heart of Magbot is a highly versatile piece of equipment that you can re-use for all kinds of projects – not just robots but also home automation devices, security alarms and much more.

If you don't fancy pulling Magbot apart just yet, you could always get another Uno – they're hardly expensive items. Or why not save some cash by building your own Arduino? It's not as hard as it sounds and we'll be showing you how to do so later on in this chapter.

When it comes to getting ideas for your projects, the internet is your friend. There are tons of great websites with examples of projects you can try. Have a look at the box on p116 for some useful URLs. Don't be afraid to borrow from other people. There's no such thing as plagiarism when it comes to building electronics – at least not at a hobby level. Other enthusiasts are keen to share their experiences and there are many great places online where you'll find people encouraging you to try out and expand or improve upon – their projects. Copying the work of others, including their circuits and their code, is a really good way to learn.

With that in mind, we've rounded up some brilliant Arduino-based projects that we reckon could be ideal candidates for you to tackle next. Maybe you'll try some of them out for yourself, or maybe you'll just use them as inspiration for a project of your own devising. Either way, it's great to explore some of the possibilities that are open to you now that you've built a robot all by yourself.

▲ Why not build a solar-powered battery charger to recharge your batteries for free?

▼ If you fancy developing another robot, try a robot tank.

SOLAR BATTERY CHARGER

Here's something you might want to do fairly early on in your electronics career. You'll be using a lot of batteries to power your projects, so it makes sense to use rechargeables. Better still, why not use a solar-powered battery recharge station to charge your batteries for free? You can buy pre-built solar chargers for about £15 but, as we've already been discovering, it's much cheaper and more fun to build your own gadgets. We made the solar charger above using a cheap 1W solar panel from **www.modmypi.com** (about £4), a battery holder and some wires. Even the stand is made from bits we scavenged from inside an old PC, including a fan grille. It's an incredibly cheap and easy way to save loads of money on batteries and electricity in the long term. The only important thing to note is that you'll

▲ Play Tetris using LED arrays.

need to include a diode in the circuit so that power doesn't discharge back through the panel when it's dark. The diode ensures that current can only flow in one direction. For more information on how to build your own version, have a look at the similar project detailed at **www.snipca.com/13144**.

ROBOT TANKS

Remote control vehicles are fun to build and operate, and the Arduino is a very good device to achieve that with. A great example of this basic robot project can be found at **www.snipca.com/13137**. The website details how to build this object using an Arduino, some motors and Bluetooth controls, and it probably only costs about £35, assuming you already have an Arduino Uno. The key components are a shield to drive the motors, gear motors, wheels, a servo and a means to connect Bluetooth into the mix. The tank body and turret are made from paper, designed in 3D and then converted to fold-and-glue printouts using Pepakura (**www.snipca.com/13138**).

As simple as it might look, this is a full four-wheel drive construction that can run at different speeds, rotates the turret, recoils and even brings red stop lights on when it halts. If you think it's overly ambitious, you could simplify it by reducing it to only two power wheels or ditching the turret. Those who think it's too easy might want to add a reversing noise and collision detection, if you can fit those using the unused two analog pins.

ARDUINO TETRIS

This isn't the only Arduino project around that enables you to play Tetris using LED arrays, but this one looks pretty cool with bi-colour output. This design uses a pair of 8 x 8 LED matrixes, though you could more easily make one using a LOL shield. This is an add-on that has lots of LEDs built into it (LOL is short for 'lots of LEDs' not 'laugh out loud' in this instance) and you can pick one up from eBay for about £10. The full build and code instructions for this can be found at **www.snipca.com/13139**. The cost of parts for this project is minimal, especially if you already have four buttons and a few resistors. The example uses the Arduino Nano, though it could easily be modified for Uno use with a bigger enclosure. Those wanting to enhance the design might want to incorporate a high score and SD card storage. What simplifies the electronics massively is that it used pre-mounted control integrated circuits (ICs) to drive the LED panels. We'll be doing something very similar in a moment in our advanced LED project.

SECURITY ALARM

Not everyone can afford their own alarms, but you can make a reasonable one from the Arduino to protect a particular entrance or window. A good example project by James Bruce can be found at **www.snipca.com/13140**. In this project, James connects the Arduino to an inexpensive ultrasonic sensor – the same modules as Magbot's ping sensor – and creates a warning using a buzzer

Copying the work of others, including their circuits and their code, is a really good way to learn

10 BRILLIANTLY CRAZY ARDUINO PROJECTS

1. **Make Android-controlled pneumatic cannon**
   www.snipca.com/13150
2. **Send an Arduino into space**
   www.snipca.com/13152
3. **Build your own Dalek**
   www.snipca.com/13148
4. **Make a 3D printed quadcopter**
   www.snipca.com/13149
5. **Wear vibrating underpants**
   www.snipca.com/13153
6. **Build an Etch-a-Sketch clock**
   www.snipca.com/13151
7. **Make a Lego CD duplicator**
   www.snipca.com/13154
8. **Play an Arduino-powered air guitar**
   www.snipca.com/13155
9. **Make a network traffic light**
   www.snipca.com/13156
10. **Design your own Daft Punk helmet**
   www.snipca.com/13157

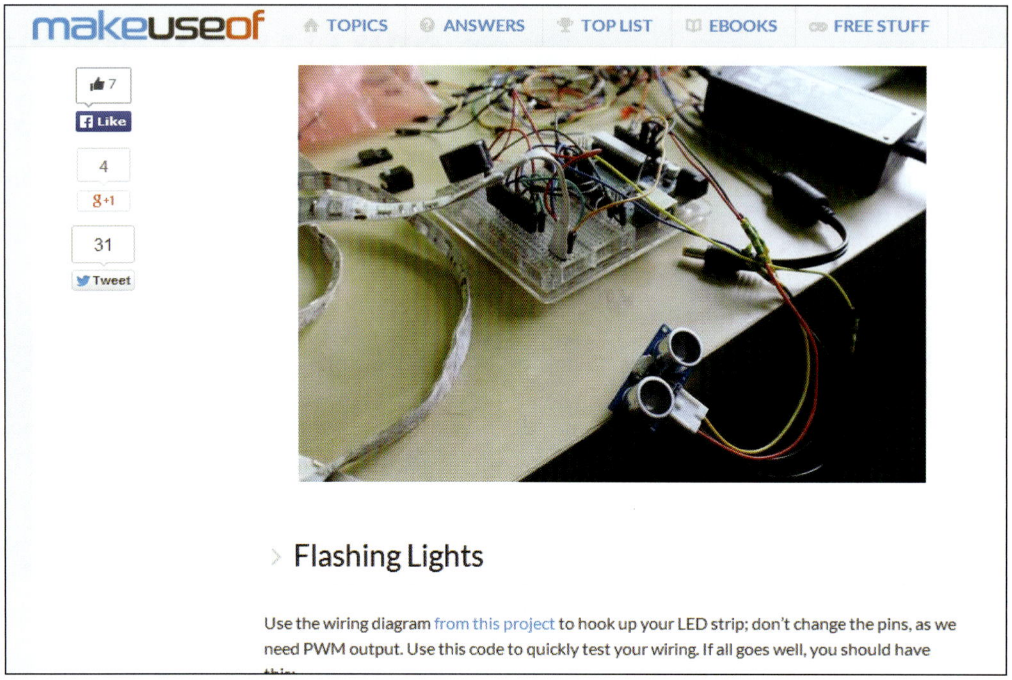

▲ Have a go at making an inexpensive security alarm.

and an LED light strip. Looking at what James did, by far the most complicated part of this is wiring the LED strip, the layout for which he borrowed from one of his other projects. The only caveat in this design is that the HC-SRO4 sensor only works up to a range of about 500cm, so it might not work in a big building or outside. Cost-wise this is a cheap project, if you leave out the LED strip, and all the coding is already done for you.

TEMPERATURE TWEETER

This project by Darren Yates is both relatively simple and cheap to do, making it ideal for anyone new to the Arduino. There are only three parts to the build if you include the Arduino Uno and no wiring to speak of. The two extra parts you'll need are the Ethernet shield (£5 from China) and the DHT11 temperature/humidity sensor (£1.72). Beyond those parts, the solution is entirely software based, and you can get the code from **www.snipca.com/13141**.

The code is kept simple by referencing a tweet library created by Markku Rossi, connecting the Arduino to the Twitter servers, even handling the necessary security protocols. Probably the biggest part of this project is creating a new Twitter account to send information out to. In this example, it transmits the temperature and humidity every five minutes. Setting up Twitter takes longer than building the project, as assembling that takes all of 30 seconds. Once you've got the Arduino tweeting, there are still plenty of unused pins to allow you to include wind speed, light levels and wind direction, if you're inclined to turn it into a full-blown personal weather station.

MOOD LIGHTING

Having lighting that always casts the same coloured light around you room can be boring. Why not make your own mood light using the Arduino and three LEDs? That might seem like a poor use of your time, but the results can be very impressive when you mix the huge range of potential colours that using a red, green and blue LED can generate when the voltage controlling them is Arduino powered. All the instructions are at **www.snipca.com/13142**. The whole assembly is mounted in a paper cube to diffuse the lights. This part we're less keen on, because it doesn't look very neat and could be very easily damaged. Instead, you could make a type of balsa lantern, like an old-style model plane, and use more robust 'doped' tissue to cover it. This is a good starter project that costs almost nothing to do.

LASER HARP

These days, you can buy lasers for just a few pounds, and hooking them up to the Arduino isn't that difficult. And who can resist a project that involves laser beams? Even if you're not an evil genius, there are lots of projects that use lasers,

▲ Who can resist a laser project? Have a go at this laser harp.

GREAT PLACES TO FIND FURTHER INSPIRATION

- **Adafruit** learn.adafruit.com
- **Arduino Playground** playground.arduino.cc
- **Dangerous Prototypes** dangerousprototypes.com
- **Instructables** www.instructables.com
- **Ladyada** www.ladyada.net/make
- **Lifehacker** www.lifehacker.co.uk
- **Make** makezine.com/category/electronics
- **Make it @ Your Library** makeitatyourlibrary.org/electronics
- **Make Use Of** www.makeuseof.com

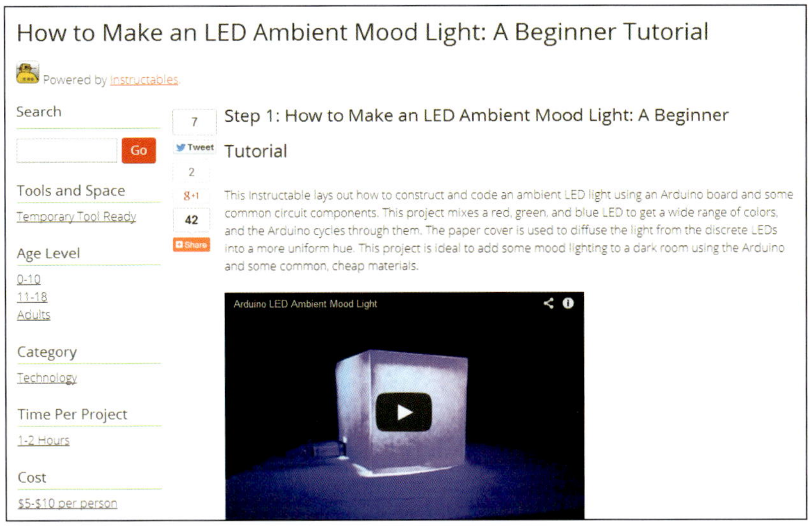

▲ **Why not make your own mood light? The results can be very impressive.**

often for security triggers or even accurate distance measurement. But a great project to let you play with coherent light is to make a laser harp. The project can be found at **www.snipca.com/13143**.

ULTIMATE REMOTE

Remember our experiments with infrared remote control back in chapter 4? We used a very well-written software library created by a fellow called Ken Shirriff. The same library is used in Magbot's code, too. On his blog (**www.snipca.com/[illegible]**), Ken comprehensively details how to build an Arduino IR controller. He documents the very straightforward circuits you need to send and receive infrared, along with the library code to drive NEC, Sony and Philips equipment. He also documents how you can add other protocols, should you wish, and even how to build a universal remote that will emulate any given controller. This project is very simple, but has the possibility to make something very complicated if you wish. You could easily use it to design a sender and receiver for IR signals so that, for example, a PVR could be remotely operated in another room or even over the internet.

ADVANCED ROBOTS

Back in chapter 5, we explained that building a robot with legs is much harder than building one with wheels. Well, that was before you made Magbot. Now you've mastered robot-building at this level, it could be time to take things up a notch and start looking at some more advanced constructions. You'll find dozens of potential projects of this type online. The one at **www.snipca.com/13146**, for example, uses a clever DIY design that features four legs but only requires two servos.

If you don't feel confident enough to build a whole new type of bot just yet, how about taking some time to refine and enhance Magbot himself? One of the features we wanted to include but didn't have the time was robot-to-robot communication. Magbot already has the ability to communicate basic sentiments ('happy', 'sad', 'dance1', 'dance2' and so on), and he also has a built-in infrared receiver. So if, in theory, you built two Magbots, it would be relatively easy to customise the code and the hardware so that robots could recognise and communicate with each other. Why not give it a try?

GOING FURTHER STILL

Hopefully some of the examples we've offered here will have provided you with a few ideas of your own. In the rest of this chapter, you'll find some further projects you can tackle, should you so wish. We're going to start off by having some more fun with the LEDs

A great project to let you play with coherent light is to make a laser harp

that came with our component kit. We'll also demonstrate how to make that DIY Arduino we mentioned earlier, and show you a great project where you can use Magbot in conjunction with a Raspberry Pi computer to add a wireless video feed to your robot's abilities.

Elsewhere in this chapter, you'll find some tips for planning your own projects, including a guide to an excellent free tool that you can use to help you design circuits. We'll also explore some of the accessories that you might want to consider investing in as you get more serious about your hobby, and we'll even show you how to start soldering.

So there you have it – even though you've finished building the main project in this book, there's still loads to explore, plenty to learn and tons of fun to be had from that pile of components on your workbench.

▲ **This temperature tweeter is fairly cheap and easy to set up.**

ADVANCED LED PROJECTS

We show you some great new tricks you can try out with LED circuits

WHAT YOU'LL NEED

- An Arduino Uno board
- A USB cable
- A computer
- 1 x four-digit seven-segment display
- 1 x shift register
- 8 x LEDs
- 8 x 220 Ω resistor
- Loads of jumper wires
- A breadboard

Back in chapter 3, we had some fun with LEDs, including making a 'Knight Rider' swooshing array. Well, now it's time to build on what we did there by making some slightly more complex LED-based circuits. In the steps that follow, we'll make and program a four-digit display like those you find on many digital readouts, and build a more sophisticated array using a shift register.

For all of these examples, we'll be using components that came with the components kit from our shopping list in chapter 2, so if you bought this or something similar, you should already have all or most of the parts needed. If not, the components we're using aren't that expensive and you'll easily be able to pick them up online for just a few pounds.

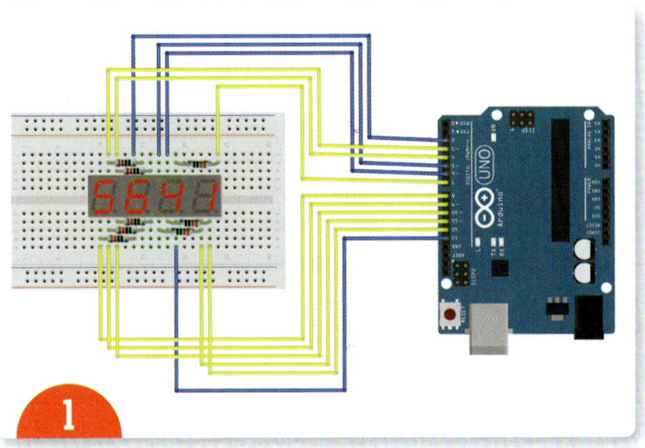

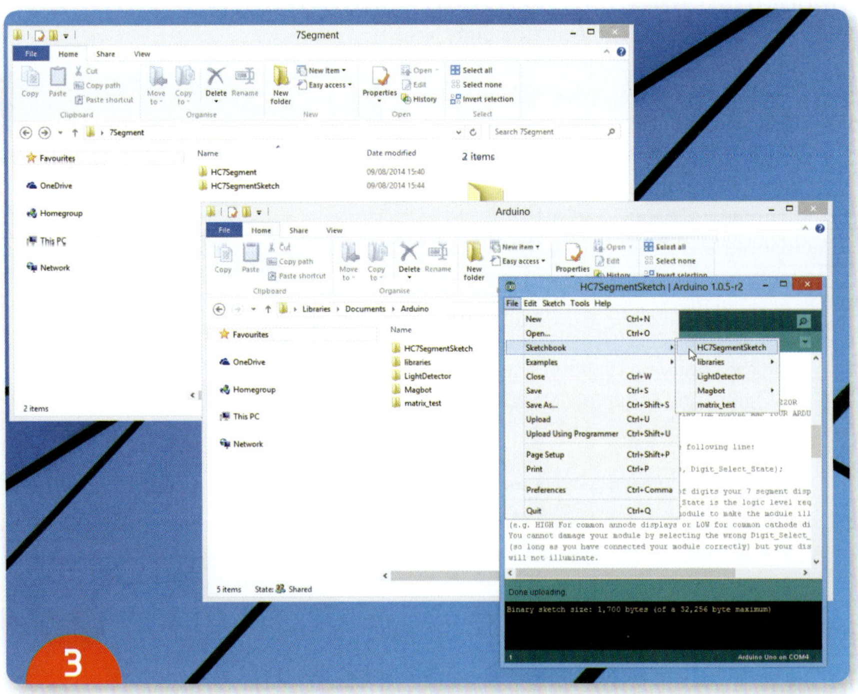

TIP

In our example, we used a single shift register to control eight LEDs using just three pins. But you can link multiple shift registers together to output even more components. See Example 2 at www.snipca.com/13163, where 16 LEDs are controlled by three pins.

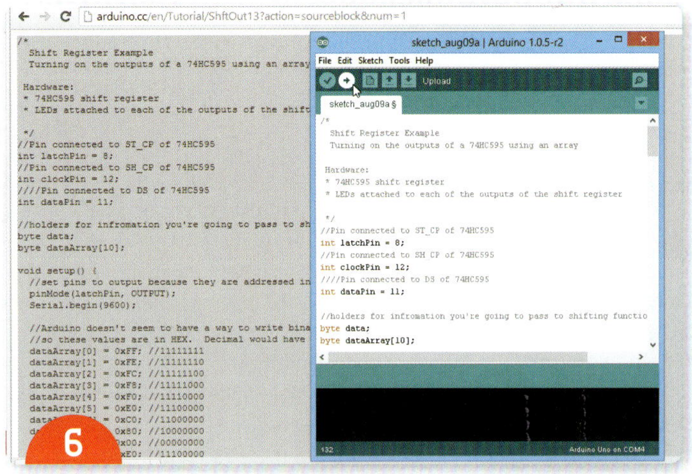

1

Here's the full diagram for the four-digit seven-segment display circuit. It looks pretty complicated, but that's mostly just because there's so much wiring involved. If you look on the back of the seven-segment module you'll see 12 pins – six on the top and six on the bottom. You'll need some female-to-male jumper wires. Tear off two strips of six wires from your ribbon and connect the female ends to the pins on the seven-segment module. Hold the module so that the decimal points are on the bottom, then plug the top row of wires into sockets G14 to G19 in sequence. Plug the bottom row of wires into sockets E14 to E19.

2

Finish off your circuit as shown in the previous diagram. All eight of the resistors we're using are 220 Ω ones. These must go into the right sockets, so plug these in carefully. The real trick is remembering which wires go where. We've separated them into yellow and blue so that you can see which connections are protected by the resistors (the yellow ones), but you can use any colours you like. Connect the other ends of the wires to pins 2, 3, 4, 5, 6, 7, 8, 9, 10, 11, 12 and 13 on the Uno. If you mix these up, the digits won't come out right on the display. The final circuit should look like the one in the photo.

3

Go to **www.pcpro.co.uk/links/robot** and download the file HC7Segment.zip to your desktop and extract its contents. Navigate to your Arduino folder and in Windows open an Explorer window (press Win+E on your keyboard) and navigate to C:\Users\Yourusername\Documents\Arduino. Drag the HC7SegmentSketch folder directly into the Arduino folder. Drag the HC7Segment folder into the Libraries folder. Close the Arduino IDE software if you have it open, then restart it and click File, Sketchbook, then HC7SegmentSketch. Browse through the code to see what it does. Then, when you're ready, upload it to your Uno and watch as the number on the display increases by one every second.

4

Okay, once you've finished playing with the seven-segment display, we're going to try something else. Back in chapter three when we made our 'Knight Rider' array, each of the six LEDs we used needed to be connected to its own pin on the Uno. This is somewhat wasteful, particularly if you're building your array into a robot, where every pin counts. So instead we're going to use an integrated circuit (IC) like the one shown. This is an 8-bit shift register (part number 74HC595), and it can let you control up to eight outputs at a time while only taking up a few valuable pins on your Uno.

5

Here's the diagram for our array circuit. Again, it looks a little complex, but in reality the most complicated bit is getting all the wiring right. Look on the shift register and you'll see a small semi-circular notch in one end. This end needs to go on the left in our diagram. The legs on the shift register connect to each of the eight LEDs through a 220 Ω resistor. Connect the power up from the IC to the upper power and ground rails, then connect these to the 5V and GND pins on your Uno. Finally, connect the three upper legs to pins 11, 8 and 12 on the Uno, as shown.

6

On your PC, open a web browser and navigate to **www.snipca.com/13162**. Click anywhere on the code in the browser window, then press Ctrl+A on your keyboard to select the entire sketch. Now press Ctrl+C to copy it. Open your Arduino IDE software and press Ctrl+V to paste the code into a blank sketch. Save this sketch if you like and have a browse through to see what it does. Then, connect your Arduino via USB and click the Upload button. The LEDs will blink a couple of times, then they should start cycling from right to left and back again in a pattern.

PLANNING YOUR OWN PROJECTS

Find out how to start designing projects of your own and discover a great free tool that can help you plan it

WHAT YOU'LL LEARN

- **What you need to consider before starting a project**
- **What tools you can use to plan a circuit**
- **How to design a project using a program called Fritzing**

Over the course of this book, you'll have worked on a number of projects by following the instructions we've provided. But at some point – if you haven't done so already – you'll begin to think beyond what we've covered here and start coming up with your own ideas for projects. Perhaps you want to try something similar to one of the ideas we showed you at the beginning of this chapter. Or perhaps there's something of your own devising that you'd like to try out. But once you've had your moment of inspiration, what do you do next?

The key to any successful electronics project is planning. You'll need to work out what components you need and how they should fit together in order to achieve what you want. And you'll probably want to try things out with your components to see whether your ideas will work in the real world as well as on paper.

▲ **Fritzing is a free, open-source application that lets you graphically design electronic circuits.**

To start with, we recommend keeping it simple. Don't try to build a two-legged robot that can juggle live kittens as your first solo project, for example. Come up with something that's more easily achievable within your experience range and budget. Preferably restrict it to components you already have – that way you won't have wasted any money if the project doesn't work out.

Once you've settled on a subject, the next thing to do is sketch it out. Professionals and experts use circuit diagrams to plan their projects, but these can be tricky to work with if you don't already know all the different symbols and conventions involved. Instead, we recommend using something called Fritzing. Developed by the University of Applied Sciences in Potsdam, Germany, Fritzing is a free, open-source application that lets you put together designs for electronic circuits of all kinds. The big difference is that it does so graphically; that's to say, it uses recognisable images of the components you're using, rather than symbols or words.

TIP

Fritzing is beta software and has a few quirks. It's worth clicking View and deselecting 'Align to grid'. Also, note that scrolling with the mouse wheel while the cursor is over the main window will zoom in and out of the image instead of scrolling up or down.

Fritzing effectively provides you with a virtual box of electronic bits and pieces – an unlimited supply of diodes, capacitors, resistors, wires and more – that you can use to build circuits. It even comes with virtual breadboards, Arduinos and more. By making your prototypes onscreen first, you can see exactly how everything will fit together before you commit to physically building your project, trying different things out and making any necessary changes as you go. You can save and print your diagrams, too. Fritzing also provides schematic and printed circuit board views. You won't need to use these when you start out, but as you progress they can help you learn more about how proper circuit diagrams work.

Over the next few pages, we'll explain how to start using this brilliant tool yourself. And if the images that the program produces look familiar, that's because we used Fritzing throughout this book to create the diagrams for all the circuits in our projects.

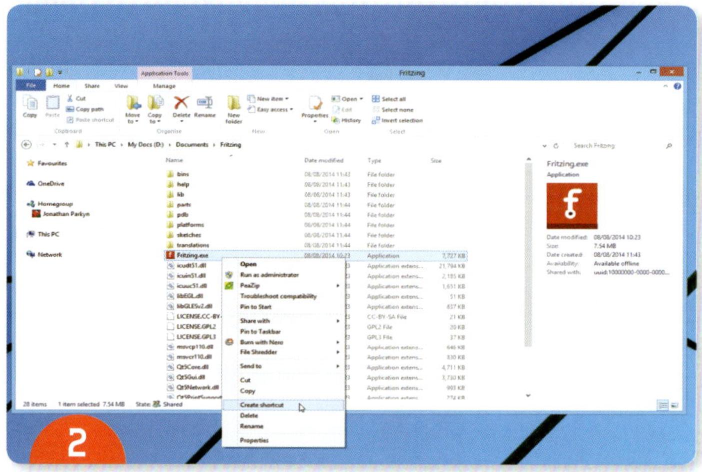

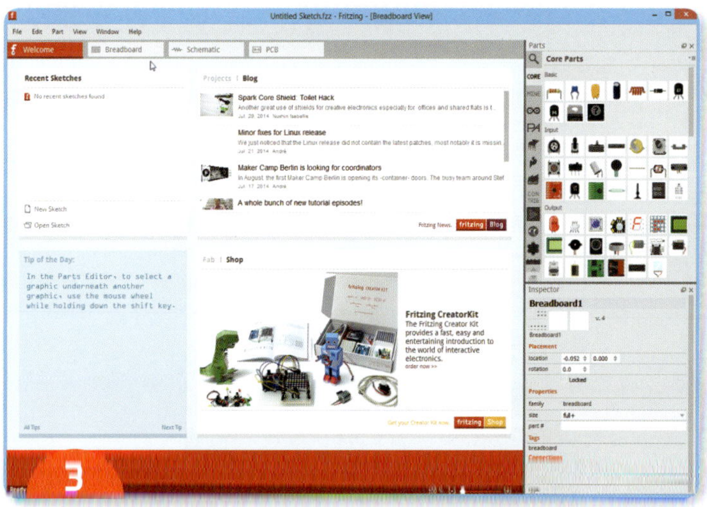

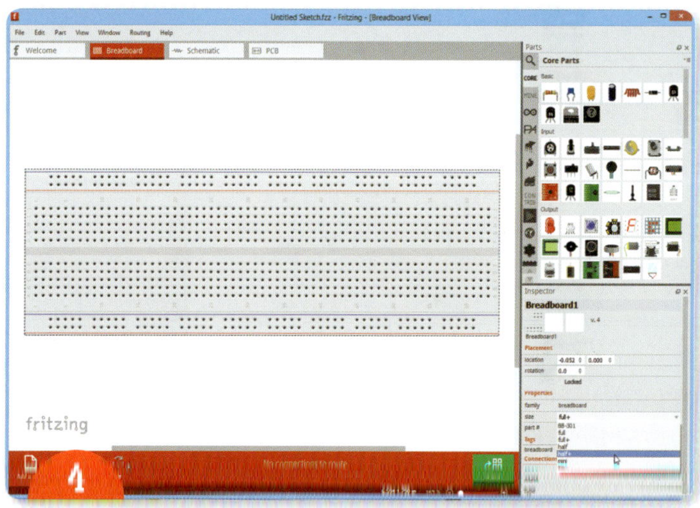

1

To get Fritzing for yourself, open a web browser and type **fritzing.org** into the address bar, then press Enter on your keyboard. When the page loads, click the Download button. Fritzing is free but you can make a donation to the program's developers if you wish. Put a check next to the amount you wish to donate or choose 'No Donation' if you don't want to pay anything, then click the Download button. Fritzing is available for Windows (32-bit and 64-bit), Mac OS X and Linux. Click on the correct version for your operating system to download the program.

2

For the purposes of this project, we'll assume you're using a Windows PC. You don't need to install Fritzing as you do with most other programs – you just need to run the EXE file whenever you want to launch the application. Locate the ZIP file you downloaded in the previous step, then right-click it and select 'Extract All'. This will unzip the program to a folder in the same location as the ZIP file. We recommend moving this folder to your Documents folder and renaming it 'Fritzing'. Then, right-click the Fritzing.exe file within it and select 'Create shortcut'. Drag the shortcut to your desktop for easy access.

3

Let's design a very simple project with Fritzing to show you how the application works. Launch the program via the shortcut you created and you'll be greeted by a welcome screen. Towards the top of the window you'll see a set of four tabs – Welcome (the screen you're on), Breadboard, Schematic and PCB. For the time being, click on the Breadboard tab. This is where you can design circuits graphically. Fritzing will have already added a breadboard for you. It will probably be a full size one, but we can change this to a half-size breadboard like the one we've been using for the projects in this book.

4

Click on the image of the breadboard itself to highlight it. Now, look at the lower right-hand corner of the program window. Here, you'll find an area called the Inspector. Any items you highlight in the main program image will be listed here. In this case, it should say 'Breadboard1'. Underneath, you'll see some attributes. Under the Properties section, click where it says 'full+' next to the size attribute. Select 'half+' from the dropdown menu, and the image of the breadboard in the main program window will change to a half-size model. Now we have the right breadboard, let's add some components to it.

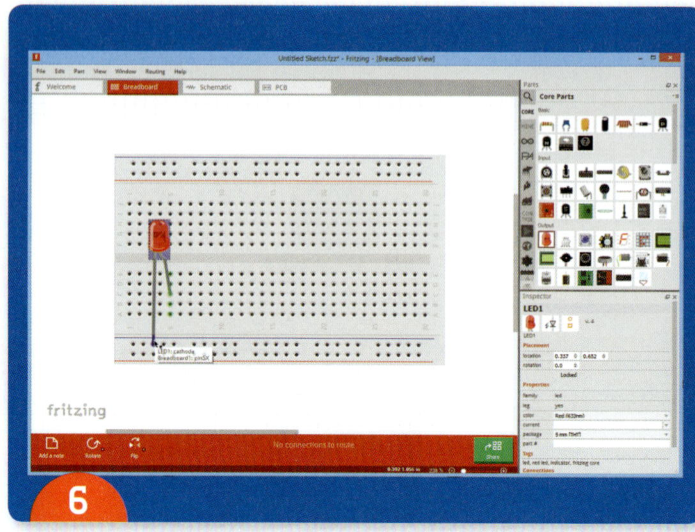

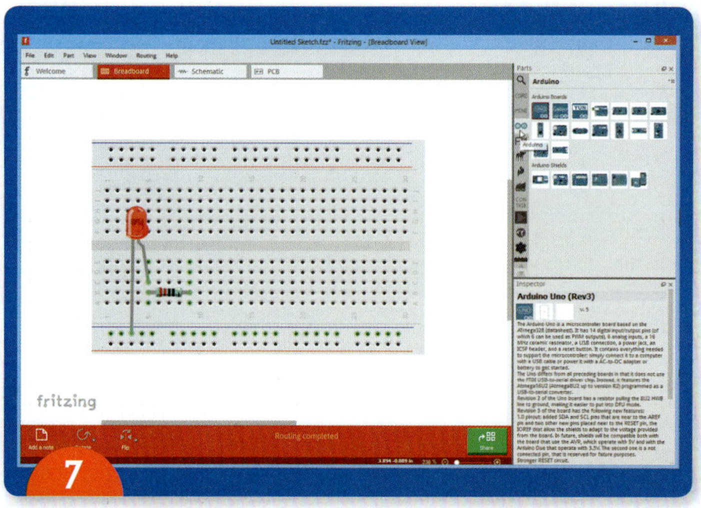

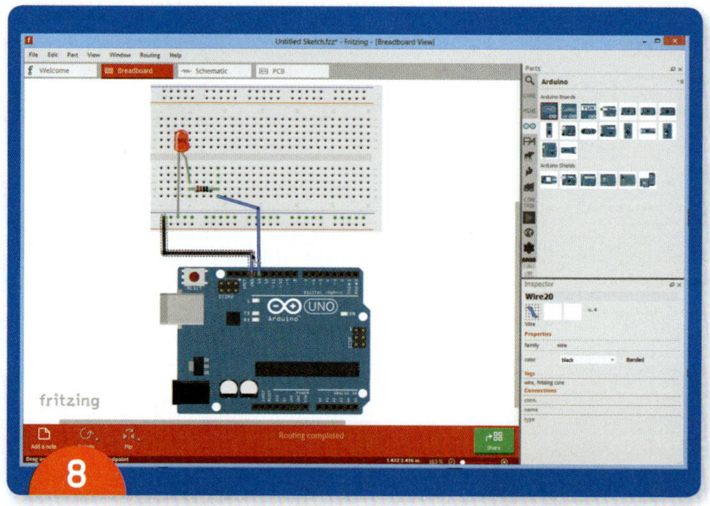

5

Look just above the Inspector on the right-hand side. Here, you'll find the Parts list – your virtual box of components. In the main area of the Parts list, you'll see little icons representing different components. By default, Fritzing shows the Core Parts list, which are commonly used, unbranded components, such as resistors and sensors. Scroll through using the right-hand scrollbar and you'll see many familiar items. Move your mouse over each icon, and the Inspector pane will tell you what it is. Under 'Output', the first icon is of a red LED. Click this and drag it onto your breadboard.

6

Drag the LED to roughly where you want it. From there, you can click each individual leg and drag it to the socket you want. Let's say you want the anode in socket C5 but the cathode connected to the lower ground rail. Hold your mouse cursor over a leg and a label will appear telling you whether it's the anode or the cathode. Drag the LED so that the anode is in C5, then click and drag the cathode to the lower ground rail. You can change the colour of the LED by highlighting it and selecting a different colour from the dropdown menu in the Inspector.

7

Drag a resistor from the Parts list to sockets B5 and B9. We want a 220 Ω resistor here and our 'real' resistors are blue with five bands on them. Click the resistor to highlight, then look in the Inspector and select '5' from the Bands dropdown menu and 220 Ω from the Resistance menu. Now, look at the Parts list again. Down the left-hand side are some icons in grey. These are other categories of parts. Click the Arduino symbol (the loop with – and + symbols in it) and, after a moment, the Parts list will change to display a selection of different Arduino boards.

8

Click and drag an Arduino Uno (Rev3) from the Parts list into your diagram, and drop it just below the breadboard. You might have to zoom out at this point. To connect wires between components in Fritzing, all you need to do is click your starting point, then drag to your destination. Here, for instance, click socket A9 on the breadboard and drag to pin 13 on the Uno. Now, click the GND pin on the Uno and drag to the lower ground rail. You can change the colour of a wire via the Inspector and add bendpoints to help make the diagram clearer by clicking in the middle of a wire and dragging.

ADVANCED ACCESSORIES

If you're going to start building more electronic projects, here are some other components and tools you might need to get started

To keep costs low, we limited our shopping list in chapter 2 to the bare minimum needed to build Magbot – and we listed even fewer items for those making Budgetbot. Not only did we restrict the components, but also the tools, devices and other accessories we recommended you got together, keeping your attention – and your finances – focused strictly on what was needed for the task at hand.

But if you're planning on taking your hobby further, you'll undoubtedly need to think about expanding your arsenal. There are numerous key electronic components that we haven't even touched upon just because they weren't needed for either Magbot or any of our practice projects. So we're going to take a moment to explain what some of these are and how you might use them.

Similarly, there are lots of useful tools and equipment you could consider for future projects, so we'll be explaining about these, too. And, of course, there are many ways to expand upon the Arduino microcontroller, so we'll show you some of these as well.

Capacitors are used to store an electric charge and filter signals.

ADVANCED ARDUINO ACCESSORIES

As you might expect given Arduino's popularity, an entire market of accessories and add-ons has sprung up around the platform. Some of these are official products from Arduino itself. But the vast majority are items made by third-party manufacturers, designed to expand the functions of the board in some way or another.

Arduino tends to stick to making variations on the form factor of the board itself, along with a few shields and adaptors, most of which we've already touched upon elsewhere. It also makes an Arduino starter kit, which comes with an Uno, a breadboard, a projects book and a box of different components. At around £65, this is somewhat expensive, however. For a full list of Arduino's first-party products, go to **www.snipca.com/13164**.

As for third-party accessories, these can range from something simple like a case to house the board in, right up to add-ons that allow you to program the microcontroller wirelessly. What you actually need will depend very much on the project you're wishing to attempt, but an enclosure would make a sound investment for most people, as it will help to protect your board. These don't have to be expensive – the average enclosure on Amazon costs around £5. Make sure you get one that provides access to the pins, and look for cases designed to suit your requirements. Some are designed for different Arduino form factors or allow the attachment of

WHAT YOU'LL LEARN

- How you can expand upon the Arduino microcontroller
- What other electronic components you can use
- What other tools and equipment you may find useful

Depending on your project, a Bluetooth module can be useful for wireless communication.

A larger-sized breadboard can allow you to build more complex projects.

8 Further projects

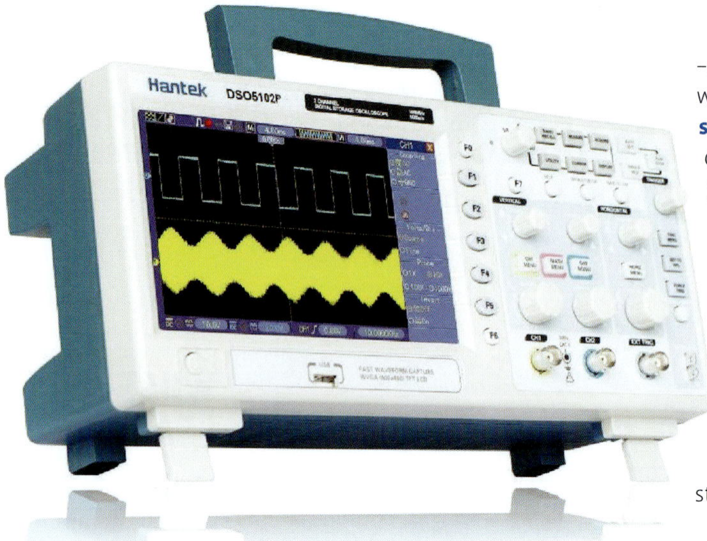

▲ **An oscilloscope isn't essential until you start getting really serious.**

shields, for instance. Others have compartments for batteries and useful features. If you're thinking of an outdoor project, such as a weather station, you might want a weatherproof case, such as the ones made by **www.otterbox.com**. There's even an American company that makes specially ruggedised Uno clones called Ruggeduinos (**www.ruggedcircuits.com**), designed to withstand higher voltages and more stresses and strains. Alternatively, you might want to make your own enclosure – see the box opposite for more.

Other useful general Arduino accessories to have include a wall adapter and a rechargeable USB power pack. One very useful accessory we picked up for £1 at **thepihut.com** was a male 2.1mm plug to screw terminal block DC power adaptor. Basically, this allows you to attach the bare wires from any battery pack to the DC power input on the board.

Wireless accessories aren't always just a luxury. If your project involves installing your Arduino somewhere that's hard to access, a wireless programming link of some kind might be essential when you want to upload code. Wireless kit can be quite costly – you'll pay about £23 each for Xbee wireless modules from Maplin (**www.snipca.com/13166**). Wireless can also be quite tricky to configure reliably. But if you're interested, there's a very good tutorial at **www.snipca.com/13167**.

It's worth browsing through online stores to see what other Arduino accessories are available, as these can often inspire an idea for a project. Stumble upon an LCD display shield for £8, like the one at **www.snipca.com/13165**, and you might be inspired to build a stopwatch or a digital clock.

Other accessories you might want to consider include an EEPROM Data Storage Module, which provides an extra 32k byte for your project, a Bluetooth module or a mounting plate to hold your Arduino and breadboard in place while you work.

ADVANCED COMPONENTS

In this book, we've used a fairly limited selection of components – mainly just resistors and LEDs. But there other types of component you'll encounter as you start to explore the world of electronics.

One type you'll meet fairly early on is a capacitor. In fact, we'll be using capacitors in our next project, when we build a DIY Arduino on a breadboard. Capacitors are similar to resistors, in that they're often used to protect your circuits. But instead of limiting current flow by providing resistance, capacitors store up an electrical charge. The amount they're able to store is measured by their capacitance in picofarads (pF), nanofarads (nF), microfarads (μF) or millifarads (mF). One common use for capacitors is to filter or 'clean up' electric signals. Capacitors are usually made from a ceramic or metallic material and come in a variety of shapes and sizes.

Transistors are something else you'll probably need to use more as you progress further. These can amplify or switch electronic

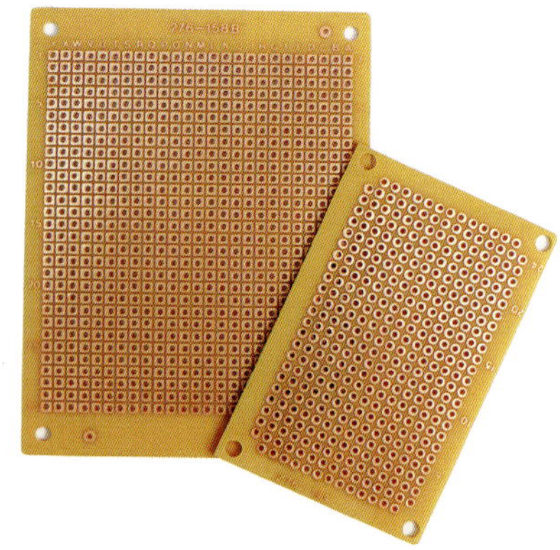

▲ **Stripboard like this replaces the breadboard when you start soldering.**

signals and power. We actually used a transistor in an earlier project – the three-legged temperature sensor in chapter 4 was a transistor.

We've touched on integrated circuits (ICs) throughout the book, too, but you'll probably find yourself using these a lot more. These are basically chips with tiny electronic circuits built into them. ICs are a cheap and easy way to add a bunch of relatively complex functions to your projects in one go, whether its memory, a timer or a way of controlling other components. The shift register we used in the advanced LED project earlier was an integrated circuit, for example, and the ATmega328 microcontroller on your Arduino is an IC, too.

Other cheap, fun components you might want to consider for your projects include

Something almost every electronic enthusiast will have in spades are crocodile clips

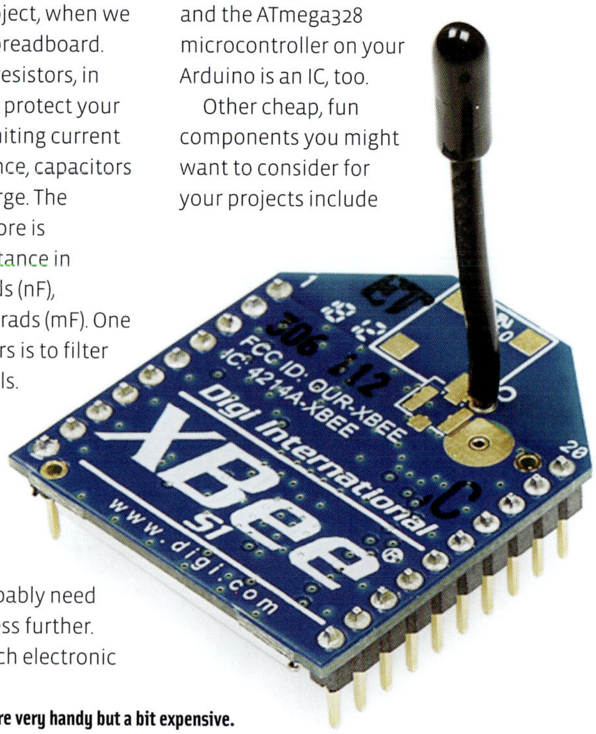

▶ **Wireless modules like this one are very handy but a bit expensive.**

motion, tilt and touch sensors. A capacitive touch sensor, like the one used in a smartphone display, should only cost about £1 from eBay, for example. And, as your circuits grow – or shrink – you might want to consider getting some different-sized breadboards. These are usually measured by the number of sockets – or tie points – they provide. Our half-sized breadboard has 400 tie points, but you can get mini breadboards with 170 tie points and full ones with 830 for a quid or two online. Even larger sizes are available, too.

BUILD YOUR OWN

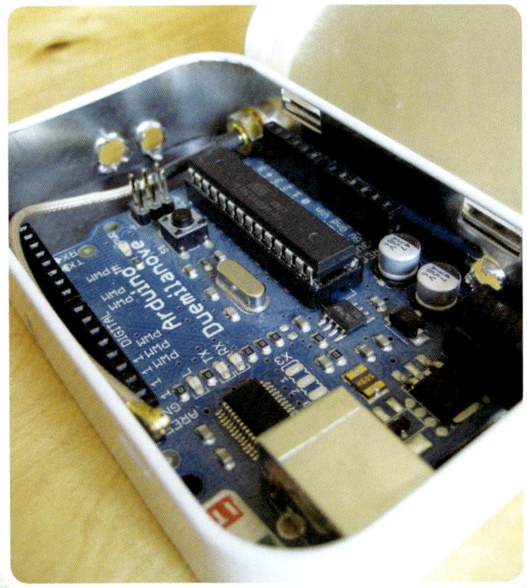

Working with electronics is all about building stuff yourself, so it makes sense to continue that train of thought when it comes to the tools and accessories you use. For example, you can buy a set of crocodile clips pre-wired for just a couple of pounds, but it's much more satisfying to build your own using raw wires, clips and insulator. Similarly, you could easily make your own Arduino enclosure, either by building something from scratch from raw bits of plastic or wood, or by recycling something else. At www.snipca.com/13169, for example, you'll find that someone has made an Arduino enclosure out of an old tin of Altoids mints. Scavenging, re-appropriating and improvising are all part of the fun!

ADVANCED TOOLS

Up until now, we've mostly stuck with tools you can find around the house – the one exception being the multimeter we recommended. As your ambitions grow, there may be a few other common household tools you can re-appropriate for your electronic projects, too. A hacksaw or mini-hacksaw is something you may well find yourself using, particularly if you start custom-building your own parts (see the box above). Equally, a drill can come in very useful for making screw holes in sheets of plastic or wood. Naturally, sharp tools like these should be used with care, and safety glasses should be worn when working with them.

Something almost every electronic enthusiast worth their salt will have in spades are crocodile clips. We've managed to get away without using them so far in this book, but it won't be long before you need to make a quick electrical connection or hold something in place so you can use your hands elsewhere. Similarly, if you've ever found it tricky to use your magnifying glass at the same time as manipulating fiddly little components, you could consider investing in a set of helping hands. This is basically a magnifying glass on an adjustable stand with a pair of clips mounted on articulated arms to hold items in place as you work. A helping hands set can be incredibly useful, and they're pretty much obligatory if you plan on doing any soldering. Cheap sets sell for less than £8 on Amazon.

▲ Arduino enclosures come in all kinds of shapes and sizes.

▲ This screw terminal adaptor lets you wire a battery pack to your Arduino.

Less essential – and much more expensive – is an oscilloscope. This is an electronic device for observing variations in electric voltages. Serious enthusiasts and professionals use these all the time, but you won't need one this early on in your career. When the time comes, you can expect to shell out up to £250 or more for a decent unit.

Before you get anywhere near an oscilloscope, you're much more likely to have developed an interest in soldering. This is basically a technique used to make permanent electronic connections using molten metal, which means you can finally ditch your breadboard altogether and start making 'real' circuits. The main tool you'll need for this is a soldering iron, but you'll also need some other paraphernalia including some solder, some blank PCB stripboards to solder things into, and a desoldering pump to remove excess solder when you get too carried away. Solder is pretty cheap, though the cost of an iron can vary dramatically – anything from about £12 for a cheap, basic iron up to £1,200 for a posh digital soldering station.

We'll be looking more at some of the types of solder and soldering irons available – as well as how to use them safely – towards the end of this chapter.

MAKE YOUR OWN ARDUINO ON A BREADBOARD

Want another Arduino for next to nothing? We show you how to build one yourself for less than £5

WHAT YOU'LL LEARN

- **How to make a breadboard Arduino**
- **What components you'll need for the job**
- **How to upload sketches to your breadboard Arduino**

One of the great things about the Arduino Uno is how cheap it is. For around £20, you get a highly adaptable, durable mini-computer that's capable of driving all manner of electronic projects. And, of course, if you go for an unofficial model or a clone, you can potentially lower that cost further to around £10. But by making an Arduino-compatible board yourself, the amount you need to spend is next to nothing. Not only that, but putting it together will help you learn some really useful things about how electronic devices work.

You can make an Arduino on a printed circuit board (PCB), but you'll need to know about soldering for that. Later in this chapter, we'll provide an introduction to soldering, but if you'd rather stick with what you know, you'll be pleased to hear that it's also possible to build an entire Arduino on a solderless breadboard, just like the one we've been using in our projects. Better still, you only need a handful of components, and many of these will be items you already have among your supplies.

Making your own Arduino clone isn't something that the Arduino company frowns upon. In fact, the people behind the official products actively encourage users to have a go at building one. There are several pages on the Arduino website (**arduino.cc**) devoted to the subject.

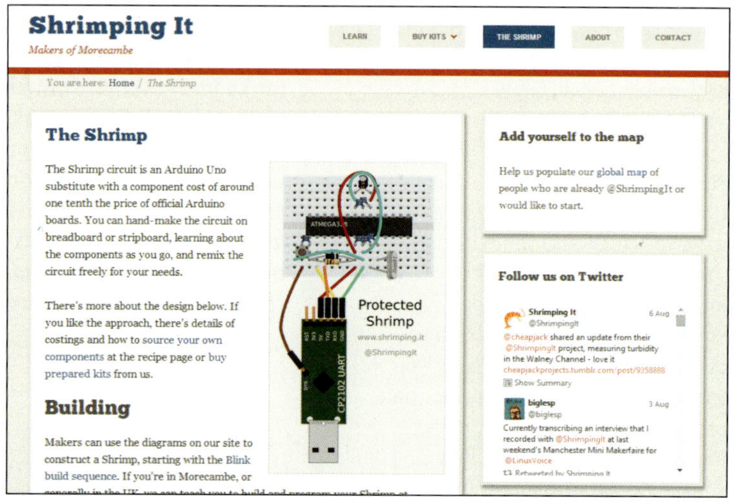

▲ **The Shrimp is an Arduino-compatible substitute.**

There are a number of different designs for homemade Arduinos, but they're all based around more or less the same principle, which is to get a raw ATmega328 microcontroller chip and insert this directly into the board.

The official Arduino website offers a number of options, ranging from a fairly complex construction designed to replicate almost everything a real board can, including the USB connection and the voltage regulator (**www.snipca.com/13128**), to a bare-bones Arduino on a breadboard that's basically an ATmega328 plus power (**www.snipca.com/13129**).

Another approach is something called the Shrimp. This is an Arduino-compatible substitute designed by a clever company in Morecambe. On its website (**shrimping.it/blog/shrimp**), the Shrimp team not only explains how to build its version of the breadboard Arduino, but it also sells all the items you'll need in kit form. While this is convenient, the website itself readily admits that you can cut costs drastically by sourcing all the individual components you need yourself from cheap suppliers.

The only drawback with the Shrimp is that you need extra hardware – namely, a USB-to-TTL UART module – in order to power the board and upload code to the microcontroller. In the steps opposite, we've provided a simpler version of our own using only a handful of components.

WHAT YOU'LL NEED

This is a shopping list of all the items you'll need to make our breadboard Arduino. You should already have many of the items in this list. The remaining components – including the ATmega328 microcontroller itself – should set you back no more than £4, or source them yourself from cheap online suppliers.

- **1 x ATmega328 microcontroller**
- **2 x 22pF capacitors**
- **2 x 100nF capacitors**
- **1 x 10μF capacitor**
- **1 x 10k Ω resistor**
- **1 x 220 Ω resistor**
- **16MHz quartz crystal**
- **2 x jumper wires**
- **6 x female-to-male jumper wires**
- **1 x LED**
- **8 x pin headers**
- **A breadboard**

TIP

The ATmega328 microcontroller on a real Arduino Uno board is actually removable. You can firmly but gently prise it out of its socket from either end. ATmega328 chips can be bought in bulk very cheaply to replace the one on your Uno in the event of damage.

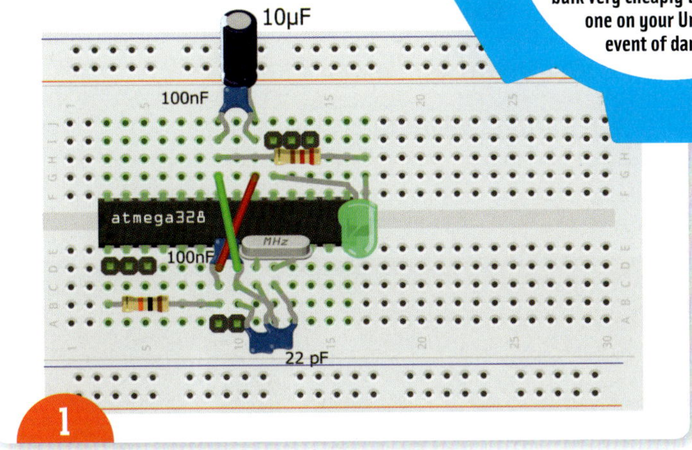

1

2

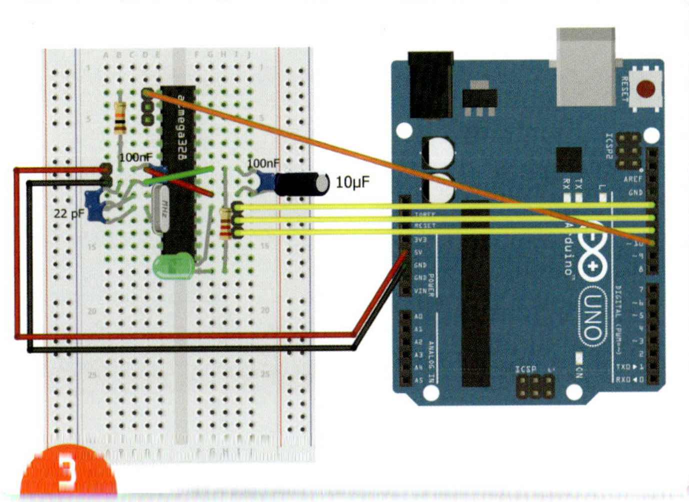

3

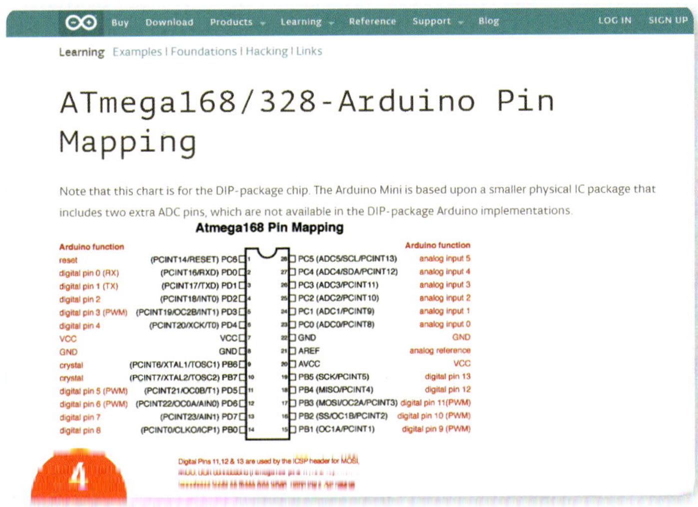

4

1

In the diagram above, you'll see how to build the breadboard Arduino circuit. You could use a mini-breadboard, but we've stuck with the half-size type we've been using throughout the book. We've labelled the capacitors so you know which go where. The 10k Ω resistor is the one in column B. The silver component labelled 'MHz' is the quartz crystal clock. The important thing is to insert the ATmega328 microcontroller into the breadboard the correct way round. You'll notice that one end has a semi-circular notch in it – this is the end with pin 1. Insert the legs at this end into E3 and F3.

2

Here's what the breadboard Arduino looks like in real life. The pin headers are optional – they're basically there to make it easier to hook up frequently used connections, such as power (the red and black headers on the left), but you could plug bare wires in instead. Our breadboard unit doesn't have all the features of a full Arduino – there's no reset button, no USB connection and no voltage regulator, for example – but in most other respects it will otherwise function just like a regular Uno. Because there's no USB, you'll need to connect it to a real Arduino board in order to upload code.

3

Here's how to hook up the breadboard Arduino to a real one. Use female-to-male jumper wires to connect the 5V and GND pins to the power headers, then connect pins 10, 11, 12 and 13 from the real Uno to the breadboard (shown by the yellow and orange wires). Before you can upload anything, you'll need to burn the bootloader to the ATmega328. With your two boards connected, hook up the real Uno to your PC's USB port and start the Arduino IDE software. Click File, then Examples and select ArduinoISP. Upload this sketch. Click Tools, then Programmer and choose 'Arduino as ISP'. Click Tools again and choose Burn Bootloader.

4

With the Bootloader burned to the chip, you can now upload sketches to the breadboard Arduino through your real one. Building circuits with your breadboard Arduino is easy. Since the legs on the ATmega328 chip are the same as the pins on the Uno, you can connect components to the pins by inserting wires into sockets in the same rows as the relevant legs. Unlike the real Uno, however, the pins aren't marked, so it's advisable to download a diagram of the pin mapping, such as the one shown. Go to **www.snipca.com/13132**, then print out your own copy and keep it nearby as you work.

MAKE A ROVING RASPBERRY PI CAMERA

Combine your robot with a Raspberry Pi to make a mini-Mars rover – complete with a live wireless video feed

WHAT YOU'LL NEED

- Magbot
- A Raspberry Pi
- A Raspberry Pi camera kit
- A USB Wi-Fi dongle
- A USB battery pack
- An SD card
- A computer
- Some Blu-tak
- 2 x wire ties
- 1 x cork

▲ **Your finished roving wireless spy-camera.**

Earlier on in this guide, we likened Magbot to Curiosity, the Mars rover, and now you've built him yourself, you might be able to see why. Just like Curiosity, Magbot is programmed to trundle around his environment and navigate any obstacles he encounters. Obviously, Magbot doesn't live on Mars, or have an onboard geology lab to analyse soil samples, and he doesn't use a high-powered laser to blast rocks. But there is one way that we can add another of Curiosity's features to our own robot.

Curiosity has ten different cameras around his body to help him navigate and perform scientific investigations. He is able to send a video feed back to NASA so that scientists on Earth can see what he sees. And, with the right equipment, we can add something similar to Magbot.

There are a few ways of doing this, but one of the simplest methods is to combine your existing robot with a Raspberry Pi. The two devices won't actually be communicating with each other in any way. The Pi will be handling the wireless camera side of things, while Magbot does all the navigating. As the robot moves around, a camera attached to the Pi will capture the world from Magbot's point of view, and the Pi will then broadcast the video signal over your Wi-Fi network, via which you'll be able to watch and control the image from a PC or a tablet.

Obviously, if you don't already have a Pi, you'll need to get hold of one. It doesn't matter which model – model A, B or even the new B+ model will all work fine. A new Pi should set you back between £20 and £27, depending on which model you get and where you get it from. You'll also need a Wi-Fi adaptor – these usually cost around £5 – and the Raspberry Pi camera module, which usually sells for around £20 online. Note that the camera module is a little delicate, so make sure you discharge any static electricity before handling it (touch a metal radiator) and try not to bend its cable.

You should make sure your Pi is in an enclosure of some kind, as it will be necessary to attach the computer to your robot. You'll also need some storage – an SD card – and a portable power supply for your Pi. We've opted for a rechargeable USB power pack, as they're cheap and re-usable.

Finally, you'll need a few extra bits to help you put it all together. You'll need something to mount the camera on so that it has a decent vantage point. We're using another cork as a kind of 'neck' (as we did with Budgetbot's ping sensor) and some wire ties. Once you've got all your bits and pieces together, follow the steps opposite to set it all up.

TIP

If the video feed from the Pi is upside down, you don't have to turn the camera the other way around. Instead, use the settings in the web interface to rotate the picture round by 180 degrees. There are other quality and resolution settings to play with, too.

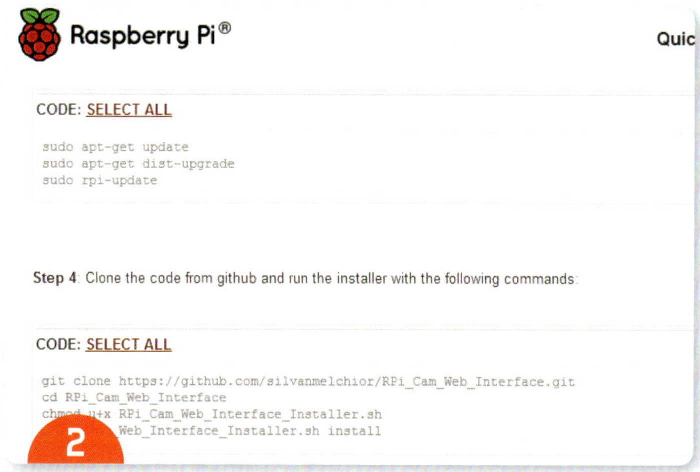

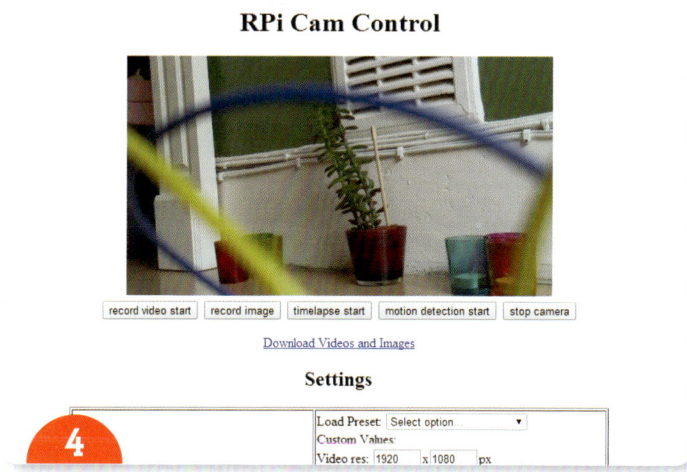

1

The camera comes with a ribbon connector flex that you'll need to attach to the CSI port on the Pi. This is the long, thin connector just behind the audio and video sockets. Gently squeeze either side of the port and pull out a small plastic clip, then make sure the contacts on the other end of the flex are facing towards the SD card end of the Pi and slide them into the port. Make sure the flex is down as far as it will go and that it's as straight as possible, then push the plastic clip back in to fasten it in place.

2

We're assuming you already have Raspian installed on your Pi. If not, do this now by downloading NOOBS (**www.raspberrypi.org/downloads**) and following the instructions at **www.raspberrypi.org/help/noobs-setup/**. Once installed, boot Raspian on your Pi, open the Terminal and enter these commands to update:

```
sudo apt-get update
sudo apt-get dist-upgrade
sudo rpi-update
```

...followed by these commands to install the webcam program:

```
git clone https://github.com/silvanmelchior/
RPi_Cam_Web_Interface.git
cd RPi_Cam_Web_Interface
chmod u+x RPi_Cam_Web_Interface_Installer.sh
./RPi_Cam_Web_Interface_Installer.sh install
```

3

Make a note of your Pi's IP address, then switch it off and unplug it from your keyboard and monitor. Insert it into an enclosure and attach it to the rear of Magbot's chassis using Blu-tak or Velcro. You'll need to cramp all of Magbot's existing circuitry up towards the front end a little to accommodate the Pi. On top of the Pi, stick your USB battery pack, but don't plug it in just yet. Then, get the cork and the wire ties and carefully attach the Pi's camera to one end, as shown. Stick the other end of the cork down to the Pi's enclosure with another blob of Blu-tak.

4

Insert the Wi-Fi dongle into one of the Pi's USB ports, then plug the USB power pack into the Pi's power socket. Now, power up Magbot as normal by connecting the 9V battery to the Arduino's power socket and switching on the motor's AA battery pack. Press Play on the remote control to set Magbot off, then turn to a computer or tablet. Open a web browser and type in the IP address of your Pi. A web interface like the one shown should open and, as long as Magbot stays within Wi-Fi range, you'll be able to watch a robot's eye view via the video window at the top of the page.

INTRODUCTION TO SOLDERING

For anyone thinking of taking their electronics hobby further, we explain the basics behind using soldering equipment and how to do so safely

WHAT YOU'LL LEARN

- **What soldering is and why it's important**
- **How to solder components together yourself**
- **How to make sure you stay safe while soldering**

Since our book is intended to be a beginner's guide to building robots and working with electronics, we've kept things simple by using a solderless breadboard for all our connections. But anyone who wants to go beyond the projects in this book and take things to the next level will, at some point, need to learn how to solder.

Soldering is basically the process of making a connection between two (or more) electronic components by heating them, then applying solder onto them. Solder is a soft metal that melts quickly when heat is applied. The molten solder forms a blob around the join, then, when it cools, it hardens and holds the components in place very firmly.

▲ **Look for 40W soldering irons with good reviews on Amazon.**

Solder is made from an alloy, which means it's actually a mix of metals. Traditionally, solder is made from tin and lead. In the EU, however, manufacturers of consumer electronics have been banned from using anything other than lead-free solder since 2006. Lead is poisonous – if ingested it can cause nerve and brain damage. You can buy both lead-free and tin/lead solder for your own projects. Lead-free solder tends to have a higher melting point, which means that it's not as easy to work with. Lead-based solder melts at lower temperatures and is much easier to use, though obviously you'll need to take great care. You must wash your hands thoroughly after touching it and you'll need to make sure you don't breathe in any of the smoke that comes off your soldering iron as you work. These aren't the only precautions you'll need to take while soldering – see the box opposite for our safety checklist.

▲ **You'll need rosin core solder.**

Solder comes in different thicknesses and types for different applications. For electronics projects, you need solder with a rosin core – also known as 'flux'. This is a resin that flows around the joint you're soldering, helping to clean and lubricate the surfaces and make a good connection.

You can get cheap soldering kits, which often include an iron, a desoldering pump (for removing badly applied or excess solder), some solder and other accessories, such as a 'helping hands' (a magnifying glass on a stand with crocodile clips) for less than £15. Some cheap soldering irons can be quite poor – look for 40W units that review well on Amazon. Good soldering irons can cost hundred of pounds. Borrowing a decent one from someone else is often the best way to start.

RULES FOR SOLDERING SAFELY

- ✓ **Always wear protective eyewear – this is absolutely vital**
- ✓ **Always place the iron back in its stand when not in use**
- ✓ **Never touch the heated tip of the soldering iron**
- ✓ **Make sure the tip of the iron never touches the power cord**
- ✓ **Always solder in a well-ventilated room**
- ✓ **Use a helping hands to hold components in place safely and help you see better**
- ✓ **Use a face mask when using lead-based solder and wash your hands**
- ✓ **Never leave your soldering iron unattended while it's switched on**

TIP

If you apply too little solder, you'll get a bad connection, so repeat the process, adding more solder where needed. If you apply too much solder, press the tip of the iron for one second until the solder has melted, then use a desoldering pump to remove the excess.

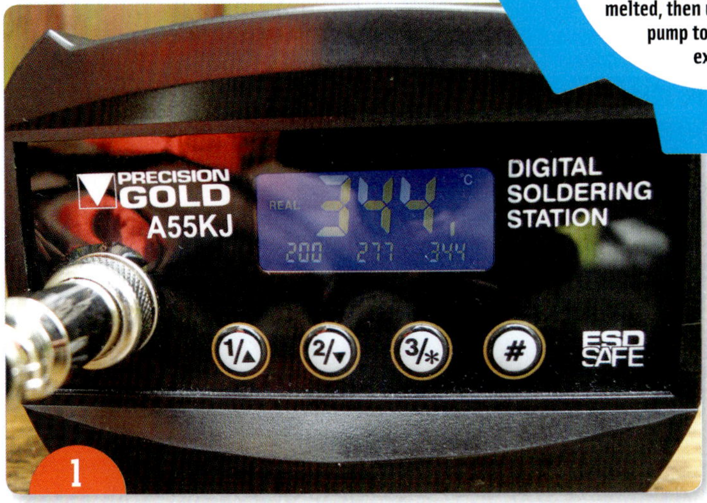

1

Switch on your soldering iron. If you're just starting out, it's likely you'll be using an inexpensive fixed temperature soldering iron. But if you've borrowed one from a more experienced (or richer) friend, you may find that it has a temperature control. If that's the case, you need to set it to a temperature that's appropriate for your project and for the solder you're using. Too hot and you could damage your components. Too cool and the solder will take a long time to melt. To give you an idea of just how hot things get, we've set ours to 344°C.

2

Leave the iron itself in its stand while it heats up and make sure the sponge in the tray is damp – if not, put it under a cold water tap and squeeze it out a little. After a minute or two, the iron should be hot enough to steam when you touch the tip on the sponge. Before you start soldering, you'll need to clean the tip. You'll probably notice that the tip is somewhat blackened at first. This is because the tip oxidises. The oxides will act as an insulator, stopping the iron from getting hot enough, so gently wipe both sides of the tip on the sponge until it's shiny again.

3

Get your components ready, but just before you begin you should 'tin' the tip. To do this, get your solder and touch it to the iron's tip, as shown. The solder will melt as you touch it and form a thin coating on the tip. Apply a little more, so the coating covers all sides. As soon as you're done, you're ready to start soldering. As you work, every so often it's worth cleaning and re-tinning your tip. Tinning improves conductivity and makes soldering easier and quicker, meaning you're less likely to damage components. It can also help lengthen the lifespan of your soldering iron.

4

In our example, we're soldering some components into a blank PCB stripboard. Put the board copper side up and poke the component's legs through the holes in the board so that they stick upwards. Now, press the tip of the soldering iron against the base of the leg of the component so that it touches the copper pad underneath, too. Hold it there for a second, then press the end of your solder to the base of the leg on the other side. Once a small amount of solder has melted, pull the solder away. Leave the iron there for another second, then pull this away, too.

IN THIS CHAPTER

HOW TO BUILD A ROBOT

TROUBLE-SHOOTING & TRICKS

If you've managed to work your way through all the projects in this book without a hitch, you're either a genius or you've been very lucky indeed. Even the most experienced electronics enthusiasts find themselves regularly stumped by problems of one kind or another, which is why we've reserved a section of our book to try and help you find solutions to the sorts of difficulties you might face while building your robot. We've also saved some space for a selection of general hints and tips that didn't fit anywhere else in the book, but may well prove useful as you take your hobby further.

TROUBLESHOOTING TRICKS

We offer a selection of troubleshooting tips for your robot as well as general problem-solving advice

WHAT YOU'LL LEARN

- How to fix Magbot if he's not working properly
- How to cure motor and sensor problems
- How to solve errors in the Arduino program
- How to work out what might be wrong with a circuit

It won't all be smooth sailing when you work with electronics. There are often dozens of different ways that even the simplest of projects can go wrong. Usually, the first thing to do is check the power (see the battery tip opposite). If that's not the problem, move onto the rest of your hardware and make sure everything's connected correctly. And if that seems okay, have a look at the sketch to make sure all the code is right. Most of the code in this book has been supplied for you, so it should be fine, but it's still worth a look. Below, we've split our advice into two sections. First, are some specific troubleshooting tips for solving problems with Magbot. Then, we'll move onto some more general advice for your Arduino and electronic projects.

TIP

If you're experiencing problems and you're running on battery power, one obvious thing to check is that the batteries themselves have enough charge. Your multimeter will soon tell you this if you press its probes onto the positive and negative terminals.

TIP

It's possible to damage pins on the Arduino Uno by passing too much current through them. If you think this might be the case, try using another pin and editing the code so it specifies the other pin, too. If your project works after doing this, it's likely the original pin is dead.

PART 1 - MAGBOT TROUBLESHOOTING

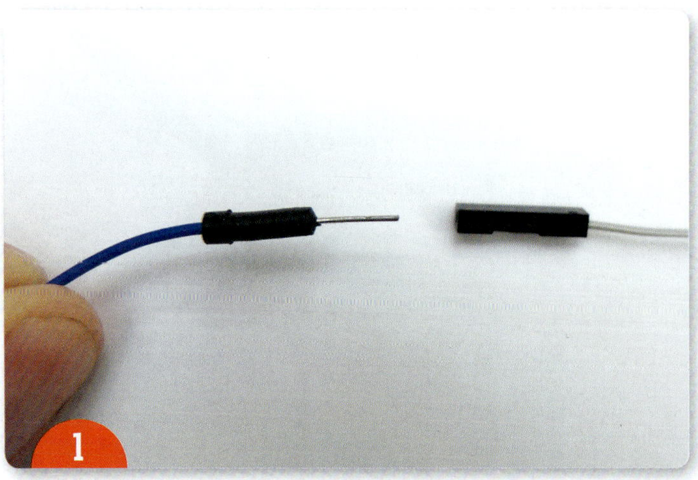

It's possible that you may encounter problems while physically putting Magbot together. Cheap chassis kits can often be fiddly to construct and they're frequently accompanied by ineffectual or misleading instructions. Don't be afraid to improvise if needed. Another problem you might encounter is that you don't have enough long jumper wires among your supplies. If the wires are too short, try repositioning the various bits on Magbot's back – the important thing is that the ping sensor is as far forward as possible. Also, you can extend any wire by fixing one of your female-to-male wires to its bare end – use some tape to hold the connection together.

The way the wires are connected to the motor shield defines the direction in which the wheels will turn, and it's all too easy to connect two or more of the wires the wrong way round, resulting in incorrect movement. If Magbot keeps going backwards in a straight(ish) line, this means both his motors are wired in the wrong way round. If Magbot keeps going round and round in tight circles, this means that one of his motors is wired in the wrong way round. Rather than turning the motors the other way around, you can simply switch the red and black wires in the screw terminal until you get Magbot moving forwards in a (more or less) straight line.

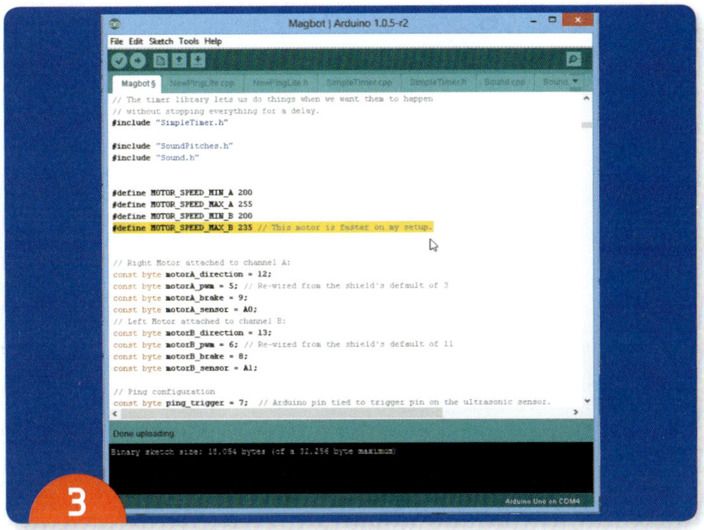

It's quite likely that Magbot will be turning either left or right in a wider arc as he travels forward. Unfortunately, this is because the cheap DC motors we're using aren't very reliable and are often imbalanced. When one motor is more or less powerful than the other, this can prevent the robot from moving in a straight line. If the left motor's maximum speed is faster than the right one's, for instance, Magbot will veer to the right as he drives. It's possible to compensate for this a little by hacking Magbot's code. Open his sketch in the Arduino IDE software and scroll to the section shown.

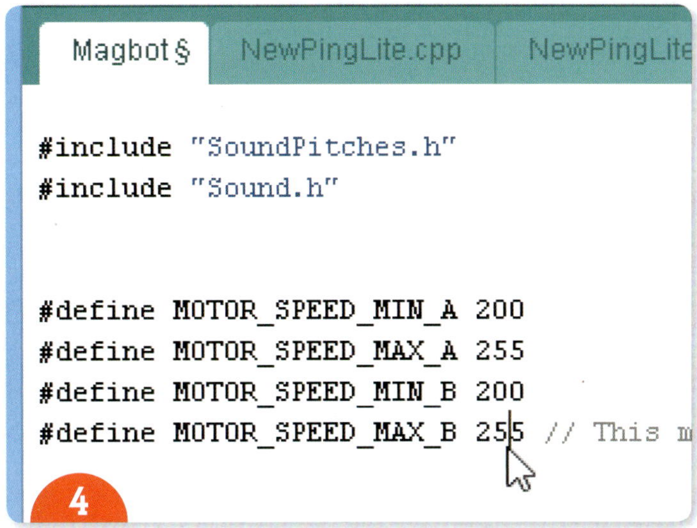

In the highlighted section, you'll see that, by default, motor B (the motor connected to terminal B on the motor shield – usually the left-hand motor) has its maximum speed limited to 235, while motor A (the right-hand one) has a maximum speed of 255. This is because in our setup the left motor was faster than the right one, so we compensated for this by reducing the left motor's maximum speed. Start by changing this to 255, too, then connect the Arduino and re-upload the sketch. This will show you how both motors work together at the same speed.

Next, look underneath the robot and make sure that none of the wires coming from the motors (or any other wires for that matter) are making contact with either of the wheels or the caster, as wires can get in the way and prevent wheels from spinning freely. Try threading the wires through the chassis to get them out of the way. You may also want to try removing the speed board holders – these are cog-like plastic things that come with some chassis kits – as these are usually pretty useless. Finally, check that the caster is moving freely. If not, give it a squirt of WD-40 or similar to lubricate it.

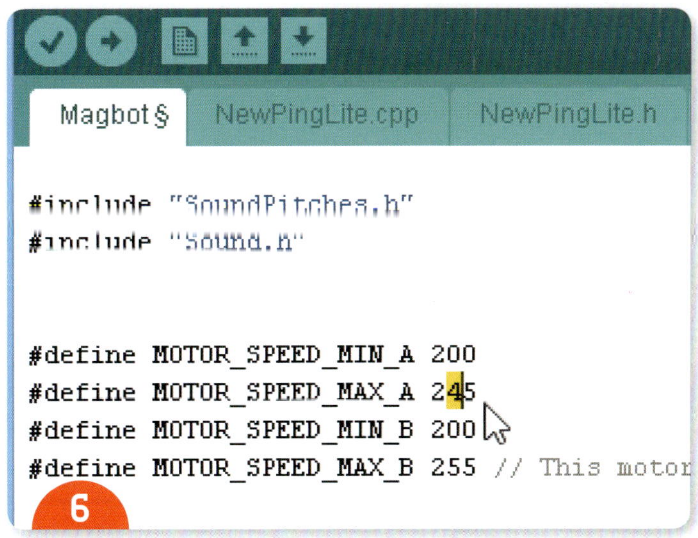

Now, try Magbot again and see how straight he moves. If he's still veering one way or the other, open his sketch again and scroll to the section we looked at in step 4, then reduce either the right (A) or left (B) motor's maximum speed to try and compensate. Re-upload and try again. Keep doing this, refining the maximum speed slightly until you're happier with the way Magbot is moving. You may also want to compare how he moves on smoother surfaces. Bear in mind that you'll almost certainly never be able to get your robot moving in a perfectly straight line unless you invest in better-quality motors.

9 Troubleshooting & tricks

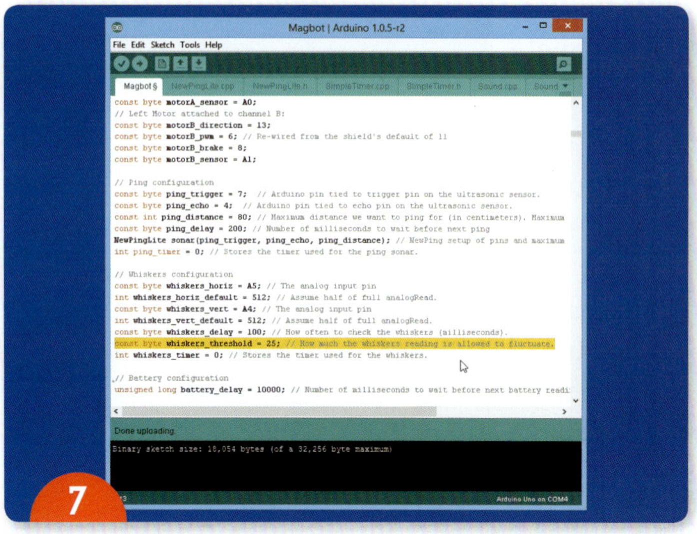

If Magbot keeps making the 'damage' sound and moving backwards, this is likely to be because his whiskers are too sensitive and they keep registering contact with something even when they haven't hit anything. As with the motors, the way to solve this is to tweak the code. Fire up Magbot's sketch in the Arduino IDE, then scroll down to the 'Whiskers configuration' section. You'll see a line of code that says `const byte whiskers_threshold = 5;` – this is the amount the reading from the sensor is allowed to fluctuate. To make the whiskers less sensitive, change the number here to a higher one – try 25 – then re-upload and see if it's fixed the problem.

If your robot keeps making the 'block' sound and moving backwards, even when there are no obstacles in its path, this is likely to be because something – usually a wire – is caught in front of the ping sensor and causing Magbot to incorrectly assume there's something blocking his way forward. Make sure there's nothing in front of the sensor and try again. If, on the other hand, the robot seems to keep driving headfirst into walls, doors and so on, it could be that the ping sensor is angled wrongly and the robot isn't able to judge distances. If the sensor is pointing upwards a little, angle it downwards and vice versa.

PART 2 - GENERAL TROUBLESHOOTING

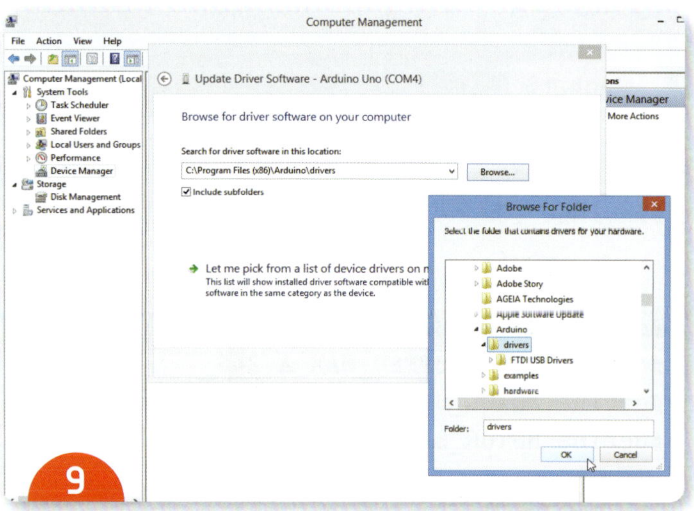

If the device driver fails to install when you first plug your Arduino Uno into a Windows PC, open Device Manager as described above and look under 'Ports (COM & LPT)'. You should see an entry for the Arduino Uno with an exclamation mark or question mark next to it. It may also be listed under 'Other Devices' or 'Unknown Device'. Right-click the Arduino Uno entry and select 'Update Driver Software', then click 'Browse my computer for driver software'. Click Browse, then navigate to the file named arduino.inf. In most cases, this will be found in C:\Program Files (x86)\Arduino\drivers. Click OK and Windows will complete the installation.

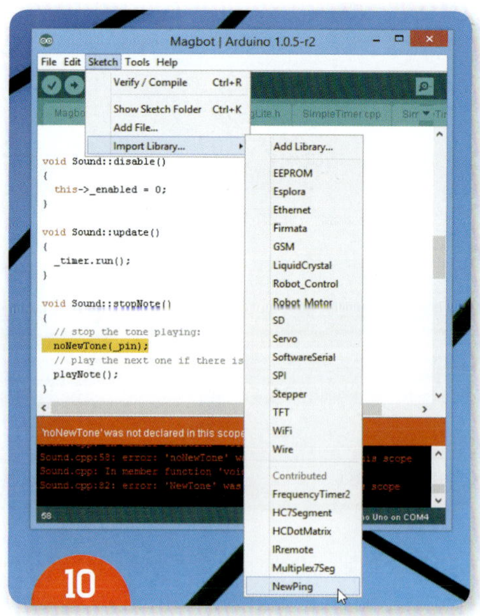

If you get an orange error message in the bottom of the Arduino program window when you try to upload a sketch to your Uno, there's something wrong with the code itself. In the projects we've covered in this book, the most likely issue is that the code is referencing a software library that isn't installed. If the library was one you installed yourself, double-check it's where it should be by clicking Sketch then selecting Import Library. At the bottom of the list, you should see a section of libraries you've installed. If the one you need isn't there, follow the instructions within the project to try adding it again and restart the IDE program.

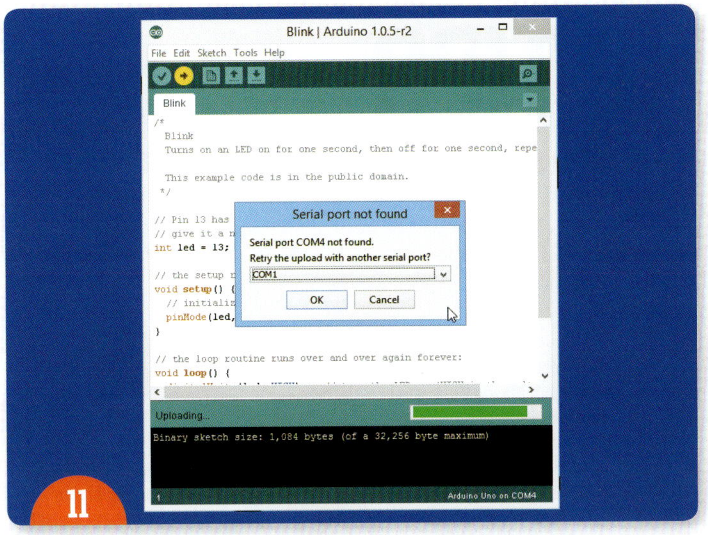

Sometimes, when you connect your Uno and click Upload, you might see a message telling you that the 'Serial port was not found'. If this is the case, before doing anything else, try unplugging the Uno, then reconnecting it to the USB port and trying again. Sometimes this is enough to solve the problem. If not and you're using Windows, click Tools, then Serial Port in the Arduino IDE software to see which port the Uno is attached to. Then, open Device Manager as described in step 9 and look under 'Ports (COM & LPT)'. Make sure the COM port matches the one listed in the Arduino IDE program. If not, change it in the IDE.

If a sketch doesn't work when you upload it, the most likely cause is that one of the connections in your circuit is wrong or missing. The best thing to do is unplug your Uno from either the PC or power supply, then run through all your connections methodically. First, make sure all the relevant components are connected to the correct pins on the Uno. Then, follow all the power and ground connections to make sure the circuit is closed. Check all the resistors to make sure they're the right values and connected in the right rows. If you still can't establish a problem, remove all the components and try making the circuit again from scratch.

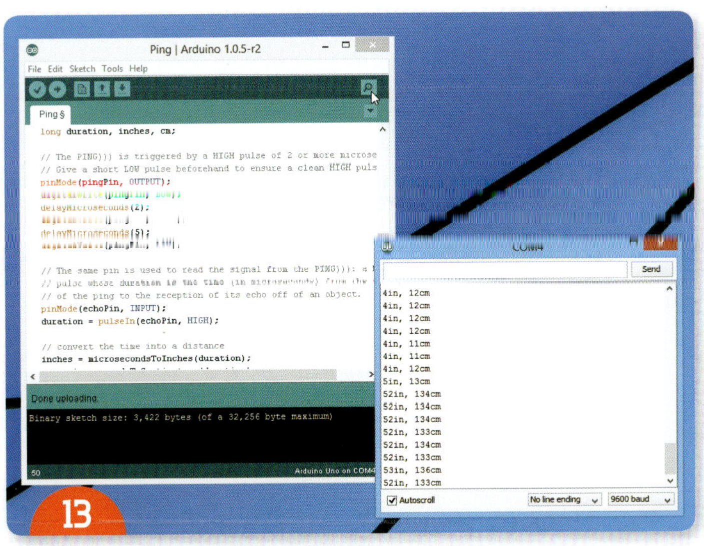

If you're still having problems getting a project to work, the serial monitor can sometimes help you establish a problem. You should also check through the circuit for any components that feel hot to the touch and sniff the air to see if there are any odd smells. Also, look closely – is there any smoke? All of these are symptoms of a short circuit and, if you notice any of them, you should disconnect your power supply immediately. Check your connections and components again, as one of them is almost certainly incorrect and you may find that you'll need to replace any components damaged by the short.

If your Arduino Uno isn't recognised at all when you plug it into a PC, it's possible the board may be faulty. Check to see whether the green power light (shown) is on or off when plugged in. If it's off, try unplugging it from your PC and powering the Uno with a battery. If the power light is still off, try removing the ATmega328 chip. Unplug all power and use a small flat-head screwdriver to prise the chip out of its header at either end, making a note of which way round it's seated. Now, try connecting the battery again. If the power light is still off, the board is almost certainly dead.

FURTHER HINTS AND TIPS

Find out how to get more from your electronic projects with these expert tricks and techniques

WHAT YOU'LL LEARN

- Clever hacks and customisations you can use
- Ways to stay on top of complicated projects
- How to take your knowledge and skills even further

You've reached the very last section of this book. And those who've made it this far will have learned a great deal by working through all our projects. But there's still plenty to learn and loads more possibilities to explore. So before we go, we're going to offer one last selection of tips for those who are planning to continue their robot-building career and start building amazing new projects of their own. Over the next few pages, you'll find a mixture of general advice about how to approach your projects in a safe and organised manner, as well as a few random hints and cool tricks that didn't fit anywhere else in this book. We'll show you how to customise components, make quick connections, enhance your multimeter and much more.

TIP

As an alternative to electric tape or hot glue in tip 4, you could use shrink wrap – heat-sensitive tubing that shrinks when you apply heat (such as a hairdryer). Put it over a join and heat it, and it will insulate the wires and help

TIP

Even once you've graduated to soldering, we highly recommend making your project on a solderless breadboard before you make it permanent on a stripboard or PCB. That way, you can test that it works and iron out any bugs before you commit to building the permanent version.

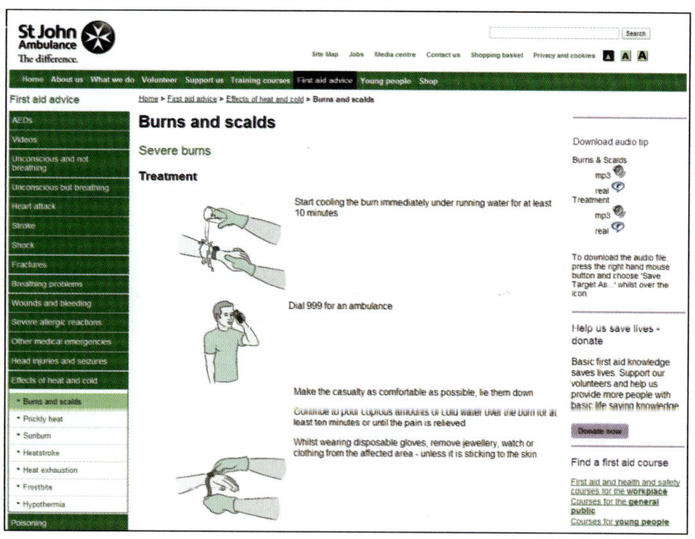

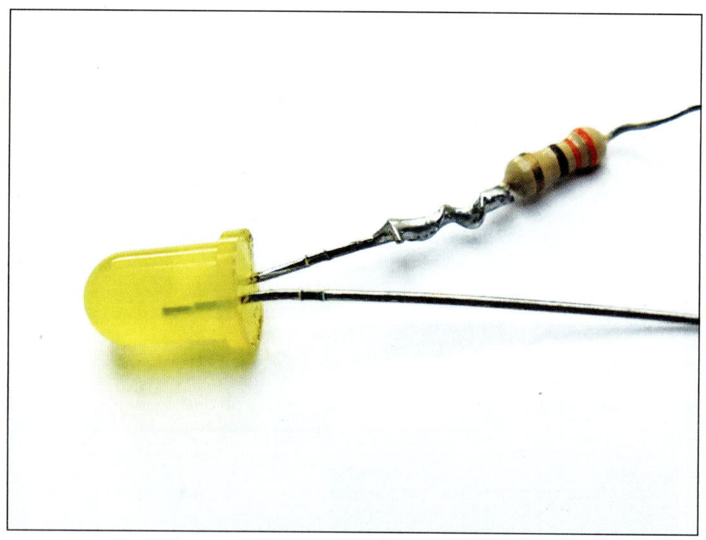

1 STAY SAFE

We've said it before, but we'll say it one last time – electricity can be dangerous! We've covered safety elsewhere in this book (see chapter 2), but make sure you take all the necessary precautions when you work on your projects. If you're working on projects with children, make sure they understand all about safety, too. As well as knowing how to prevent accidents, you'll need to know what to do if one ever happens. Visit the Electrical Safety First website (**www.snipca.com/13179**) for advice on what to do if someone is suffering from an electric shock. The St John's Ambulance website (**www.snipca.com/13180**) has more general first aid advice, including what to do for burns.

2 HACK COMPONENTS AND TOOLS

Working with robots and electronics is all about making your own things and improvising, so you should feel free to adapt and customise the equipment you have to suit your own needs. You could stick strips of Velcro on things like battery packs that you frequently find yourself needing to fix to other surfaces, for example. Or how about making something like the component in the picture above? It's basically a hacked LED with a 220 Ω resistor stuck to one leg. That way it can be plugged straight into a circuit without having to worry about adding a separate resistor for protection.

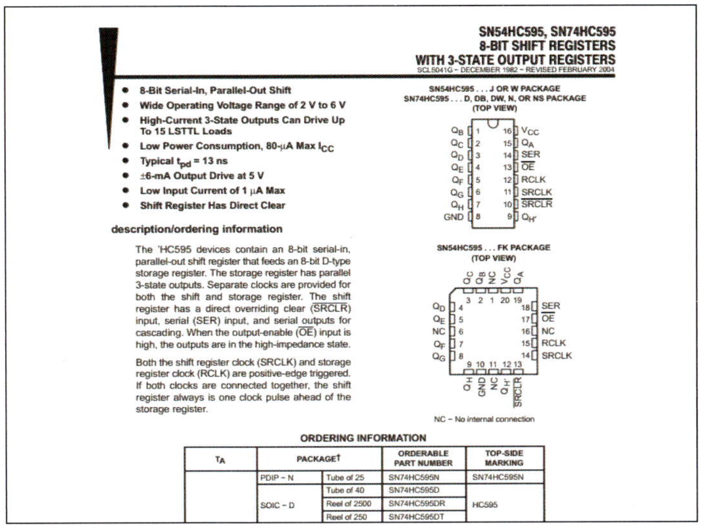

SN54HC595, SN74HC595
8-BIT SHIFT REGISTERS
WITH 3-STATE OUTPUT REGISTERS
SCLS041G – DECEMBER 1982 – REVISED FEBRUARY 2004

- 8-Bit Serial-In, Parallel-Out Shift
- Wide Operating Voltage Range of 2 V to 6 V
- High-Current 3-State Outputs Can Drive Up To 15 LSTTL Loads
- Low Power Consumption, 80-μA Max I_{CC}
- Typical t_{pd} = 13 ns
- ±6-mA Output Drive at 5 V
- Low Input Current of 1 μA Max
- Shift Register Has Direct Clear

description/ordering information

The 'HC595 devices contain an 8-bit serial-in, parallel-out shift register that feeds an 8-bit D-type storage register. The storage register has parallel 3-state outputs. Separate clocks are provided for both the shift and storage register. The shift register has a direct overriding clear ($\overline{SRCLR}$) input, serial (SER) input, and serial outputs for cascading. When the output-enable ($\overline{OE}$) input is high, the outputs are in the high-impedance state.

Both the shift register clock (SRCLK) and storage register clock (RCLK) are positive-edge triggered. If both clocks are connected together, the shift register always is one clock pulse ahead of the storage register.

SN54HC595 . . . J OR W PACKAGE
SN74HC595 . . . D, DB, DW, N, OR NS PACKAGE
(TOP VIEW)

SN54HC595 . . . FK PACKAGE
(TOP VIEW)

NC – No internal connection

ORDERING INFORMATION

T_A	PACKAGE†		ORDERABLE PART NUMBER	TOP-SIDE MARKING
	PDIP – N	Tube of 25	SN74HC595N	SN74HC595N
	SOIC – D	Tube of 40	SN74HC595D	HC595
		Reel of 2500	SN74HC595DR	
		Reel of 250	SN74HC595DT	

3 CHECK DATASHEETS

We haven't really covered datasheets in this book. But if you plan to take your interest in robot-building and electronics any further, at some point you'll find you need to refer to them. Datasheets are basically instruction manuals for electronic components. They list lots of useful details and specifications, like the one shown. You can usually find a component's datasheet by typing its part number plus the word 'datasheet' into Google. The trouble is, datasheets are usually written with professional engineers in mind, so you'll also need to learn how to read them. Sparkfun offers a good explanation of how datasheets work at **www.snipca.com/13181**.

4 CONNECT WIRES WITHOUT SOLDER

We managed to get away without using a soldering iron at all to make Magbot and, while you'll eventually need to start soldering at some point, there'll be moments when all you want to do is quickly make a connection between two components. But what if you need to connect two bare wires? Well, there are a number of ways to do this without soldering. You could use a crocodile clip to hold the ends together, for example. Or you could twist the wires around each other, then wrap them in electrical tape. If you have one, you could use a glue gun instead of tape.

5 SALVAGE WIRE FROM NETWORK CABLES

Recycling stuff is definitely the way forward when it comes to building your own electronics projects, and wire is a prime example of something you can re-appropriate for your own use. In this book, we've used lots of nice pre-prepared jumper cables, but the truth is that you can use almost any wire you can lay your hands on. A common tip amongst enthusiasts is to use an old network (Cat-5) cable. Clip the connector off and carefully remove a section of the outer insulation, and you'll find eight differently coloured sets of decent quality wires in four twisted pairs. You can clip these to the lengths you need.

6 KEEP THINGS NEAT

One of the secrets to successful electronics is staying organised. In terms of your workspace, that means keeping your components and tools tidy and well-organised so you always have access to what you need when you need it. But the best engineers extend this discipline to the circuits they build. When you're making something temporary, for example, it's okay to leave long wires and have components sticking up on long legs, but when you're making a purpose-built circuit you should trim the wires to fit and make sure resistors, LEDs and other components are almost flush with your breadboard, as they are in the image shown.

7 MAKE USE OF YOUR MULTIMETER

Your multimeter has a wide range of handy uses, both for your electronics projects and for general use around your home. We've already explained elsewhere that you can use it to test the batteries for your robots and circuits, for example, but you can also use it to test the battery in your car, as well as light bulbs, fuses and more. Most cheap multimeters come with a pair of bare probes, so you could consider investing in a set of clips that you can attach so that you can fix the leads to components you're testing without having to hold them. These cost about £2, or you could make a set yourself!

8 GET LOTS OF PRACTICE

It sounds obvious, but the best way to learn more about making robots is to practise as much as you can. And you can learn a lot by experimenting with simpler electronics projects, like the practice projects we worked through in the early part of this book. You'll find loads of ideas for new projects online. We already looked to the web for inspiration back in chapter 8, so start with some of the projects on the websites we recommended there. Don't just practise your hardware skills – remember to work on your programming technique, too. There are loads of C++ tutorials online, like the one at **www.snipca.com/13188.**

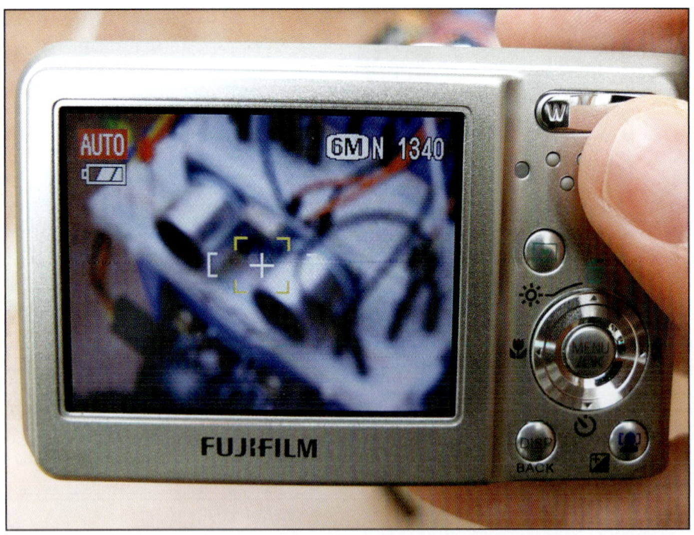

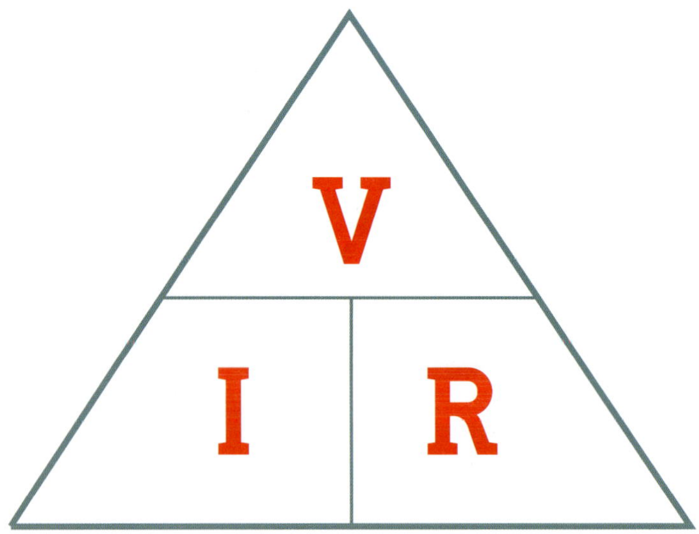

9 TAKE PHOTOS

A lot of the projects you'll work on will end up being dismantled once you've finished them, so their component parts can be reused in your next big project. It's kind of sad, but it's the nature of hobby, as people rarely have a limitless supply of components at their disposal. So it's a good idea to take photos of the things you build, and maybe even upload them to a blog so that other people can see what you've made. Don't just take photos of your successes, either – documenting your failures can be just as useful, as you'll learn just as much from your mistakes.

10 USE OHM'S LAW

We mentioned Ohm's Law early on in this book and this is something that you'll need to start using more as your ambitions grow. For example, if you're building a circuit and you need to know what value resistor to use, you can use Ohm's Law to calculate it for you. Remember, R = V/I, so divide the voltage by the current required to work out what resistance you need. If the LED you're using needs a voltage of 3V and a current of 15mA (milliamps), for example, divide 3 by 0.015, which gives you 200. Therefore, you'll need a 200 Ω resistor.

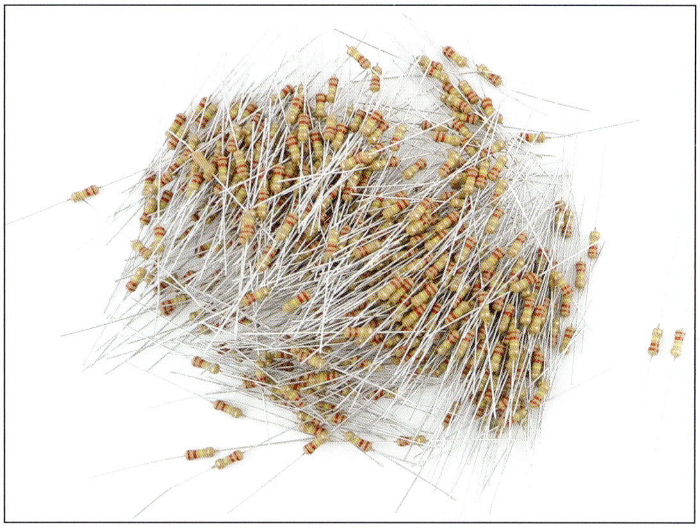

11 USE THE NEAREST VALUES

Quite often when you're working with electronics, you'll make a calculation, but you'll then need to round the value up or down to the nearest value that matches the components you're using. In the example we just gave, our Ohm's Law calculation gave us a resistance figure of 200 Ω, but it's unlikely that you'll actually have a 200 Ω resistor among your components. Instead, you can round this up and use a 220 Ω resistor, which is a much more common value. This might seem like you're fudging it, but accuracy isn't always vital early on.

12 STICK BREADBOARDS TOGETHER

As your horizons grow, inevitably your projects will, too. And you may eventually find that, for your increasingly complex circuits, you need more room than your current breadboard can provide. We've used a half-size breadboard in this book, as it's the ideal size for Magbot, but there are lots of different sizes – both larger and smaller – available. However, if you already have a couple of breadboards hanging around, you might not need to buy a larger one. Most breadboards are expandable. They come with little notches on all four sides, which allow you to slot two or more together to make one big one.

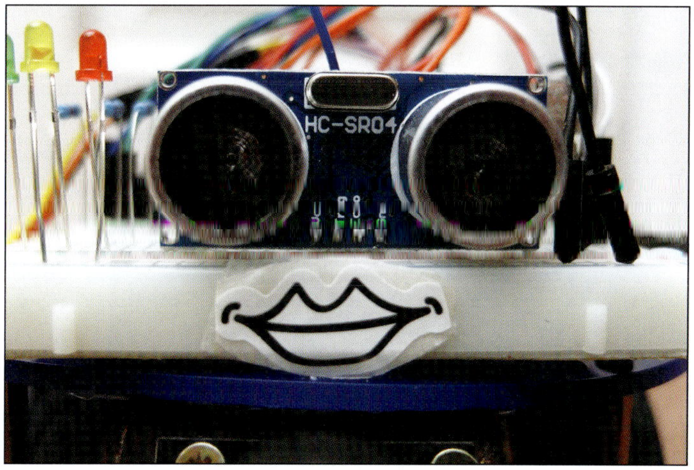

13 MAKE THINGS YOU'LL USE

When it comes to building your next big project, we recommend making something that you'll actually use. There's a lot to be said for practising on projects that let you build cool things, like the laser harp we saw in chapter 8. But you'll get an immense sense of satisfaction from building something that you'll actually end up getting a lot of use from. If you're a keen gardener, for example, you could consider making a soil moisture detector to tell you when your plants need watering. It's simpler than you might think – all you really need is a couple of galvanised nails. See **www.snipca.com/13184** for more.

14 HAVE FUN

The final piece of advice we'll offer is simply to enjoy what you do. Obviously, you'll always need to be careful and keep half a mind on safety. And, yes, you'll need to be systematic and organised in your approach – you'll need to follow instructions carefully and double-check everything you do. Admittedly, there's a lot to learn, too, and solving problems can seem very frustrating at times. But making electronic devices of your own, particularly robots, can be an enormous amount of fun, not to mention hugely rewarding. So take what you've learned from this book and go wherever you want with it. Whatever you make next, we're sure you'll have a blast!

GLOSSARY

Not sure what that technical term means? Don't be baffled by jargon – find everything you need to know in our handy glossary

A

AC
Short for alternating current – an electric current that constantly changes direction. Mains electricity is an AC supply.

Alkaline cell
A type of commonly used battery.

Alligator clip
See crocodile clip.

Ampere
A unit of electrical current, often shortened to Amp or A.

Analog
Also spelled 'analogue'. A signal that's constantly varying, as opposed to a digital one, which is either 'on' or 'off'.

Anode
The positive electrode, leg or terminal of a device or component.

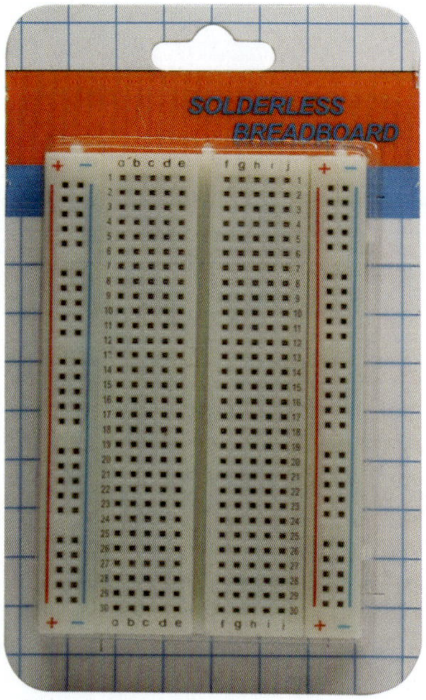

▸ Use a breadboard to create circuits without soldering.

B

Battery
A power source that uses an electrochemical reaction to create voltage.

Binary
A numbering scheme where there are only two possible values for each digit – 0 or 1.

Breadboard
A plastic board with sockets for connecting electronic circuits without the need for soldering.

Byte
A unit of data that consists of eight bits.

C

C++
A commonly used programming language. The programming language for the Arduino platform is based on C++.

Calibration
The process of adjusting a device to the correct setting or value.

Capacitor
An electronic component capable of storing an electrical charge. The amount of electrical charge that a capacitor can store is its capacitance, measured in Farads.

Cathode
The negative electrode, leg or terminal of a device or component.

Charge
An amount of electrical energy.

Chassis
A (usually mobile) framework or enclosure onto which you can mount components.

Circuit
A combination of interconnected components through which an electrical current can flow.

Class
In computer programming, a class is a set of related objects that share common characteristics.

Closed circuit
A closed circuit is one where there is a complete path for current to flow.

Code
A term used to describe text that's written using a computer programming language, such as C++.

Comment
A block of text included by the programmer within a program's code to help you understand what's going on.

Compile
The process of transforming the source code written in a programming language into an executable program.

Conductor
An object or material that allows current to flow, such as a wire.

Constant
A term used in programming to describe a value or data that doesn't change over a given amount of time, unlike a variable.

Contact
Two pieces of electrically conductive material that pass electrical current when touched together or stop the current flowing when opened.

Conventional current flow
A concept of the direction current was